The Transparent Brain in Couple and Family Therapy

Why should family therapists care about brain research? Are there invisible connections between the breakdown of our relationships and the breakdown of our cells? To answer these questions, author Suzanne Midori Hanna paints pictures of ancient principles coming together with contemporary research as a context for why basic concepts of neuroscience are relevant to couple and family therapy. She illustrates the reciprocal nature of the body and relationships in a book that simplifies and demystifies brain science for therapists. Using the latest findings from affective and cognitive neuroscience, she highlights six brain-friendly family therapy approaches and introduces the concept of **biological empathy**. This analysis enables practitioners to harness the power of mindfulness toward brain development and interpersonal healing. Client-friendly language allows busy therapists to educate without jargon. Applications of family therapy begin with the self of the therapist and advance through the interpersonal layers of attachment, pair-bonding, and community.

Chapters include topics on:

- Whole body awareness
- A narrative approach to neuroanatomy and physiology
- Five basic principles of neuroscience
- Basics of trauma treatment

- Male/female brain differences in couple therapy
- The ancient concept of tribe and a community frontal lobe.

Each chapter summarizes with principles and guidelines for clinicians. Numerous illustrations make the brain transparent, while surveys, worksheets, and tables make therapeutic process transparent. The last chapter illustrates concepts and interventions through a full-length case story and applies addiction treatment as a case study for program development. *The Transparent Brain in Couple and Family Therapy* includes case examples from all walks of life, highlighting heroic acts of survival. Clinicians can use five basic principles of neuroscience to bring relief more quickly, for more people from more diverse backgrounds. It is a revolutionary read and a must-have reference for any mental health professional.

Suzanne Midori Hanna, PhD, is a marriage and family therapist with over 30 years' experience as a clinician, educator, and program developer. She is a Clinical Member and Approved Supervisor of the American Association for Marriage and Family Therapy. She has been a faculty member, program director, and program developer for three COAMFTE-accredited programs in Wisconsin, Kentucky, and California. Her specialization in integrative family trauma treatment is the result of 20 years working with African Americans in Kentucky and California. She has authored *The Practice of Family Therapy* and co-edited with T. Hargrave *The Aging Family*. Her practice includes family therapy, consultation, training, and evaluation to nonprofit organizations who serve veterans and disadvantaged trauma survivors. She is also an instructor for Amridge University and a senior scholar at the Hiebert Institute.

The Transparent Brain in Couple and Family Therapy

Mindful Integrations with Neuroscience

Suzanne Midori Hanna

Routledge
Taylor & Francis Group

NEW YORK AND LONDON

First published 2014
by Routledge
711 Third Avenue, New York, NY 10017

Simultaneously published in the UK
by Routledge
27 Church Road, Hove, East Sussex BN3 2FA

Routledge is an imprint of the Taylor & Francis Group, an informa business

Library of Congress Cataloging in Publication Data
Hanna, Suzanne Midori, 1950–
    The transparent brain in couple and family therapy : mindful integrations with neuroscience / authored by Suzanne Midori Hanna.
        pages cm
    Includes bibliographical references and index.
    1. Couples therapy.   2. Family psychotherapy.   3. Couples—Psychology.   4. Neurobiology.   I. Title.
    RC488.5.H3372 2013
    616.89'156—dc23

                                                        2013008651

ISBN: 978–0–415–66225–3 (hbk)
ISBN: 978–0–415–66226–0 (pbk)
ISBN: 978–0–203–07250–9 (ebk)

Typeset in Minion
by RefineCatch Limited, Bungay, Suffolk, UK

SFI Certified Sourcing
www.sfiprogram.org
SFI-00453

Printed and bound in the United States of America
by Edwards Brothers, Inc.

To my 11 nieces and nephews: I am humbled and amazed at your talents, wisdom, compassion, and heroism. Thank you for lighting my way. May you take the spirit of our ancestors, and with it, heal the wounds they were unable to heal, celebrate the transformations they were able to make, and live to see your own lives as the miracles that they are. You take the concept of numinosum to the highest peak. I love you all.

Contents

List of Figures, Tables, and Boxes

BOXES

Preface

In 1990, the President of the United States issued a proclamation designating 1990–2000 the decade of the brain. In 1999, I heard Dr. Carlos Sluzki speak about why family therapists should care about brain research. At the time, I didn't know it would come to this! In just a few short decades, we have traveled from a world of fighting disease as an isolated biological process to a world in which we see transparent connections between the breakdown of relationships and the breakdown of our cells. As the evidence continues to accumulate, the practice of family therapy has never been more relevant.

DISCIPLINES AT A CROSSROADS

Currently, we see many disciplines at a crossroads. There are specialties and subspecialties coming together and crossing old boundaries to revolutionize traditional thinking about human development and mental health processes. Descriptions of these appear in Chapter 1. Affective and cognitive neuroscientists deconstruct diagnoses in the DSM-V, using their knowledge of emotional regulation and stress. These analyses may lead to new practices that are based on biosocial processes instead of settling for a list of behaviors without social context. In addition to these possibilities, social neuroscientists are studying the interplay between interpersonal processes and our chemistry. My colleague, Paul Zak (2008), studies the "neuroeconomics of trust," which transcends traditional disciplines in the exploration of human behavior and neuropeptides. As these disciplines talk and share the territory of the brain, one thing has become clear. The brain is but one player in a much larger drama. Thus, neuroscientists now focus on the *whole body*. After centuries of the old mind-body split, now, it seems there is no way to separate the two. When the brain is transparent, communication with the rest of the body appears before our very eyes!

Perhaps the name most associated with this crossroads is Daniel Siegel (2012), who developed interpersonal neurobiology as a multidisciplinary conceptualization of attachment, physiology, and health. For the past 15 years, he has brought together the thinking of east and west to form a community of scholars who have made the physiology of attachment look like an art form. This book is full of their fascinating contributions.

So, where do family therapists enter the scene? For a long time, many have had gut feelings about the reciprocal nature of body and relationships. Now, existing evidence not only validates our hunches, but helps us know exactly how to use these relationships for greater successes in our work. Would we like a client to have a little more dopamine? There are interpersonal strategies in Chapters 4 to 8 that can induce more dopamine without taking a pill. In my clinical work with couples and families, there is only one thing better than witnessing a breakthrough in which some impasse has dissolved, or some relationship wound has healed. That one thing is to have it happen more often, with more people, from diverse backgrounds, more of the time. Because I love breakthroughs, I am obsessed with efficiency and effectiveness. Can I bring relief more quickly? Can the results of my work have long-term effects? The world of neuroscience helps any psychotherapist who is on this quest.

WHY NEURO? WHY NOW?

With all this progress, what are the most relevant findings for clinicians? Does the next step of progress require complete retraining, or is it possible to build on what we already have? To improve outcomes, traditional models of mental health and family therapy practice must be informed by the latest research. However, the latest research places great emphasis on social process. That makes it easier for family therapists who already learn about theories of human development based on ecology. Thus, social process is biological process. The time for family therapists to embrace their ecological roots is now. The possibilities for making unique contributions with systems and interpersonal process are endless.

In some ways, we need to see how the body is a person, too. During any session, the body is remembering things outside the awareness of the mind. Like an extra member of the family, these bodies have their own story to tell. Thus, this is a "call to arms" for family therapists to improve their practices by reuniting mind and body functioning, after centuries of separation by western disciplines. In this regard, the practice of marriage and family therapists (MFTs) has a rich history that can make this transition a celebration of our most basic principles. For example, when Jay Haley studied the practices of Milton Erickson, he learned how Erickson's work was informed by his personal history. As a farm boy in Wisconsin, he was stricken with polio during adolescence. Paralyzed, he would sit and look out the window every day, wondering what it would feel like if he could just move his finger again. He began to imagine this simple goal and spent lonely hours focusing his mind on this goal (Rossi, 1983).

We can now understand that when his finger began to move, and then his hand, he was reaping the benefits of mindfulness, one of the popular practices that is linked to brain health. Erickson gave us a taste of what he learned about the mind-body connection, but there was so much more than we could digest at the time. Caught up in the art of what he did, there was little dialogue about the physiology of all those interesting hypnotic suggestions.

Thus, the age of the brain has made the line very thin between art and science. Family therapists have become acquainted with emotionally focused couples therapy (EFT), one of the most researched of all couples therapy approaches. At the same time, its emphasis upon primary emotion can paint an artful scene of how one can address attachment issues in the repair of marital conflicts. In this work, we see that art and science are not opposing views, but complementary partners that strengthen various parts of the brain.

Nevertheless, this book will simplify and demystify science. It applies the latest findings of neuroscience in light of six brain-friendly family therapy approaches. Practical steps and creative innovations help practitioners achieve greater success in their practice. Most important, wellness of the therapist is a path to greater clinical success. Clinicians find exercises that help them tune in to their nervous system in new and healthy ways. Sometimes, tuning in to the affect of clients in body-oriented ways can help change brain circuits. Future and current practitioners will learn simple techniques that harness the power of mindfulness to foster brain development and interpersonal healing.

In addition, the use of client-friendly language helps busy therapists who want to integrate neuroscience in ways that resonate with everyday experiences. A number of charts and diagrams help the reader create down-to-earth narratives that explain the latest scientific and humanistic principles of intervention. The end of each chapter has principles or guidelines as a summary for clinicians.

Chapter 1 provides a whirlwind tour through the global panorama of eastern and western ideas that are coming together as part of the crossroads of neuroscience. Readers have the opportunity to stop and sample the flavor of each historical moment during the human search for health and well-being. The final stop explores the history of mental health treatment and how family therapists fit into the big picture.

Chapter 2 is an unconventional lesson in anatomy and physiology. Using a narrative perspective, miracles of the body are cast as an epic drama of survival. We learn about the brain as only one character in the plot. We see how our chemicals have a mind of their own. Some are sneaky and fast-acting. Others are slow and gradual. Just like people, they have their quirks.

Chapter 3 will review the basic principles that dominate our current understanding of neurophysiology. These principles orient practitioners to 1) the whole body, not just the brain, 2) survival as a biosocial process, 3) attachment as a primary element in everyone's survival story, 4) circuits of meaning and memory that fire off electrochemical energy, and 5) the concept of transformation as the goal of family therapy.

Chapter 4 explains how to use whole body awareness to prepare the self of the therapist for brain-informed relationships with clients. Here, there are illustrations of how attachment theory can guide our approach to joining and engaging clients.

Chapter 5 is an introduction to the basics of trauma treatment. In the absence of advanced training to help those with complex traumas, this chapter describes the beginning steps toward healing that all practitioners should know. There is an urgent need for practitioners to become trauma-informed. Perhaps no other condition has plagued our service men and women like combat stress. This chapter provides a map for trauma-informed service that can help clinicians manage the minefields of emotional dysregulation from overwhelming experiences.

Chapter 6 reviews what neuroscience is saying about male and female differences. There are some surprising discoveries from an array of professions, from medical anthropology to social endocrinology. These studies are a prelude to three cutting-edge approaches to couples therapy that illustrate how to tune in to the emotional circuits in the body. Readers can review an analysis of their similarities and differences as they see examples of brain-friendly practices.

Chapter 7 addresses family therapy innovations that speak to transformations in body and brain through addressing the tribe. The concept of tribe is an ancient one that makes a comeback in three cutting-edge approaches that address attachment injuries from within and outside the family. Follow these models like explorers on an expedition to find the holy grail of healing by involving family and social network in changing the physiology of the brain.

Chapter 8 assembles interventions from previous chapters and relates them to a full-length case story. Then, these approaches form the basis of a proposal for program development. Using substance abuse treatment as an example, the proposal will review the physiology of addictions and how this knowledge could revolutionize the field of addictions treatment.

The objectives of this book are to:

1. Create a historical and theoretical context for why the basic concepts of neuroscience are relevant to couple and family therapy.
2. Explain the neuroanatomy and physiology of interpersonal process in a practitioner-relevant way.
3. Describe five principles clinicians can use to make their practice brain-informed.
4. Describe intervention strategies in couple and family therapy that attune to basic processes of the whole body.
5. Illustrate how neuroscience informs the treatment of substance abuse and program development.

Because our brains have parts that process memory, threat, consciousness, and well-being, this exploration brings us squarely to the center of our work as relationship-centered mental health practitioners. As these connections become transparent during interpersonal process, a number of options emerge for transforming stuck cases i~*~ fluid cases through interventions that focus on the basics of survival and attachment.

In addition to a focus on *whole body*, I borrow a concept from McFarlane's (2002) successful work with schizophrenia. He suggests that the symptoms of these disturbances are *biosocial* in nature. Assessment can address *biosocial* elements, and interventions can target *whole body* outcomes. All told, I am a better practitioner for learning about science in a way that compliments the *art* of therapy. There is a depth to my empathy that sees inside the body.

My journey is far from over, but, at this stage, I invite you to join me on an adventure into this amazing world of neuroscience as it applies to couple and family therapy. MFTs already have many brain-friendly practices. A review of these in later chapters will provide a foundation from which to build a biosocial bridge to whole body practices.

ACKNOWLEDGMENTS

There are so many people who have made this book possible. My tribe has grown substantially during the professional journey that has taken me from a young, research-avoidant clinician to a passionate devotee of neuroscience. I must reach back all the way to Madison, WI, where I stumbled into medical family therapy opportunities and grappled with the intersection of family therapy and Alzheimer's Disease (AD). I thank those families for opening their lives and their homes to our home-based family therapy program. Yours were the brains that were part of a career-defining moment as I witnessed your love, compassion, dignity, and grace with the ravages of AD. Drs. Mary Coleman and Riann van Zyl in Louisville gave me the chance of a lifetime to learn from public health voices that cared about the brains of the disadvantaged. Thank you for valuing the contributions of family therapy students in the context of primary care. The mentoring I received from you in the science of clinical practice remains with me to this day. To the students who have joined me in these adventures of the brain, I owe a tremendous debt as I learned from you how vast the ocean is and how much courage it takes to go where others fear to tread. Thank you for your courage, thirst for knowledge, patience with me, and invaluable help. In particular, Drs. Rik Rusovick and Calvin Thomsen provided much hands-on help as all these ideas began to percolate some years ago.

The tribe at Routledge has been especially kind to me. I am so grateful to Anna Moore for her faith in this project and her ability to keep the rough stone rolling until it was polished enough. Thank you for your guidance and analysis as we pulled everything together. Marta Moldvai has been a tremendous help sorting through the content and making it better. Your support has sustained me during some long hours and times of self-doubt. Thank you for coaching me on to the finish line! Many thanks to Rebecca Willford for guiding our project through production and to Sarah Fish for her dedication, patience, and competence as we completed the finishing touches.

To my tribe at home, I thank you for all the meals, errands, favors, listening ears, and understanding while I went into hibernation. Our bonds span houses, neighborhoods, cities, and states, as blood and non-blood kin. I can't imagine doing this without the love and support you provided every step of the way. My love to you for the joys and sorrows of each that we make our own. You take the concept of tribe to a divine level.

1

Journey to the Center of the Brain

It is not wrong to go back for that which you have forgotten.

African proverb

My ancestors are with me. For this, I am truly grateful. They have given me my genes and my DNA. They have also given me my social environment, culture, and family. Regardless of the hardship they may have sent my way or the obstacles I must now overcome, I stand in awe of the gifts they have given me—the human capacity to survive, problem-solve, and thrive. At center stage is the power of interpersonal process. First, we learn to survive as babies with the essential help from our family and caregiving network. Later, we contribute to the survival of the species as we form bonds outside these circles and reproduce. Those who do not reproduce contribute to survival of the species through creation of community and social supports (Small, 2011; Kropotkin, 1902).

This capacity for survival is a central element in the fascinating journey that leads to the center of the brain. Every day, millions of molecules pass through the brain like commuters in the train stations of New York City and Tokyo. These molecules carry bits of chemical and electrical information. Brain structures sift, file, and organize this information to help us survive. As humans, our capacity for complex, higher order thinking has added a myriad of detail to the tasks of survival. Paradoxically, our complexity can lead us on detours that actually distract us from good health and mental health.

Oops! In that last statement, my language separated the mind from the rest of the body. Excuse me while I overcome centuries of fragmented thinking! Whose idea was it to separate our physical and mental health? Our brain from the rest of our body? For centuries, this conceptual guillotine dominated the study of western medicine and health (Damasio, 1994, 2010). Now, thanks to modern technology, we can see our wholeness through computer screens and scanning machines. Our nervous system is an extensive highway that begins in our heads and runs to every extremity. The traffic flow on this highway can be as exciting as the best science-fiction thriller or a high-speed car chase. After all, much of its work is about threat and survival, the elements of good drama. Understanding the drama of this *whole body* activity is a road to greater success for helping professionals who want to bring more relief to more people.

In addition, whose idea was it to separate the person from their relationships during treatment? When the brain is transparent, we see the important links between the nervous system and all other systems, including interpersonal systems. This network forms an *ecology of survival* that reveals the biological impact of interpersonal process on brain development. With these discoveries, family therapists and their like-minded colleagues have cellular evidence as to why humans are wired for interpersonal process and why we crave relationships throughout our lives. Crave? Does that word sound too strong? What about Ed, the neighborhood hermit? He doesn't look like he craves relationships. Wait until Chapter 5. Van der Kolk (2003) has some interesting things to say about trauma attachment. Trust me—a knowledge of this craving makes couple and family therapy more relevant than ever, especially for people like Ed.

Ultimately, advances in neuroscience bring greater clarity as to why "mental health" is really "interpersonal health." Besides closing the gap between mind and body, the new breed of neuro-scientists shows us that relationships are the basis for survival or destruction at the molecular level. When family therapists engage more fully in a dialogue with neuroscience, there will be affirmations for current practices, discoveries for greater effectiveness, and new opportunities to advocate for the ecology of survival. For humans, their social ecology keeps them alive (Berkman & Syme, 1979; Berkman & Glass, 2000; Small, 2011).

During the dawn of the family therapy movement in America, Gregory Bateson (1979) began talking about the relational nature of the brain. This matches research that reveals how babies are wired to track interpersonal process from the moment of birth. Mind is social. The tabula rasa (blank slate) model of the human brain is becoming obsolete. For humans, survival is intensely interpersonal and relationships really are a matter of life and death. We have known for years that marital quality predicts a host of health problems including wound healing (Kiecolt-Glasier et al., 2005). Thus, as we go back and get some basic family therapy concepts, let us also see how to expand these concepts into a

> For humans, survival is intensely interpersonal and relationships really are a matter of life and death.

marriage with the latest brain research. Not only are my ancestors with me, I stand on the shoulders of those family therapists who came before me. Many were ahead of their time. Now, we have new tools to fully appreciate their visions.

STEPS TO AN ECOLOGY OF SURVIVAL

Along with the relational brain, Bateson taught family therapists about elements of communication. Clinicians of the day seized on distinguishing content from process. Emerging from a world in which psychoanalysis reigned supreme, they knew about the content of dreams and free associations. Thus, communication process seemed the neglected element in treatment and they set to work introducing the importance of relational dynamics as the focus of treatment. In their new world, it was no longer important to focus on <u>what</u> a couple was fighting about. The bigger issue, it seemed, was <u>how</u> they fought and whether they could learn new patterns. To this day, family therapy programs teach these concepts and help students focus on the process. As the field evolved, attention to content considered themes and issues that are central to an individual's phenomenology. For example, during conflict, each person's interpretation of the other would come forth as part of the ecology. Treatment became a dance of new meanings and behaviors. These levels of communication have been the focus of analysis for decades of family therapists.

As an extension of these fundamental concepts, I suggest we expand this paradigm to include the *substance*, or biology of relationships. Interviewing skills that ignore the primacy of significant relationships actually chop off an important part of the neural network, instead of mobilizing the whole. This contextual lobotomy limits therapeutic activity to the therapist's world. What the therapist sees and thinks is what you get, even in the most client-centered approaches. Instead, it is possible to embrace clients' rich interpersonal resources. In the person's biological world, images of relationships stream through the brain every second.

The behavioral part of these relationships became the foundation of early family therapy training (Hanna, 2007). Then, some of this perspective sank under the weight of mainstream psychosocial assessments in the workplace. Our practice environments too often privilege reason and cognition to the exclusion of affective, interpersonal, and physiological processes. Neuroscience teaches us that the latter are the central ingredients of individual development. In this book, we will discuss how content, process, <u>and</u> substance can become a triangle to guide intervention strategies and treatment plans.

It is no longer enough to merely talk about raw emotions like fear, shame, hurt, and humiliation. These byproducts from pivotal family interactions become part of a powerful flood of hormones, chemicals, and electricity tied up in neural networks. Regardless of how a person may appear, these networks may contain private, puzzling, triggers. The extreme case of these triggers involves the body's response to trauma. In Chapters 5, 6, and 7, we will describe detailed strategies to help couples and families overcome the effects of trauma. Ecologically, these emotional rivers may have been blocked from running their natural course through our bodies. Usually, they are held back by the floodgate of a "civilized" society that invites us into gendered and cultural scripts (e.g., big boys don't cry; girls should be everything "nice"). For many reasons, these pools of emotion may become stagnant breeding grounds of confusion or quicksand to be avoided at all costs.

And what of the costs? One example from the world of endocrinology suggests that tears are an important part of our body's natural system of balance. Stress hormones are secreted through our tears to avoid a toxic build-up of waste in our systems (Ishii et al., 2003). Because of this one bit of knowledge, I can gather intake information that helps me assess whether the body might be storing some debris that is part of an emotional dead end in which the body stays stuck in an extreme state of high or low activation. These states can unplug the prefrontal cortex (PFC), the rational part of the brain. Each pool or patch of quicksand is part of an interpersonal network in the brain. With an eye to the role of physiology in relationships, later chapters will discuss interventions that address both dimensions. There, practitioners will learn how to address these priorities through brain-friendly strategies for couple and family therapy. Embedded in these powerful principles are keys to facilitating an energized healing process, self-regulation, and ultimately, secure attachments.

On a personal note, over the past ten years, my study of neuroscience has had some surprising effects. Mysteriously, I pay more attention to cave men, babies, and animals. Neuroscientists are in love with them. They talk about them all the time. Metaphors related to these noble groups pop into my mind during clinical sessions. Thankfully, most of my clients are dog lovers. Other metaphors spin off of these as I spend more time thinking about basic survival processes. My brain has become contaminated with the lofty ideas of E.O. Wilson (1998), a Harvard scientist who hopes that, someday, we will find a unifying theory to connect all disciplines into one grand scheme. I try to wrap my mind around this hope

> Mysteriously, I pay more attention to cave men, babies, and animals. Neuroscientists are in love with them. They talk about them all the time.

and sometimes a parallel between social process and brain process will leap out of my head. When you find one of these, you may think it a leap of insanity, rather than faith. Oh well. Please bear with me. I leave them for you to explore as a way to engage your right brain.

So, all aboard! This book is a journey that will uncover the center of the brain, where relationship quality is a dominant force. Ironically, many brain-friendly practitioners are not trained to be "relationship friendly." They are often psychoanalytically trained. Thus, neuroscience needs family therapists and family therapists need neuroscience. To begin, we can gain insight into brain basics with a bit of time travel to distant lands where the human race began its quest for survival. Let us invoke the spirit of the ancestors and go back to get what we may have forgotten. The world of the healing arts is full of monumental discoveries that have changed the way industrialized cultures view their bodies, their health, and their mortality. As we shift into *whole body* awareness, we will see how connections between head, torso, and extremities relate to health and illness. On this journey, we will see how the western world got caught up in studying each part of the body at the expense of the whole, and how the eastern world seemed to err in the opposite direction. We can learn from their mistakes. Taking the strengths from each side of the globe puts us squarely in the realm of neuroscience today. As we move through time, you may conduct a self-assessment as to what traditional ideas have been most influential in your thinking. As we walk the walk of those who have gone before us, we can decide whether to tinker, brainstorm, or even overhaul our approach to couple and family therapy.

IN THE BEGINNING

For early humans, the drama of survival involved more than just food, clothing, and shelter. Disease and illness plagued us from the beginning. Over many centuries, our major civilizations addressed disease in ways that acknowledged balance, life force (spirit), and energy. Ancient artifacts contain records of shamans and religious ceremonies as a way to bring about healing. These involved family and community. The process often included herbal treatments and various potions. For western, Hindu, and Chinese traditions, ancient practices were rooted in spiritual and supernatural beliefs of the time. Disease was a curse from one or more gods. The following are a few highlights that illustrate how western knowledge of human anatomy and physiology evolved over the past 5,000 years.

ca. 4000 B.C.   Ancient Sumerians reported the mind-altering effects of the poppy plant.
ca. 2700 B.C.   In China, Shen Nung developed acupuncture.
ca. 1600 B.C.   Egyptians recorded one of the earliest dissections.
ca. 1300 B.C.   Hindus began developing their Ayurvedic system of medicine.

As the limitations of these practices emerged, the human capacity to envision how life could be led to a striving for greater understanding of the physical. The western world pursued study of the body and its levels of organization. This led to the following developments:

ca. 400 B.C.	In Greece, Hippocrates developed theories about how illnesses came from natural causes in the environment, rather than as a punishment from the gods. His new approach took center stage in the west. He believed the brain was the center of our intellect.
ca. 387 B.C.	Plato believed the brain was the center of our thoughts.
ca. 335 B.C.	Aristotle believed the heart was the center of our thoughts.
ca. 150 A.D.	In Rome, Galen, a prolific scientist, surgeon, and philosopher, made numerous contributions to our knowledge of anatomy. His dissections led to a wealth of information about circulatory, respiratory, and nervous systems.
ca. 400 A.D.	During the decline of the Roman Empire, Galen's work was lost. However, earlier translations of his work into Arabic led to major influences upon Islamic medicine. These allowed his work to resurface in the western world.

For the next 1,000 years, scientists dissected, named, and studied each nerve, muscle, and organ in the human body. Medical practitioners began to develop a certain status within many societies. Then, a medical calamity occurred. Picture a world in which 30–60 percent of the entire population dies in a few short years. This isn't just one or two of your neighbors, but nearly half of everyone on your street. Sounds like science fiction, but it was the Black Death of the Middle Ages (1348–50 A.D.). Historians agree that this plague affected every sector of society and led many to question what certainties in medicine they had taken for granted. Western medicine continued to study anatomy and physiology, but we were besieged by pandemics across the continents of

Europe, the Middle East, and Asia. Perhaps it was this legacy of loss that heightened the value of technology when Janssen invented the microscope in 1590 A.D., setting the stage for the advent of germ theory.

Prior to these developments, our view of the body was limited to what we could see with our naked eye. This area of study, *gross anatomy*, was no match for the plagues of the Middle Ages. By the time the famous philosopher René Descartes (1596–1650 A.D.) was musing over distinctions between the substance of mind and the substance of body, others were marching headlong into technologies that made the body more transparent. However, Descartes left his mark for hundreds of years through a deal he struck with the Church. They would let him deal with the body as long as he stayed out of the mind. With the Church safeguarding all things mindful, Descartes died just a few years before van Leeuwenhoek described cells and bacteria under the microscope in 1675 A.D.

As the western world evolved into the Renaissance, it must have been exhilarating to witness modern technologies that could put an end to the tragic and monumental losses of the Black Death. The study of the brain, with its diverse structures and functions, also accelerated as an extension of these discoveries. Gross anatomy gave way to many subdivisions such as regional anatomy, cell physiology, neurophysiology, and immunology. As these discoveries brought tremendous relief from the trauma of disease, it is easy to see how the west became captivated by these rapid advances in epidemiology. Scientists opened up a universe of microbiological worlds that were previously invisible. Now, the body was a collection of atoms, molecules, and cells, adding another layer of knowledge to the world of tissues, organs, and systems.

Meanwhile, in the east, the study of the body and disease took some similar and some different directions. Ancient Chinese documents describe medical records used by shamans, who would offer prayers to ancestors and appeal to the graces of the gods. However, by 256 B.C., practitioners broke away from the realm of the supernatural and began to specialize as physicians, surgeons, and dieticians. There was a focus on natural elements and how they related to the body, such as air, wood, fire, earth, and water. The well-known concept of yin and yang conceived of opposing forces that brought about balance within the body. Current practices of acupuncture apply these concepts of balance.

The medical system in India, termed Ayurveda, developed during 1400–1200 B.C. Evolving from practitioners who were both priest and physician, ancient texts from this tradition are among the oldest in the world. In these traditions, there is a focus on balancing body, mind, and spirit (Patwardhan, 2008). The use of herbs, diet, massage, breathing exercises, lifestyle changes, and a striving for harmony in the universe are typical of treatment strategies using Ayurvedic medicine. Records from India reveal that practitioners from Greece, Egypt, and China visited India to learn this approach and took this knowledge back to their

> When we examine emotion through the lens of basic energy, balance becomes an imperative.

own cultures. Underlying these approaches is the belief that humans and their external environment are connected through invisible forces. This premise is also a central tenet of Chinese medicine (Hong, 2004). In Chapter 2, we will see how the physiology of emotion relates to the quest for balance within and between the elements of nature. When we examine emotion through the lens of basic energy, balance becomes an imperative.

The Chinese were also developing their own technologies. Some credit the Chinese with the first known example of inoculation for smallpox in the sixteenth century (Buck, 2003). Medical training flourished into specialties such as internal medicine, pediatrics, and ophthamology. However, in the early eighteenth century, advances came to a halt as political regimes began to discourage new knowledge. This brought transitions that led to a mix of traditional and professional Chinese medicine. Over the next centuries, a lack of rigor and creativity resulted in poorly trained practitioners, and a decline in the previous progress (Hong, 2004).

By the nineteenth century, Christian missionaries introduced the advances of western medicine and the government made attempts to adopt these new approaches, once the public health benefits became obvious. India and China also suffered tremendous losses from the Black Death. However, there was great public opposition to western ways, as traditional medicine brought satisfactory results in many cases, and even superior results for those conditions that western medicine could not cure (Hoizey & Hoizey, 1993). Modern-day China reports that traditional practices still account for approximately 40 percent of all medical care. In India, 60 percent report a continued use of Ayurvedic medicine. These traditional approaches maintain a focus on some elements that used to be considered abstract and elusive by western standards. However, their focus on aspects of spirit, life force, and energy resonate with people around the world, including many in the west. Because of this resonance, there is now an Office of Complementary and Alternative Medicine in the U.S. National Institutes of Health that conducts research to explore the benefits of these practices.

As these traditional practices continue around the world, studies in neuroscience are now revealing the vast connections between body, mind, and spirit. The fact that our nervous system is electrical and chemical in nature brings some of our knowledge full circle with ancient health theories about the role of energy in the body. These remind us that there are primitive and complex

> **The fact that our nervous system is electrical and chemical in nature brings some of our knowledge full circle with ancient health theories about the role of energy in the body.**

operations that work together for our survival. The universe is full of invisible electrical and chemical forces that affect our health in tangible, observable ways.

These chemical forces took center stage in research at Georgetown University. Scientists made Nobel-prize-winning discoveries about neurotransmitters and neuropeptides. As chemical messengers, they flow through our bodies with information about emotion. These signals have selective effects on our bodies, from the immune system to our state of mind. Candace Pert (1997) discovered opiate receptors that are like magnets contained in numerous cells of the body. These magnets attract chemical messengers who are sent on their way when we experience an emotion. When these receptors find the substances they are created to attract, the substance "binds" to the cell. Pert aptly refers to this as "sex on a molecular level," and her research has revolutionized what we know about emotions and health (Pert, 1997, p. 23). Chapter 2 reviews information about messenger molecules that are relevant to our work with couples and families. Chapter 5 describes how these relate to the physiology of trauma. Chapter 6 will apply this knowledge and address the neurophysiology of marriage as we are coming to understand it.

State-of-the-art research now includes a new field, *psychoneuroimmunology (PNI)*. It is the study of links between nervous system, endocrine system, emotions, and health. Within a whole body perspective, health now includes the biological, emotional, and interpersonal. PNI examines marriage and health, social support and health, stress and health, attachment and health, etc. (Ader, 2007; Lincoln et al. 2010; Mays et al., 1996). Alongside these advances, cultures of the world were coming to terms with the realm of consciousness that enables *Homo sapiens* to engage in complex thought. More than any others in the animal kingdom, humans have a capacity for complex thought that can be a blessing and a curse. As neuroscience continues to influence many branches of science, we will see psychotherapy, as we have known it, apply basic ideas from east and west that are whole body in scope and integrative in practice.

The final stop on our journey allows us to revisit the story of mental health treatment through the ages. Here, the intent is for practitioners to step back and see themselves as part of a larger drama in the history of the world. The transition that went beyond gross anatomy into the study of "invisible" cells sets the stage for psychotherapists to include physiology in their narratives of relationships, meaning, and emotion. As these pivotal discoveries change our narratives about symptoms and behavior, they become as historic in our day as the invention of the microscope.

FROM RELIGION TO MEDICINE TO PSYCHOTHERAPY TO FAMILY THERAPY

A number of historians argue that the ancient social stigmas of mental illness have never changed. First, people were thought to be possessed by demons. In Greece, as Hippocrates argued for the physiological basis of mental disturbances, treatment strategies became more physical, from drilling into the brain, to diets that might bring about balance of basic body fluids such as blood, phlegm, bile, and black bile. In most countries, the stigma, isolation, punishment, and shame that attended those with mental illness continues to the present day. In America, there were the Salem Witch trials that invoked explanations of demonic possession. In Europe, hysteria was thought to be caused by a "wandering uterus." Eastern cultures would hide the troubled person, avoiding dishonor to the family. Patterns of institutionalization and deinstitutionalization suggest that societies around the world have been largely unsuccessful in finding satisfactory services for those with disturbing behaviors (Foerschner, 2010).

It is easy to see how Sigmund Freud became a lighthouse in this sea of darkness when he introduced his "talking cure" in the nineteenth century, with a focus on dreams, free associations, and the unconscious. The complexity of mental process that Freud outlined in his psychoanalytic theory brought the concept of mental health to a new level of enlightenment. Instead of hysterectomies, women could hope for relief from their emotional symptoms through psychoanalysis. The age of somatic medicine would now make room for more abstract explorations of the mind. Concurrently, other physicians explored biological solutions to mental disease. These efforts lead to lobotomies, psychoactive drugs, and electroconvulsive shock therapy.

In the wake of these explorations, the field of family therapy developed throughout the 1960s as an interpersonal response to mental illness, marital discord, family disruption, and child behavior problems (Hanna, 2007). It was a time when disciples of Freud practiced lifetime psychoanalysis, and psychiatric facilities found relief for their patients with the evolution of pharmaceuticals. Mavericks from these existing professions turned their attention toward the primacy of the family. They changed the emotional ecology of family relationships. Many family therapists have no idea that Salvador Minuchin was ahead of his time when he conducted an early study with diabetic children, drawing their blood as they observed parents' discussions behind a one-way mirror. What he found from measuring levels of blood chemicals convinced him that family process affected children's biology. He continued to explore anorexia in similar ways (Minuchin et al., 1978). These studies would be mainstream PNI by today's standards. Researchers in family intervention have made structural family therapy one of the most researched of all family therapy approaches. From heroin addiction to conduct disorder, changing the family's ecology improves a number of health problems (Stanton & Todd, 1982; Henggeler et al., 1999; Liddle, 2000; Sprenkle, 2002).

Following Minuchin's discoveries, an array of clinicians developed a subspecialty in medical family therapy (McDaniel et al., 1992; Rolland, 1994; Hanna, 1997). Here, there was attention to the family as a resource in the treatment of physical ailments, from asthma to heart disease. If not a resource, the family had genetic history that was important. At the very least, family might be a potential hindrance to successful treatment. In this case, intervention could lessen obstacles and challenges to a patient's recovery. A great deal of this work was a collaboration with family medicine physicians. This medical specialty requires education in the social and behavioral aspects of illnesses. Engel (1977) coined the phrase *biopsychosocial*, referring to the nature of an ideal assessment by a family practitioner. Currently, family therapists work at the cutting edge with pituitary disorders (Laws et al., 2013), cardiac diseases, and many chronic illnesses (McDaniel et al., 1997).

Thus, for the average medical family therapist, biology has been a familiar component of clinical cases for over thirty years. However, for mainstream practitioners, many settings did not provide the opportunity to explore biology, aside from the use of drugs. When Siegel (1999) published his first edition of *The Developing Mind: The Neurobiology of Interpersonal Experience*, many family therapists took note of the validation his work provided for our field. As a child psychiatrist, he was interested in early attachment experiences and research findings about optimal brain development. He reviewed numerous studies in attachment, memory, cognition, and emotion. The outcome was a seminal work summarizing brain development and the impact of interpersonal process (Siegel, 1999, 2012). His focus on *attachment theory* research does not require that a practitioner leave a cherished family therapy theory behind. Instead, it becomes a guide to understand the content, process, and substance that will refine and improve all family-centered work. Chapter 3 summarizes the vast ocean of neurobiological research on attachment theory.

A LOVE STORY: FAMILY THERAPY, ATTACHMENT THEORY, AND NEUROSCIENCE

Playing "hard to get," U.S. family therapists were initially hesitant to embrace the British influence of John Bowlby's seminal theory of attachment and loss (Bowlby, 1969). Although he explored family environment and its affects on child well-being, the innovators in family systems interventions sought an identity separate from psychoanalysts. However, the past two decades have closed this gap. Attachment theory, well known for its influence upon the practice of Emotionally focused couples therapy (EFT), provides a map for human survival that resonates with findings of neuroscience (Johnson, 2002; Siegel, 1999).

It was only a matter of time before American family therapists would make their peace with John Bowlby. After all, one of the first family therapy sessions on record was that of Bowlby with parents of a young patient (Bowlby, 1949). Though their language was full of strategy and directives, pioneering family therapists sought secure attachment for their clients. It was called *differentiation* or *permeable boundaries*, but on closer examination, these concepts represented interpersonal processes that were the seeds of attachment (Minuchin, 1974; Bowen, 1978). Especially when it came to microprocesses of the therapist-client relationship, family therapists rebelled against traditional, removed, diagnostic interviews. They called it *joining* or *engaging*, but regardless of the name, verbal and nonverbal behaviors centered on resonance and attunement (Satir, 1972). Third and fourth generation family therapists seek attunement with their families. They want safe havens for their clients. In addition, the focus on strategy and intervention evolved to include the importance of meaning and experience in the construction of a client's reality (White &

Epston, 1991; Hargrave & Pfitzer, 2003). For decades, family therapists promoted an array of therapeutic approaches that honor the world views of clients and facilitate interpersonal transformations in their lives. Chapter 4 describes some of these basic elements with examples of how they attune to the brain.

By the advent of the twenty-first century, family therapists became integrated into many mental health treatment settings. State licensing agencies in the U.S. recognized family therapists as legitimate providers. At the same time, Freud's work on the mind and the widespread use of psychoactive drugs would separately address mind and body, but without any true integration of the two. As a bridge between many realms of thought, neuroscience provides new knowledge at the interface of mind, body, and relationships (Sluzki, 2007). We now have neurological evidence as to why family system interventions are so important. Family therapists and their like-minded colleagues stand at the doorway of opportunity as rich biological data speaks to the power of significant relationships. In some respects, modern day psychotherapy has had its own form of "gross anatomy." Clinicians construct a world from data that is observable or reportable in the therapy session. While various theories attempt to make sense of the behavioral, few have biological evidence to support them. However, with new technologies, this may change.

In the world of couples' research, we have already seen how Gottman and colleagues conducted physiological monitoring with couples who reported violence. As they discussed an area of disagreement, heart rate variability and other signs of emotional activation provided a picture of biology (Gottman et al., 1995). Developmental scientists can view attachment happening in real time. A baby's head lights up on a computer monitor when hearing a human voice (Lloyd-Fox et al., 2012). That makes a powerful statement about the substance of relationships. What would happen if a client's brain was attached to a computer monitor and the family therapist could watch patterns of neuronal firing during a therapy session? Such a scene is not far away.

Already, researchers can detect the neural correlates of empathy (Preston et al., 2007).

To prepare for these amazing advances, this book makes the brain transparent through diagrams, maps, and metaphors. If we keep these invisible processes in mind, the educated practitioner can achieve a new level of empathy—*biological empathy*. As we emerge from the world of gross anatomy and fragmentation, we now come full circle. The wisdom of the ancients existed in a world that sensed energy, biology, and spirit. The integration of all three allows us to be fully present with our clients. New information on the conscious/unconscious mind can help us individualize treatment. Family and social network can play an even greater role in brain development. Sigmund Freud would not be surprised, Carl Rogers would be pleased, and Salvador Minuchin is cheering us on (Minuchin, 1987).

> If we keep these invisible processes in mind, the educated practitioner can achieve a new level of empathy—*biological empathy.*

GETTING STARTED: THE CLINICIAN'S JOURNEY

Our time travel has brought us to the present. We have the best of east and west. We see how intelligent and creative people used their complex brains to envision how our health treatment *could* be. When family therapists introduced the language of cybernetics, systems, part/whole, interactions, and sequences, who knew we would return to the root world of this language—biology? In addition to this irony, who knew that neuroscience could make a convincing case for much of the "art" of couple and family therapy?

Now, take a few moments and think about your own journey. What is your story of professional development? Did you begin with some basic traditions and expand on those as more information came available? How did you get here? What traditions do you cherish and bring with you? What ideas have you left behind? Who helped you along your journey? Did you have setbacks? How did you overcome them? We each have a history that mirrors the history of the world. Humans fearlessly engage in trial and error, vision and setback. We are resilient. We are compassionate. In fact, historians illustrate how the twenty-first century is the least violent of any in recorded history (Pinker, 2011). We dream, and we follow our dreams. What is your place in history? Hopefully, this book will help you get there. The following chapters explore many clinical possibilities in detail. It's time for travel into the future. Before entering any foreign country, it is helpful to learn some basic language and follow a few travel guidelines, based on what we've learned from history. We're almost there . . .

MASTERING THE LANGUAGE: NEURO THIS AND NEURO THAT

The explosion of interdisciplinary neuroscience research has produced a list of terms that cross many disciplines. These scientists are skilled at making up names that are not in any dictionary. My opinion is that they are trained to be as precise as possible and, accordingly, carefully capture the smallest distinctions. As they communicate with each other, they may put the rest of us to sleep, especially with the exotic names and acronyms of chemicals. To balance this, the style of prose in this book may seem elementary to some. It stems from the intent to create client-friendly narratives that will streamline the translational process for practitioners. An essential part of a practitioner's job is to make sense to the lay person. Throughout this book, the use of formal scientific terms is joined with lay language and metaphors that might be more client-friendly. Hence, in the title, just plain "neuroscience" suggests the broadest realm of brain research.

However, understanding professional domains is also important for clinicians who hope to move beyond the basics. The following is a topic-centered glossary that maps a few concepts, disciplines, and practices within the broad field of neuroscience. Then, the end of Chapter 2 will provide a glossary of basic anatomy, chemistry, and physiology. Chapter 8 will summarize clinical activities and interventions that appear throughout the book.

The Neuros

Affective neuroscience. The study of brain process related to emotion. Some scientists now use the term affect rather than emotion. *Affect* refers to basic states in the body, such as fear and anger, that are necessary for survival. *Emotion* refers to contextual responses that may be a combination of affective states.

Cognitive neuroscience. The study of how mental processes develop in the brain. This may include information-processing models, linguistics, cognition, the impact of abnormalities, memory, learning, and problem-solving.

Interpersonal neurobiology. A term coined by Daniel Siegel (1999), that he uses to name his interdisciplinary study of brain processes that acknowledge the central influence of human relationships upon brain development, health, and healing. He draws from anthropology, sociology, and psychology.

Neuroanatomy. The study of all the parts of the brain.

Neurobiology. The study of the living brain.

Neurochemistry. The study of all brain chemicals and their properties.

Neuroendocrinology. The study of interactions between the brain, glands, and hormones including what they do and how they do it.

Neurophysiology. Learning how all the parts work together. *Physiology* requires a knowledge of anatomy, including all the chemical substances that make their unique contributions to the ecology of survival.

Neuroscience. The most generic of all. This is any research and study about the brain and nervous system, including functions, injuries, diseases, interpersonal processes, and human development.

Psychoneuroimmunology (PNI). The study of links between nervous system, endocrine system, emotions, and health.

Social neuroscience. The study of how biological process and social process are related. A number of researchers examine relationships between theories of social behavior and hormones, neuropeptides, and brain regions.

Other "Ologies"

Cultural anthropology. The study of cultural, economic, and political diversity in the world.

Developmental psychopathology. The study of processes leading to child and adult symptoms, behaviors, and mental health conditions.

Evolutionary biology. The study of how life has evolved on the earth. There are many subspecialties within this, such as the study of genes, microbiology, prehistoric life, and environmental ecologies.

Medical anthropology. A subspecialty of cultural anthropology that addresses health-related practices in cultures, biological adaptations of groups for survival, and the social ecology of health (McElroy & Townsend, 1989).

Social endocrinology. In-depth study of hormones, behavior, and social environment. Most of this is about testosterone, oxytocin, and estrogen in both genders.

Practices

Family therapy. A generic term for accepted mental health practice that highlights 1) the profession and practice of licensed marriage and family therapists (MFTs), 2) the emphasis on family-focused psychotherapeutic processes that address couple interaction, parent-child interactions, sibling dynamics, and child well-being, and 3) family psychoeducation that involves family and social network in the treatment process.

Multifamily Psychoeducation Groups (MFGs). The term used in this book for the specific form of family psycho-education developed by McFarlane (2002). In federal documents, the approach is also called Multifamily Psychoeducational Groups (MFPGs) and Family Psychoeducation (FPE).

Couple therapy. A generic term for treatments involving marital and dyadic conflict, domestic violence, sexual dissatisfaction, attachment injuries, courtship, mate selection, and divorce adjustment.

Mindfulness. The practice of focusing the conscious mind on various elements related to healing. Like a mental laser beam, the intense focus of the mind on an image, scene, or part of the body stimulates physiological change. A cluster of practices use this principle, such as felt sense exercises, meditation, guided imagery, and focusing. Research tracks the effects of these activities and documents changes within the body and comparisons between groups.

Somatic Experiencing®(SE). An approach to trauma healing developed by Peter Levine (1997, 2010) that uses felt sense exercises, medical biophysics, and polyvagal theory to use the body's own energy in healing trauma.

Concepts

Biosocial. A term used by McFarlane (2002) to describe the circular interplay of biology and family/social process in the treatment of schizophrenia.

Ecology of survival. A term in this book for the content, process, and substance of interpersonal interventions as they relate to the basic processes of survival.

Health disparity. A condition or disease that occurs in certain groups at a disproportionate rate. For example, Native Americans experience post-traumatic stress syndrome at twice the rate of the general population. In California, young African American males receive a diagnosis of conduct disorder more often than other groups.

Whole body. A term in this book that replaces mind/body, body/mind, etc. from other sources. The head, torso, and extremities are regions of the body that continually interact, striving for balance and health.

TRAVEL GUIDELINES FOR THE PRACTITIONER

1. **Learn from history, your own and others'.** The "big picture" perspective of history teaches us that even when we think we know something, developments somewhere in the world are about to expand on what we think. During the horrible black death of the Middle Ages, the average citizen couldn't see that small steps were adding up to monumental discoveries. Remember how far we've come compared to how it used to be.

2. **Never say "never."** The language of possibility is uniquely human. Your own history is already a combination of surprises and serendipity. Trust that these will always happen. The greatest advances in the history of the world have come from someone asking, "What is possible?" "How can we do it better?"

3. **Basics first.** The outer, progressive, rational part of our brain comprehends the modern world, with its video graphics, iPhones, and smart cars. However, it will not function well if our basic needs are neglected. The inner,

middle, basic part of our brain thinks that we are still cave men and women. Threat is threat. Under stress, it doesn't know the difference between a lion chasing us, or the stock market falling. It doesn't compute the difference between ancient and modern. Joy is joy, regardless of whether it is addiction or love. Stress hormones and those of joy flow accordingly. Mammals and babies teach us about these basics and explain the meaning of our behavior in light of basic process. So-called irrational behavior in the eye of some beholders makes perfect sense through the lens of protection and survival. This is particularly true of people burdened by trauma reactions.

4. **Integrate.** Content, process, and substance cover a wide range of concepts, strategies, and interactions. Content can include survival goals that range from overcoming disease to gaining a secure attachment. Process is social and interpersonal process related to achieving survival goals. Substance is what happens to the body and in the body during threat, survival, and problem-solving. All human experience has a physiological component. A thought is a physiological event. Affect is a physiological state. Social process provides the most complex stimulation for the brain. Recent research suggests that a higher rate of social interaction lower the risks of disability in older people (James et al., 2011).

5. **Honor the invisible.** The five senses are important to scan the environment and make immediate sense of our conscious world. Beneath these is a survival drama that includes unconscious and subconscious capacities in the body. These are different than the psychoanalytic use of the words. Here, unconscious processes do not require conscious effort. They include breathing, blood flow, hormone secretion, and memory storage. Subconscious processes include routine actions that we do without thinking, but are accessible to awareness when the need

arises. They include affect, meaning, and memory retrieval. Neuroscientists have technical debates about terms related to consciousness. However, here, they simply denote familiar distinctions of human awareness. The best example is love. Love is a combination of the content, process, and substance between people. Some aspects of it are conscious and some are outside our awareness, such as the neurophysiology of love. However, because of the physiology of memory, we know it when we feel it and we resonate with its importance in our lives (Hargrave & Pfitzer, 2011).

Now, with language and travel tips close at hand, we're ready to enter the world of the brain. If the details become tedious, just skip over them. You can always go back later and use them as a reference. Instead, examine the miracles of life from all angles and then remember to return to the big picture: What is your place in history?

2

A Miraculous Biological Drama

What is important is invisible to the eye.

Saint-Exupréy, 2000

In Chapter 1, we see that humans have spent thousands of years in search of more answers about the brain and what it means to be human. So, what is the brain? In typical family therapy fashion, it depends on who you ask. Gross anatomy reveals lobes and functions of the brain (see Figure 2.1). With white matter the consistency of soft butter, these lobes find strong protection under a series of tough membranes (dura), fluids that lubricate and cushion, and finally, the hard shell of the skull. This is what we knew 100 years ago. Then came the electrical brain, the chemical brain, the cognitive brain, the emotional brain, the social brain, and the psychosomatic brain. Historically, *psychosomatic* referred to a whole body, multidirectional network of information. Turns out, the brain is one player in a much larger drama. Pert (1997) discovered that the brain was "a bag of hormones" (p. 139). Endocrinologists now realize that the brain is like a giant gland, transmitting two-way messages to distant lands in the form of hormones. In fact, Chopra (1997) refers to the *mobile* brain as our ability to have consciousness throughout the body, not in the head alone. This is how *mindfulness* and *felt sense* exercises have become increasingly relevant. A later section describes these

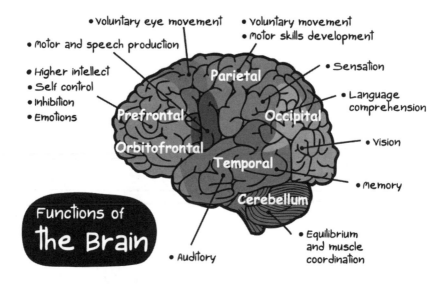

Figure 2.1 Lobes and functions of the brain.

skills. Each of these "brains" will become transparent as we learn the story of survival that grows from a single, fertilized egg.

This drama is an epic journey that has a cast of characters in the millions—cells, chemicals, and bundles of *neurons* (brain cells) take on different shapes, sizes, and personalities. There are also lobes, glands, organs, and systems. A special relationship between characters is an *axis*, like the *hypothalamus-pituitary-adrenal axis (HPA-axis)*. This axis explains how an organ like the liver, far away from the brain, can still be affected by emotion. Our travels take us to neurons who live everywhere, not just in the brain and spinal chord. There are thousands of them in the heart and digestive tract (*gut*). Instead of the old phrase, "It's all in your head," we now say, "It's all through your body."

Meanwhile, back at the ranch, the study of *right and left hemispheres* in the head has moved into the deep relationships between these two complementary spheres. Attachment theorists are interested in the right brain and depression researchers wonder why the left brain is more activated during sadness. They also report that when there is dominant side injury, depression is more prevalent. When there is a non-dominant side injury, manic behavior is more frequent (Sweeney, 2009). Although there is increasing discussion about variations in stereotypic descriptions of each hemisphere, most scholars still recognize these characteristics:

Right or non-dominant hemispheres will more likely 1) decode nonverbal communication, 2) distinguish nuances of spoken language, 3) express emotion and recognize it in others, 4) manifest spatial cognition, and 5) integrate details.

Left or dominant hemispheres will more likely 1) process verbal communication, 2) attend to literal language, 3) analyze details, 4) perceive categories, 5) activate motor responses and approach behaviors (Trevarthen, 1996).

There are also some crossovers. In one study, sadness was associated with increased activity in the left amygdala and right PFC; decreased activity in right amygdala and left PFC (Sweeney, 2009).

MacNeilage, Rogers & Vallortigara (2009) suggest that prehistorically, the left hemisphere may have focused on controlling established patterns and the right specialized in detecting unexpected stimuli. Thus, speech and right-handedness may have satisfied the body's need for stable behavior. Then, the operations of face recognition and perceiving spatial relations might have evolved to sense predators quickly. Their theory is consistent with connections observed between the amygdala and right hemisphere.

Research continues to explore the integration of eastern and western thinking about the whole body. Yoga breathing techniques involving nasal dominance as an indicator of cerebral dominance can distinguish performance in various states of mind. A number of studies explore the effects of shifting nasal breathing to favor one hemisphere over the other. When the left nostril is more open, right hemisphere is more dominant, etc. One study shows that spatial task performance was significantly enhanced during left nostril breathing in both males and females. Verbal task performance trended toward right nostril breathing

(Jella and Shannahoff-Khalsa, 1993). Block, Arnott, Quigley, and Lynch (1989) found that males performed better on verbal tasks during left-nostril breathing and on spatial tasks during right-nostril breathing.

Rossi (2002) routinely uses activities with clients that help them shift their dominant nostril during a critical time. With a man who had been a chronic alcoholic, Rossi helped him track his cerebral dominance during times when he had the strongest urges to drink. He found after work, his right nostril was more open, suggesting that he was still in left-brain mode and presumably wanted the drink to relax. Shifting dominance with this technique has been used for years within the yoga community. Now, it is linked to patterns of EEGs, math performance, and interpersonal conflict. Clinicians help clients gain balance between the sympathetic nervous system (that which excites) and parasympathic nervous system (that which calms). They regulate all basic functions and organs in the viscera.

Take a moment now and breathe nasally. Which nostril is more open? Does it resonate with what you sense as your mental state right now? In reading this chapter, some might want to read it with the left brain and some with the right. By manually blocking the opposite nostril or lying down on the opposite side, dominance will usually shift in a few minutes. If an individual becomes anxious about grasping all the scientific details, the right hemisphere might overview the big picture and leave the comprehension of all the parts until later. If there is a pressing need to grasp the details and understand each part, the left might help to categorize and analyze the parts now.

The story that is told about our hemispheres is still developing. Since many brain structures have a right and left part, studies are only recently revealing the many combinations of regional activity that light up in brain scans. As we delve into the microbiology of it all, we can think of our hemispheres as being the stage upon which the plot develops. As each scene develops, there is a rearranging of the set to match the context. Now, the curtain goes up on the smallest parts of the drama.

THE CAST: WHO THEY ARE AND WHAT THEY DO

Our invisible transportation and communication system is electrical and chemical. These properties enable scanning machines and blood tests to help us "see" our microbiological parts. Neural networks begin with basic relationships between cells and grow into circuits, layers, organs, and systems. Communication between these levels results in our memories, consciousness, and appraisals of experience related to survival.

CELLS WITH SUBSTANCE: OUR ELECTROCHEMICAL BUILDING BLOCKS

Figure 2.2 illustrates generic neuronal relationships. What would we do without electron microscopes that magnify this activity 15,000 times? At this level, information flow is one-way. A cell receives a chemical through *dendrites* or the cell wall. This produces an electrical charge, or *firing*. Like the pony express, the *cell body* turns on or off and passes the charge to the *axon*, whose

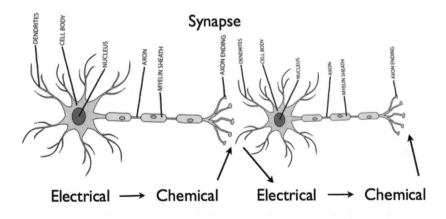

Figure 2.2 Neurons.

branches transmit chemical messages to neighboring dendrites on the next neuron. The dense branches on dendrites and axons create thousands of possible chain reactions for each cell. While we lose numbers of neurons from a peak in embryo, it is the number and density of connections that affects our abilities throughout life. This growth process in embryo contains lessons that reach far beyond the womb. As a metaphor about the ecology of survival, we pause to consider how social systems have a knack for behaving just like biological systems deep in our brain.

THE GREAT MIGRATION: STORIES OF CELLS AND CIRCUITS IN ALL OF LIFE

The brain begins with small cells, like footprints that gradually become a dirt road. With more use and traffic, it acquires gravel, then pavement, signs, and signals as it traverses more populated territory where repetition and activity is ongoing. In embryo, growth and differentiation begin as DNA directs cell division for undeveloped neurons, or *neuroblasts* who have neither axons or dendrites. These are simple in form. First, the neural plate is a sheet of cells no bigger than the tip of a match. For several weeks, they grow through cell division at a rate of 250,000 per minute! What does an embryo do with all these neuroblasts? The eventual inventory of cells will die off by half over nine months of gestation. This process of *pruning* allows energy and nutrients to benefit the strongest and most important connections, while weaker and irrelevant connections disappear. What happens next becomes an amazing process of cellular migration that has parallel processes in our social environment.

The term "Great Migration" is used throughout life sciences in a number of ways. Perhaps it is because all cycles of life and survival involve looking for proper resources. In the spirit of E.O. Wilson's (1998) invitation to join different knowledges together, a comparison of neuronal migration with other forms of migration suggests that social and biological processes inform each other and provide a way to understand each more deeply than we could by observing one alone. One example is the majestic migration of wildlife in Africa as they sense a change in pastures and water. Following their instincts above all odds, they triumph over lurking crocodiles and lightning-fast predators. They arrive at a new location with new resources that support life until the next dry season prompts a new cycle.

Neuroblasts participate in a migration that leads them to a final destination where resources exist for them to grow dendrites and axons. Their first environment lacks resources and they must travel through the chaotic webs of proliferating cells and circuits to find their ultimate destination. They travel as tiny specks across the great expanse of the embryo in heavy traffic as the neural plate kicks out trillions of new cells like a popcorn machine. Although the traffic can be intimidating, before they can specialize and make their contribution to the organism, they must make this journey.

Another Great Migration occurred in American history (ca. 1915–1970) when six million African-Americans made heroic transitions from the hostile challenges of the rural south to the unknown promises of industrialization in the north, Midwest, and west. After slavery, lacking important resources, many migrated to new locations in which there was the possibility to put down roots and fully develop their potential. Those who stayed behind specialized in their own way, in their own loca-tions. Those who migrated found new experiences and environ-ments that fostered their specialization and gave them new perspectives. Along the way, toxic environments made their migration especially difficult (racism, housing shortages, poor working conditions, etc.). However, the challenges of African Americans did not prevent them from making important contri-butions to a more diverse, complex, American society. Similarly, in biology, diversity and complexity is what makes us *Homo sapiens* (wise man).

Neuroblasts begin during the confusion of explosive cell division. Some stay close to home and become part of the brain, with its lobes, glands, structures, and sensory systems. Others are crowded out and travel a great distance to become mature neurons in the far reaches of the body, like the spinal chord and vagus nerve. Only after arriving at a specific location do they grow dendrites and axons to communicate with each other. Figure 2.2 illustrates mature neurons and their relationship to each other. In essence, a "community" develops that becomes a central communication system for survival, processing each function such as vision, emotion, language, movement, heartbeat, digestion, etc. As the developing brain sends out layers of new citizens to new places, the organism eventually has the specialization needed to benefit from the brain's amazing capacity for complexity, diversity, and creativity. In essence, neurons are "people," seeking the right resources for their growth. According to Sweeney (2009), scientists have learned that these cells are not preprogrammed to land in a certain area, like speech or cognition, where they develop their speciality. Instead, "neurons take on different characteristics *because* of their journey and their destination" (italics added, p. 74).

As with other aspects of human development, context is everything. Each brain cell has a journey that contributes to its maturity. There is a consensus among geneticists that we arrive with a certain number of genes, but the majority of gene expression is influenced by experience and environment throughout our lives (Rossi, 2002). Thus, how neurons function in their specialization depends on the success of their migration. Prenatal health warnings to expectant mothers are based largely on the fact that toxic substances interfere with the migration, arrival, and establishment of vulnerable circuits with other cells. The result can delay the full potential of each cell. However, as we will see in Chapter 3, the brain has an amazing capacity for adaptation and transformation, even in the face of disadvantage.

Likewise, even if a baby had prenatal difficulties, after birth, they are poised to continue their growth through family relationships that stimulate all five senses (Porges, 2011). Early and focused interventions can bring about increased circuitry for those who have been prenatally disadvantaged. As these circuits fire away at 9–400 feet per second, they move information through the body like racing cars. This information flows into the whole body highway as cells migrate, connect, communicate, and specialize to form the complete nervous system. After that, specialization continues with chemical messengers for intricate basic functions. Meanwhile, the heart and circulatory system develop. After these fundamental structures can support a slew of tissues, organs, and systems, the rest of the body comes along, prepared for complex interpersonal relationships.

Figure 2.3 illustrates how trillions of dendrites and axons do not physically "touch." The tiny space, or *synapse*, between the axon and the next dendrite is the site for an explosion of chemical activity as each axon has little bags of chemicals, just waiting for the electrical charge to dump them into the synaptic gap. Each

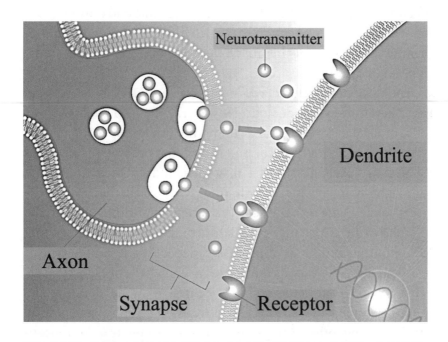

Figure 2.3 Synapse.

axon can store over 100 tiny sacks. Paradoxically, synapses are both gaps and connecting points. Their connection is through chemical transmission, not physical contact. This creates a delicate environment that requires a careful balance of elements to remain healthy. By the time we are born, neurons decrease, synapses increase. The firing along a string of neurons, or *circuit*, develops through a baby's experiences. First, neurons are neighbors, firing off in chains of activity. Next, neurons are distant relatives, sending chemicals long distances to take an array of messages to the right places.

As the cast of characters grows, the destinations of these chemicals have tiny molecules, or *receptors*, that welcome them and create the chemical reaction within the cell. Many of these are on dendrites, where they receive chemicals produced by neighboring axons. Other receptors play "hard-to-get" inside cells and can only receive those who are capable of penetrating the cell wall. In either case, these receptor cells hang out, just waiting for the right chemical to swim by. They are chemical-specific and only respond to one substance, or *ligand*, that which binds. Out of thousands of ligands existing in biochemistry, there are hundreds found in the human body.

The next step is called *binding* (see Figure 2.4). Most sources use a key and keyhole analogy. However, Pert (1997) refers to "sex on a molecular level" because, under the microscope, one can see vibrations between receptor and ligand that precede the moment of binding. Her analogy is the image of ligand and receptor finding the right note to sing, which rings a doorbell that opens the receptor as a *gate* into the cell. The receptor introduces it into the cell body where it changes the nature of the cell by either exciting or inhibiting a number of processes, depending upon the type of cell and its receptors. Sounds like a first date, doesn't it? This capacity to excite and inhibit is central to understanding the neurophysiology of attachment, love, sex, serenity, and addictions, among other things. It can also stimulate a muscle to contract or carry a message from skin or other organs back to the

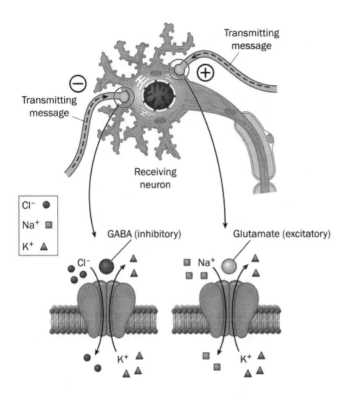

Figure 2.4 Binding.

brain. This extensive cast of characters will take its bow later in the chapter.

Wow! All this activity can happen in one thousandth of a second or 200 miles an hour (Fincher, 1981). The sequence begins as an electrical charge that creates a chemical reaction that leads to another electrical charge. We can see why scientists use terms such as "hard-wired" and "soft-wired" to help us visualize the structural and chemical properties of our energy flow. The nature of the chemical reaction from binding or the strength of electricity from firing depends on the type of sensory information that arrives, type of neuron, type of ligand, and the existing balance of chemicals in the brain at a given instant.

Now, take a moment before you continue reading. Close your eyes and take the deepest, longest, slowest breath possible. Inhale and exhale slowly. Besides your heartbeat, can you feel the slightest vibration in different locations? This is more than just blood and oxygen flowing through your arteries and capillaries. We are electrical and chemical beings. This simple exercise becomes a building block for interventions that change emotional regulation for trauma survivors, couples in conflict, and us—clinicians who work in the trenches where any strong emotion exists. This process applies to a number of interventions in later chapters. Take a moment and savor your ability to sense the energy flowing through your body, from the top of your head, to the tips of your fingers and toes. This is a conversation between your conscious mind and the rest of your body. It is called the felt sense.

UP CLOSE AND INTERPERSONAL: THE CHEMICALS OF CONNECTION

No cast of characters would be complete without those who provide the suspense and intensity of emotion. These messengers deliver punch lines, describe actions, and make meaning about the relationships in the drama. Axons are versatile, just oozing with multiple messengers that come popping out according to what type of chemical charge the cell receives. Because human biochemistry presents an ocean of detail and depth, this discussion will focus only on those substances that have the most relevance to couple relationships, child development, trauma, and addictions. This overview will prepare readers for later chapters that make transparent the particular biochemical processes that are relevant to particular clinical outcomes. However, it is not critical to grasp all the details at once. Box 2.1 provides a glossary of basic biochemistry relevant to our task. These terms provide the context for understanding one substance from another.

Box 2.1 Basic biochemistry

Elements such as oxygen, hydrogen, carbon, etc. are substances that contain only one type of *atom*.

Molecules are groups of atoms that have a neutral electrical charge. Molecules that comprise the human body are Water (65 percent), Proteins—including hair, muscles, bones, etc. (20 percent), Fats (12 percent), Minerals (1.5 percent), Carbohydrates (0.4 percent), and RNA and DNA (1.1 percent).

Ions are groups of atoms that have either a positive or negative charge, depending on the number of their protons and electrons.

Amino Acid is a type of molecule found throughout nature. There are 500 known amino acids in four categories. Twenty of these occur in humans and 9 of those are not produced in the body (*essential amino acids*), thus we must find them in our diet. Amino acids as proteins are the second largest component of muscles, cells, and other human tissues. Some single amino acids (*monoamines*) become neurotransmitters and hormones.

Peptides are combinations of amino acids in chains that become neurotransmitters and hormones. In general chemistry, they comprise 95 percent of all ligands (Pert, 1997). There are over 100 neuropeptides in the human nervous system.

Steroids are biochemical compounds that have 20 carbon atoms combined with other substances. They start out as cholesterol. Enzymes change them into their final state.

Enzymes turn cholesterol into different steroids such as testosterone, progesterone, and estrogen (Pert, 1997, p. 25).

Table 2.1 summarizes chemical messengers that connect the brain, our five senses, visceral organs, and extremities with second-by-second commands and updates concerning our well-being. The table lists the messenger, its chemical category, and what type of receptors bind with it, either at the synapse or within the cell's membrane. During interpersonal process, these chemicals may excite or inhibit a number of operations as we assess threat, determine relevance, seek resources, and find meaning. Body chemistry is intricate, versatile, and tantalizing. (Chocolate, anyone? That's a cue for dopamine).

Table 2.1 Chemical messengers

Name/Type Receptor type	Origin	Function
Acetylcholine polyatomic ion, Synapse	Brainstem, Vagus nerve Basal forebrain, Gut	Connects motor neurons to muscles Increased attention and learning
Glutamate monoamine, Synapse	90 percent of synapses in the brain	Excites synapes. Facilitates learning and memory
GABA monoamine, Synapse	Basal ganglia, hypothalamus, hippocampus	Inhibits (calms) synapses. Regulates muscle tone
Dopamine monoamine, Synapse	Substantia nigra, ventral tegmental area, Adrenal glands, hypothalamus, 50 percent of total in gut	Voluntary movement, motivation, expectation, registers rewards, learning, relationship satisfaction
Serotonin monoamine, Synapse	90 percent in gut 10 percent raphe nuclei	Mood, sleep, appetite, memory, learning
Adrenaline monoamine, Synapse	Adrenal glands Central nervous system	Prepares body for fight/flight by raising heart rate, lung capacity, muscle capacity
Noradrenaline monoamine, Synapse	Sympathetic nervous system, Brain stem, Adrenal glands	Raises heart rate, blood pressure, anxiety and attention in amygdala, sugar levels, general fight/flight abilities
CRH Peptide, Synapse	Hypothalamus	Stimulates pituitary to release ACTH
Endorphins Peptide, Synapse	Hypothalamus Pituitary	Endogenous morphine Pain relief
ACTH Peptide, Synapse	Pituitary	Stimulates adrenal glands to release cortisol
TRH Peptide, Synapse	Hypothalamus	Stimulates pituitary to release thyroid-stimulating hormone and prolactin
GnRH Peptide, Synapse	Hypothalamus	Stimulates pituitary to release sex hormones
Vasopressin Peptide, Synapse	Pituitary	Increases water retention, blood pressure
Oxytocin Peptide, Synapse	Pituitary, Hypothalamus Testes	Childbirth contractions, milk let-down, romantic attachment, empathy, trust

Estradiol (estrogen) Steroid, Nucleus	Ovaries, Adrenal glands placenta, Testes	Growth during puberty, regulates menstral cycle, sustains pregnancy, libido, mood.
Progesterone Steroid, Nucleus	Ovaries, Adrenal glands Placenta, Fat tissue	Regulates menstral cycle, sustains pregnancy, affects mood.
Testosterone Steroid, Nucleus	Testes, Adrenal glands Ovaries	Growth during puberty, libido, statusseeking, prevents osteoporosis.
Cortisol, Steroid Nucleus	Adrenal glands	Inhibits reproductive system, immune system, increases sugar and fat levels for energy, anti-inflammatory, role in emotional memory
Nitric oxide, Gas, Nucleus	Many general cells Vascular Lining	Powerful vasodilator, facilitates erections.

(Siegel et al., 1999)

In this world of chemicals, the plot really thickens. Due to so many disciplines arriving at the crossroads of brain research, new languages and terms warrant translation. Historically, *neurotransmitters* were messengers produced in the axons that had an effect on the neighboring cell through the synapse, such as serotonin. A *hormone* was a messenger produced by a gland that had an effect somewhere else in the body, such as insulin. Sounds simple enough. However, newer discoveries reveal that some substances can be both neurotransmitter and hormone. Over 90 percent of all serotonin is produced along the digestive tract (*gut*), where neurons are more numerous than in the spinal chord (Gershon, 1998). These clusters of neurons have earned the name *enteric nervous system*, because they function independently of the central nervous system. At these sites, serotonin behaves more like a hormone where it travels to various locations and helps to regulate appetite and vascular tone. However, in the brain, it is a neurotransmitter. What's produced in the brain stays in the brain. There, it travels along well-defined circuits that lead to a sense of well-being. These new discoveries occur daily and scientists constantly find exceptions that require a revision of rules, patterns, and categories.

There has also been confusion about the labels of various substances. *Epinephrine* is a stress hormone secreted from the central nervous system and adrenal glands. Along with cortisol, it is released into the bloodstream to initiate the fight/flight response to threat. The American medical establishment has adopted that name. British and International scientists use the term *adrenaline*. A reader may see both terms, depending on the source. For clinicians, adrenaline is a simple label that most lay audiences know from the popular press. This book uses adrenaline to maintain a client-friendly perspective.

For our purposes, the generic term *chemical messengers* includes a number of labeled substances that have chemical properties (type of substance) and physiological properties (how it works). Some neurotransmitters are a pure amino acid. Some are derived from an amino acid and changed by enzymes (*monoamine*). Others are chains of amino acids (*peptides)*. They are produced in the brain and have a local effect there. In addition, peptides may also travel somewhere in the body for a distant effect, like *beta-endorphins*, that have opiate receptors just waiting for them throughout the body. Opioid peptide systems have a role in motivation, emotion, attachment, stress, pain, and appetite. Therefore, under the microscope, our bodies are peppered with opioid receptors.

Other messengers are *steroids* (derived from cholesterol), *gases*, and *polyatomic ions* (molecules with more than one atom). These are considered *hormones*, not because of their chemical composition, but because they travel to other regions. The peptides that travel are also considered hormones, even though they are not produced in glands. Thus, the term hormone relates to the physiology of a substance (what happens), rather than its chemical makeup.

Another physiological distinction is how these messengers deliver their message. Are they courteous, waiting for the receptor at the synapse to "ring them in?" Or, do they just barge right in through the cell wall and make their statement without further ado? It turns out steroids and gases penetrate the cell wall and find the nucleus for an immediate effect. Amino acids wait at the synapse. Thus there are two types of receptors, one on a dendrite and one inside the cell membrane. Table 2.1 lists these distinctions. This chapter is an overview for future reference. Later chapters will describe additional details germane to a given case. In general, clinicians should have a conceptual knowledge of selected chemicals that are endogenous in the body. Then, specific insights from research can focus on how to integrate the information. In summary, the majority of chemical messengers fall into these groups:

Monoamines. Axons store these and release them at the synapse for immediate action. Then, storage bags are refilled and await the next electrical charge. Examples are serotonin, dopamine, adrenaline, noradrenaline, thyroid, glutamate, and gamma aminobutyric acid (GABA).

Neuropeptides. Some of these are the focus of increasing research regarding attachment behaviors, stress responses, and pain relief. They include adrenocorticotrophic hormone (ACTH), Thyrotropin releasing hormone (TRH), Corticotropin releasing hormone (CRH), Gonadotropin releasing hormone (GnRH), Beta-endorphins, vasopressin, and oxytocin.

Steroids. These substances emerge from the reactions of various enzymes on cholesterol. Relevant to relationships and stress reactions, some of them are estradiol, progesterone, testosterone, and cortisol.

Now it's time to take another break. Look around your room and find something that makes you smile. A picture? A person? A symbol? Better yet, is there something that makes you laugh? A story bubbles up to consciousness? If you pause long enough, your body relaxes with a sense of joy. Behind the scenes, beta-endorphins and dopamine swim through your bloodstream to relieve pain and enhance sensations of reward and well-being. This five-minute side trip has other benefits. Glutamate is the most abundant neurotransmitter and excites learning, memory, and brain plasticity. Smiling and laughing: the win-win interlude on a cloudy day. Share the memories with another person and you have a "triple crown" with oxytocin. This is a form of mindfulness.

Siegel (2010) reports the case of an adolescent with emerging bipolar symptoms whose parents opposed medication as a solution. Through his six-point plan, evaluations at three and six months showed a dramatic reduction in symptoms. One part of the plan was to learn exercises to focus his attention (mindfulness). This was based on a study of people with bi-polar diagnoses, in which researchers found that they had thin fibers in a part of the brain that secretes GABA, a calming neurotransmitter (Blond et al., 2012). Kabat-Zinn's (2006) work found that mindfulness exercises increased density in these fibers after just eight weeks. The six-point plan was:

1. Get good sleep.
2. Engage in aerobic exercise.
3. Take healthy sources of omega-3 oils.
4. Develop novel ways of thinking.
5. Have relationships with family, friends, and Siegel.
6. Learn mindfulness exercises.

What is powerful about current models of brain science is the way in which social interactions can focus more clearly on certain therapeutic directions. To increase social relationships, the young man needed a family that would support and encourage all aspects of the six-point plan. An important component of this work is providing information that will motivate parents and spouses to support a certain treatment plan and engage them in novel ways of thinking. Then, clinicians and clients can choreograph new dances based on desired chemical influences. We can even respect these messengers as "family members" in the process of therapy, like GABA. As they go about their work, they travel the highway of the nervous system and our vital organs, keeping nerve bundles, glands, and organs in close communication. Meanwhile, couple and family patterns can change, first, to support symptom relief, then, as part of a new, reinforcing pattern. According to Siegel, the focusing of attention sends energy and information through the nervous system, activating those cells that secrete calming or stimulating chemicals.

Besides these chemicals, other characters, with their diverse functions, work their magic from a variety of locations, knit together because the messengers keep them talking. In an embryo, DNA directs the specialization of organs, glands, and tissues that become primary systems in the body. Within these systems are the cops and robbers that facilitate or threaten our survival. For example, when our endocrine system runs smoothly, hormones direct healthy digestion, sexual vitality, and metabolic stability. If rogue cops should turn to robbers, a pituitary tumor only the size of a pinhead can create a range of life-changing symptoms that affect mood, vision, digestion, and blood pressure. These are often discovered only after a person has been through a series of unsuccessful diagnoses, leaving them depressed and traumatized (Laws et al., 2013). Descending from head to torso, the following is a description of these other network members along the whole body highway.

NERVES AND GLANDS: HOW THEY CALM AND EXCITE US

Human brains develop from bottom to top. Neurons move from the neural plate down and out. The great migration of neuroblasts began with the brainstem and spinal chord (*central nervous system*) and added layers from trillions of cells that divided. Figure 2.6 illustrates three regions of the brain. The first consists of the brain stem and cerebellum. The second, in the center, is the limbic region. The third is the cerebrum, which contains the lobes of the brain. Although we have all three layers at birth (brainstem, limbic, neocortex), there is still a lot of work to do. Under the skull, the neocortex must add *myelin sheath*, from the cerebellum, over the top, toward the forehead. This fatty covering improves the speed and accuracy of each electrical charge. Formation is not completed until ages 23–25, just about the time that American auto insurance companies report that driver risk decreases (Laird, 2011)! The frontal lobe is the last to receive its completed myelin sheath, another indication of how dependent humans are compared to other animals. In addition, the hippocampus does not retain long-term memories until ages 2–3. This is why we have no concious memory of our birth. Included in these layers are other structures that are part of the survival drama.

Neocortex Region

Outermost top and sides of the head, under the skull, it is more advanced than any other creature. The sky is the limit as it mediates more complex information-processing functions, perception, thinking, reasoning, and imagining. It has four lobes and some important subdivisions that interact with other regions (see Figure 2.1).

Occipital lobe. Located in the back of the head, this area processes visual information. The optic nerves that link this lobe to the eyes cross right at the intersection of the thalamus and hypothalamus, one of the busiest places in the brain.

Parietal lobe. Located on top of the head, behind the center line, it enables movement and motor skills. Processes temperature, pain and touch.

Temporal lobe. These are underneath the ear in each hemisphere. They enable memory, hearing, language, and emotion.

Frontal lobe: Prefrontal cortex (PFC). Located behind the forehead and top front of the head, it performs executive functions, such as conscious memory, judgment, planning, sequencing of activity, abstract reasoning and dividing attention. There are several stress reactions that will restrict operations of the PFC.

Frontal lobe: Orbitofrontal cortex (OFC). This area is located just behind the eyes and is involved in impulse control, sense of self, reactivity to surroundings and mood. Damage to this area causes personality changes. Schore (2005) suggests that the OFC depends on stimulation from the emotional connections of the attachment figure in the form of eye contact, face-to-face communication, and affective attunement.

Insula. Tucked away under the sides of where the OFC and temporal lobes meet, a small lobe about the size of a silver dollar lays against the limbic region. The insulae seem to be involved in consciousness and emotion (Damasio, 2012). Of particular interest is the link to internal body awareness (*interoception*), much like the felt sense activity of focusing the conscious mind toward internal experience. There may be a relationship to addictions and internal sensations.

Corpus Callosum

This is a band of tissue that arches over the limbic region and under the lower cortex (anterior cingulate). It is involved with communication between left and right hemispheres.

Basal Ganglia

This group of structures involves the putamen, caudate nucleus, globus pallidus and the upper area of the midbrain below the thalamus. It surrounds the deep limbic region just under the cortex. It is cut away in Figure 2.5, but you can imagine it to be like a pair of ear muffs on either side of the thalamus, then curves around clockwise to join the amygdala. It appears to set the body's anxiety level, promotes motivation, and facilitates pleasure and ecstacy (Amen, 1998). From the midbrain, the *substantia nigra* sends dopamine to the *striatum* as part of reward stimulation, as in addictions, praise, or even money (Izuma et al., 2008). The substantia nigra and *globus pallidus* also ooze with lots of GABA to calm us.

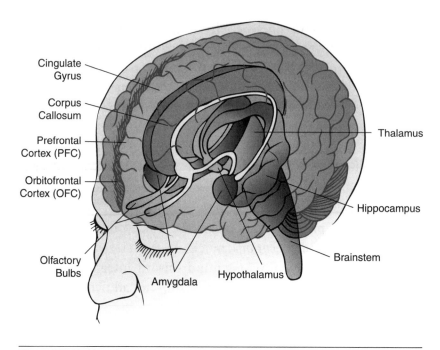

Figure 2.5 Limbic region.

Cerebellum

Located on the back side of the brainstem, this cauliflower-like section manages coordination, balance, and movement. Recent studies also note implications for some emotional processing issues after injury or disease in this area (Schmahmann, 2004).

Thalamus

These nerve bundles come in two walnut-sized lobes that join in the middle. They sit between brainstem and neocortex, with very extensive interfaces as a gateway for sensory information to regions of the cortex, amygdala, and hippocampus (see Figures 2.2 and 2.6). This structure is Grand Central Station for all sensory information, directing heavy traffic to these other areas. However, there is one exception. Sense of smell goes to the amygdala first (see Figure 2.5). All other senses are sent to the thalamus first for processing. Some speculate that smell was an important sense in prehistoric times and was part of a "first responder" system set up in the body that enabled the amygdala to signal quickly to imminent danger. One theory is that the thalamus is central to a sense of conscious experience (Siegel, 2012).

Deep Limbic Region: Friend or Foe, Good or Bad

Inside the temporal lobes, perched on top of the brain stem, a collection of characters conducts some of the most lively dialogue in all the brain. With messengers coming on and off stage from five senses, vagus, and cortex, the landscape of survival unfolds at one of the busiest intersections of the body, commonly known as the *limbic system*. No other area processes so much information, from so many sources, coming and going in so many directions. Within the skull, it sits at the center, just behind our nose and nasal passages. Slightly above this and behind our eyes is the *orbitofrontal cortex (OFC)*.

Neuroscientists began calling the limbic system the emotional center of the brain. However, in recent years, that term has become problematic for those who argue that this area does not function as a system in the same way as the *nervous system*, or *digestive system*. The structures here are multitaskers who have their hands in many areas of neurophysiology, not emotion alone. As the activities of neurophysiology become more transparent, we see the formation of sensory data, memory, meaning, and emotion on a wider stage in the body, and not limited to a single construct within the realm of a few glands and structures. Thus, many neuroscientists refer to this area as the limbic region, limbic structures, or limbic network. It seems that *limbic network* involves communication and transformation of all substances that enter this space. Once this location has worked its magic, blood and axons carry hormones to many parts of the body. Like radioactive elements, receptors located in designated locations scoop these cells up and bind. From rational thought to sexual abandon, the limbic network has something to say and do about many functions in the body. Since the field of family therapy has a long tradition with the process of metacommunication as a clinical process, perhaps we can think of the limbic network as a meta-system, continually negotiating transactions with all other systems.

As a region, it is centrally located and coordinates the activity of higher and lower brain structures and links to widely distributed areas in the brain. It processes survival states, emotion, motivation, and relationships (Siegel, 2012; Levine, 2010). It is like the U.S. Department of Homeland Security with many components that read, analyze, and process information related to safety. This includes early attachment experiences that lead to safety or anxiety in a developing child.

Amygdala. The amygdala is the "watchdog" of the whole body, regardless of whether the threat is an *attachment injury* or an auto *accident* (Johnson et al., 2001). These are two almond-sized bundles of neurons that sit atop each right/left hippocampus with special sensitivities to danger, fear, and anxiety. If anything goes wrong, the amygdala is the first to evaluate. It is well developed before birth and can sense fear from inside the womb (Cozalino, 2006). After birth, it works closely with the thalamus, hypothalamus, septal nuclei, orbital frontal cortex, cingulate gyrus, hippocampus, and brain stem, processing information from them about the well-being of the person. Given their role with fear and aggression, four amygdala outnumber two marital partners, if attachment injuries have become prominent in a marriage. There are two pathways for responding to threat. One by-passes the PFC altogether (Fight! Run!) and the other consults as part of an executive committee with the PFC and hippocampus. Smells go directly to the amygdala and can influence emotional and endocrine reactions through the hypothalamus. This may explain the effects that essential oils and ingestion of addictive substances have from nasal administration. When a person "snorts" cocaine, glue or other inhalants, the effect goes immediately to the amygdala and disengages its fear and anxiety.

Hippocampus. This structure also has a right and left as arcs curve between the inside of the temporal lobes and the limbic region. It helps control cortisol production and works to orient toward visual-spatial interactions in the environment. It stores and retrieves factual information and details related to events and one's sense of self (*autobiographical memory*). It becomes part of the executive committee with the amygdala and PFC. The hippocampus plays a critical role in short-term memory, a necessity to establish long-term memory patterns. Ultimately, memory storage is transferred to other areas of the cerebral cortex, and the location of encoding of these memories may be a function of the type of memory. Established memories involve association areas in the frontal lobe and parieto-temporo-occipital association cortex (Sweeney, 2009).

Hypothalamus. This lima-bean-sized cluster of cells has one of the densest blood supplies in the body. The most important function of the hypothalamus is to link the nervous system to the endocrine system via the pituitary gland. It masterminds the master gland and directs everything that the pituitary does to maintain balance in the body. They even share some blood vessels to maintain the capacity for quick action. As the chief of staff, it consults regularly with the amygdala, always on guard for the first signs of trouble. As part of the HPA axis, it facilitates fight/flight responses through secretions to the pituitary that trigger messengers that travel to the adrenal glands for release of stress and sex hormones (see Figure 2.8). Despite its size, it is the emotional center of the brain, lighting up in numerous studies that use brain scans.

Pituitary gland. This small gland is the size of a garbanzo bean and sits in a little cup that is part of the skull. Technically, scientists do not include it as part of the original "limbic system." It is a *gland* (not a bundle of nerves), with cells that produce hormones. However, it is almost like a Siamese twin to the hypothalamus, with acute sensitivity to blood flow from it. Although the master gland, as we can see, the hypothalamus takes on its share of the work, guiding the pituitary at every turn. Of the many hormones released by the pituitary, those most relevant here are beta-endorphin and those that stimulate other glands to release testosterone, estrogen, adrenaline, and noradrenaline. During activation of the HPA Axis, the pituitary keeps the adrenal glands hard at work.

Brainstem

This busy intersection is more like a major highway interchange composed of multiple lanes and numerous on and off ramps from many directions. There are three main divisions from top down, the *midbrain, pons,* and *medulla* (see Figure 2.6). In the midbrain, the raphe nuclei release serotonin to the striatum and *nucleus*

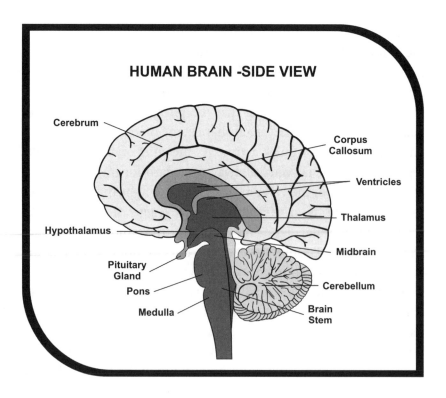

Figure 2.6 Brainstem.

accumbens. The *ventral tegmental area (VTA)* in the midbrain releases dopamine to the PFC, *nucleus accumbens,* and hippocampus. Some theorize that this involvement with a memory center may intensify any reward as a possible addiction, even attachment (Zellner et al., 2011). The VTA activation also relates to other rewards and motivation. It may also play a role with the amygdala in avoidance and fear-conditioning. Brain recordings demonstrate that VTA neurons respond to novel stimuli, unexpected rewards, and cues for rewards such as the anticipation of drug administration. Fisher et al. (2006) documented VTA reactions to falling in and out of love, much like attachment and loss, or addiction and withdrawal. In the pons, *raphe nuclei* produce serotonin and send it throughout the cortex.

Twelve cranial nerves. Branching off the pons and medulla are twelve cranial nerves. These receive unprecedented attention in Porges' (1995, 2001, 2007, 2011) *polyvagal theory,* in which he provides a basis for the neurological primacy of attachment. In this theory, he demonstrates how cranial nerves orchestrate a newborn's capacity for social engagement from the moment of birth (see Figure 2.7). Chapter 3 provides a summary of his work. These nerves play important roles in all the communication processes in the head that babies need to survive. The one exception is the *vagus nerve* (wanderer, vagabond), which makes a quick exit from the medulla and heads south.

Vagus nerve. The vagus, cranial nerve (X), has a right and left branch off the medulla, descending into the torso (see Figure 2.7). As the second longest nerve in the body, it connects the medulla with major organs through an extensive web that snakes through the viscera, gut, and intestines, gathering information from them and sending those pictures back to the brain. The heart connection is noteworthy because the vagus can inhibit (or calm) our body functions. It slows our heart rate and contributes to affect regulation (Beauchaine, 2001). In a large corporate office building, the vagus would be the network of security cameras placed at key locations that beam images back to command central (Insula,

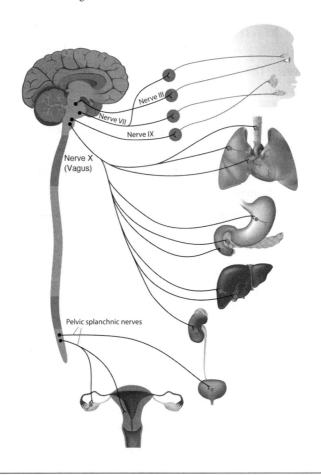

Figure 2.7 Vagus nerve.

thalamus, amygdala). Nearly 90 percent of its work is one-way, from the visceral organs to the brain. Only 10 percent of its fibers send messages down. Outside our consciousness, the vagus and brain are monitoring well-being, including the threat of internal processes. Although our vernacular often uses the term *stress*, our bodies use the term *danger or threat*, because survival is our highest priority.

The vagus reached a degree of notoriety in the family therapy world when Gottman and colleagues explained that vagal tone relates to measures of heart rate variability, a measure of children's emotional reactivity (Gottman et al., 1997). Previously, the vagus had become the darling of neuroscientists who conduct PNI research and other mind-body studies of health (Porges, 1998). Whipple and Komisaruk (2002) reported interesting findings in a study of women with spinal chord injury. As a by-pass to the spinal cord, the women experienced orgasm through stimulation of a vagus-cervix pathway. Areas of activation in the brain were similar to those documented with the usual spinal chord pathway. It is also famous for its utility as a site to connect heart pacemakers, due to the many fibers that connect to the heart. Thus, the vagus, with its varied and extensive connections to viscera, is another way in which the brain is in the body. When someone experiences "butterflies in the stomach," that's the vagus nerve sending "gut level" information to our conscious mind.

Adrenal Glands

Sitting on top of the kidneys in the middle of the torso, this pair of thumb-sized glands secrete sex hormones and stress hormones. If we wonder about low libido for some clients, these are partners in crime with relationship stresses. The adrenals are of critical importance during puberty and they pump cortisol on a daily basis because of its role in digestion and blood sugar, even when there are no signs of stress. They continually help regulate nutrition, digestion, sex, and safety through the hormones they secrete. Imbalances in the body come about because many of these hormones are multitaskers. When they are overworked in one area, it compromises functioning in another. These are part of the HPA axis that is responsible for the fight/flight responses to threat. Respectively, these pathways assess danger and enable us to take action against it. However, experience, context, and trauma may lead to a breakdown in our ability to accurately assess and take action. This leads to adrenal overload. Neuroscientists now agree that affect and emotion are tied to our ability to assess threat (Evans, 2002; Siegel, 2012). The world of appraisal, memory, meaning, and emotion has significant effects on the adrenals. As with any superstar, it is only a matter of time before the body's need for balance and harmony cry out for a change.

HPA AXIS: SUPERSTARS DURING STRESS

Figure 2.8 illustrates the HPA Axis and how activation affects other systems. Through our five senses, long and short-term

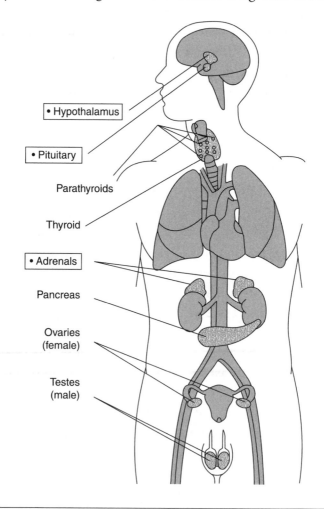

- Hypothalamus
- Pituitary
Parathyroids
Thyroid
- Adrenals
Pancreas
Ovaries
(female)
Testes
(male)

Figure 2.8 HPA Axis.
Adapted from *The Merck Manual Home Health Handbook* (Wiley, 2011)

memory, amygdala, and OFC, we appraise social and physical stimuli for their potential threat. These can be split-second analyses that excite or inhibit our actions. When our appraisal says to act, the HPA axis begins a complex loop of hormones that prepares the body for fight/flight responses. Here, fight/flight is a unitary construct because physiology is the same for either action. The chemical cascade begins after limbic structures determine threat. They prompt the hypothalamus into action. These signal the pituitary to send one of its eight hormones through the bloodstream to stimulate adrenal gland production of adrenaline, noradrenaline, and cortisol. Cortisol tells the liver to dump its stored glycogen, which converts to sugar. Other functions increase levels of fat in the system. This is how liver functioning becomes activated during stress. When there is no physical discharge of energy to use this extra sugar and fat, they accumulate in other parts of the body. Couch potatoes, beware!

If we imagine being chased by a bear, the HPA axis gives us a fighting chance. It shuts down any systems that are not needed at the moment of emergency—immune system, digestion, even the PFC. Arnsten (2009) notes a great deal of evidence attesting to the fact that the HPA axis is very sensitive to stress exposure (amygdala). He suggests that "mild acute uncontrollable stress" leads to a dramatic change in cognitive abilities. This research leads to explanations as to how stress can lead to PFC changes as part of mental illnesses. As traumatologists have suggested, proper treatment depends more on the therapist learning about "what happened," instead of assessing "what's wrong." Chapter 5 reviews details of how a knowledge of the physiology of stress and trauma can inform family therapy.

SNAPSHOTS OF THE WHOLE BODY

As we leave the anatomy and physiology of the transparent brain, we can take a number of images with us. We have traveled from the head, where we have two hemispheres and many lobes of the neocortex, to the limbic region with its collection of nerves that come bundled in various shapes and sizes, through the brainstem with its reward centers and branches, out the vagus nerve as it wanders and looks for messages to send home, and finally, to the adrenal glands that pump their chemicals out to all important organs. Flooding the entire system are cascades of chemicals from top to bottom that calm, excite, reward, and communicate. They seek out their matching receptors. We get a charge out of them!

And so, what is the brain? It is a whole person inside a body that wants to survive against all odds. This person survives through attachment to others for safety, love, and emotional regulation. Communication inside and out are specialties of this person. Family therapists can be lighthouses when the winds and waves threaten attachment and interfere with our chemical messages. Balance and harmony are the goals. All of this so the species will survive. All of this because the ancestors have spoken.

3

Human Development
Prehistoric, Microscopic, Biographic

> We shall not cease from exploration, and the end of all our exploring will be to arrive where we started and know the place for the first time.
>
> T. S. Eliot

So, how does a family therapist make sense of neurophysiology in daily practice? Generally, family therapists look at interpersonal not biological contexts. Pioneering family therapists were mavericks from other mental health fields who "invented" an interpersonal approach to mental health problems and eschewed biology and medicalization (Hanna, 2007). Now, with the proliferation of voices from neuroscience, there are unifying themes that contribute to the integration of these worlds. Scientists who study emotional regulation suggest that many diagnoses could be reclassified according to brain activity when viewing behavioral and emotional process under the microscope (Gross & Munoz, 1995; Gross, 1998). This would provide a new lens for traditional diagnostic categories. While this may not change political and financial dependence upon the DSM-V and its iterations, it may change clinical discussions to help clients benefit from the best of both worlds. From birth, emotional regulation is a developmental and interpersonal process. Brain-informed narratives normalize symptoms by invoking the inheritances of our ancestors and the complexity of contemporary lifestyles. Pain and intensity of symptoms makes sense when cast as the collision between these two worlds.

Part of the excitement about neuroscience is a new transparency that links attachment processes with biology. Neurophysiology co-creates attachment narratives by tracking adaptive biosocial process. Instead of labeling symptoms, clinicians can explore layers of development At biosocial levels, this includes questions about the body, a person's survival strategies, formative relationships, patterns, and aspirations. Here, these unifying themes form five principles that practitioners can use to integrate neurophysiology into their work.

PRINCIPLE ONE: THINK WHOLE BODY

Leaving Descartes and the conceptual guillotine behind, clinicians can now sense layers of neurons throughout a person. The body is the mind. The body is an information-processing network with a mind of its own (Pert, 1997, p. 185; Levine, 2010; Ross, 2008). Messengers, receptors, circuits, glands, and organs work according to the logic of the body, which is a dialogue about survival between many parts. Processing signals and sensations from the inside out, the whole body uses its collective intelligence in search of balance, stability, and health.

Collective Intelligence

Siegel (2012) notes that there is no agreement on a definition of the mind. He suggests that *mind* emerges from energy and information flow (electricity and chemicals) as they intersect with interpersonal process. The body's *collective intelligence* is a set of dialogues scripted around the neurophysiology of experience, emotion, meaning, memory, and action. Circuits that underlie this sequential information-flow become a state of being and a state of mind anchored in various parts of the body. For example, trauma-focused neuroscientists consider the whole body as a storehouse of biological memories shaped by experience (van der Kolk, 2000). Levine (2010) states, "The body has its reason, which reason cannot reason" (p. 157). However, biological memories can become transparent through use of the *felt sense*.

Felt Sense

The five senses begin our interactions with others, but we also have a *felt sense*, the signals about how the body feels. Beyond the autonomic nervous system, babies report their felt sense when they communicate distress. Toilet training depends on a toddler further developing the felt sense. Throughout life, we are consciously aware of hunger, thirst, and fatigue. However, beyond these basic physical needs, our felt sense registers emotional process and can become a mechanism for balancing the nervous system (Levine, 2010; Ross, 2008; Heller & La Pierre, 2012). As a therapeutic tool, focused attention to the body from the inside out brings forward important information about where the body is storing significant experiences.

Now, take a moment and remember the exercise in Chapter 2 (p. 38). It provides a beginning experience with the felt sense. Repeat it now, with these additional dimensions. First, there is awareness of energy and arousal states in the body. Where are they? Do they feel comfortable or uncomfortable? Once awareness emerges, locate and focus on a positive location. Stay with it. Savor it. What sensations do you feel? Does it "say" anything? By noticing a positive location, a helpful message travels from that location to the brain. It may only be a tiny spot, such as the feet or a finger. Focus on that spot. Take some breaths and just sit with that place. Neurons fire in certain circuits that are desirable as future resources for resilience. This is known as grounding (Levine, 2010; Ross, 2008; Heller & La Pierre, 2012).

The felt sense, five senses, and the body's capacity for affect, meaning and memory lay a foundation for collective intelligence.

Affect, Meaning, and Memory in the Body

Neurons are firing early in development. The amygdala is fully developed by the eighth month of gestation (Cozalino, 2006). Circuits in the autonomic nervous system develop basic survival responses ready to come "online" from the moment of birth. Then, circuits connect through repetitive cycles of interaction with family and attachment figures. The body's arousal states are the first signs of *affect*. Conceptually, many neuroscientists distinguish between affect and emotion. Affect is a physiological state related to survival. Emotion develops as interpersonal development becomes more complex. However, the terms are often used interchangeably. Thus, infants begin with the capacity for affective states. For instance, a baby cries, receives food, soothing, or other responses from family, and the felt sense registers bodily sensations of change, no change, calm, uncertainty, comfort, distress, joy, etc. This affective process of *arousal-appraisal* is the beginning of *meaning* (Siegel, 2012). When a pattern repeats, circuits strengthen and expectations form. This is the beginning of *memory* as infants anticipate something familiar, based on history. Well-being is a cluster of sensations tied to basic survival needs. Thus, meaning begins as good feeling in the body.

> The body has its reason, which reason cannot reason. (Levine, 2010)

Affect expression for a newborn is just the tip of an iceberg consisting of sensing basic physical needs, engaging those who have the resources, receiving the resources, and appraising whether those are sufficient. If so, the reward structures signal, "good, safe, etc." If not, threat structures signal "bad, fear, etc." Porges (2011) suggests if repeated efforts at social engagement fail to get results, we move to more primitive means, *fight/flight*, and hope for the best. If these strategies fail, the extreme shutdown is called *freeze*. In the animal world, some animals die suddenly from the body's extreme freeze mode, without any injury from a predator (Porges, 2007; Levine, 2010). As humans develop, this basic sequence becomes more complex as appraisal mechanisms process a range of stimuli. From the basic good/bad or safe/unsafe paradigms, children begin making subtle distinctions between various body states and various stimuli. For example, the "bottle" state may feel "good," but in a different way then the "mother smiling" state. When the bottle and mother smiling states become joined, the circuits that develop from these associations may signal "attachment."

The affect that develops from these associations becomes a signal with its own physiology. Fear tells us to run. Anger tells us to fight. After birth, these circuits cross all senses—what we see, hear, feel, taste, and smell. These associations become the first emotions we feel toward the first caregivers that provide the resources for survival. If we fast forward to the field of developmental psychopathology, we might see that some trauma survivors may have bodies who have not encoded the experience of safety or survival. Thus, the cortex and temporal lobe may "know" that the person survived, but the endocrine system or the amygdala may not "know." Body systems come to resemble a "family" in which information flow can be stuck or transferred to members according to context. Family therapists can easily transfer their knowledge of cybernetic communication to the neurophysiology of survival.

The work of Ekman (2007) identifies basic emotions and corresponding facial expressions that appear to be universal across cultures. Gottman's work on marital interaction includes Ekman's schema for coding emotions that relate to the predictors of divorce (Buehlman et al., 1992). Ekman suggests that humans are born with the capacity for certain affective states related to survival. They are joy, distress, anger, fear, surprise, and disgust. Even in cultures that discourage free expression of emotion, analyses of facial expressions reveal fleeting, micro-second flashes of these basic facial expressions during the research task. Clinically, it is possible to identify these emotions and track them back to basic survival issues. In emotionally focused couple therapy (EFT), Johnson (1996) identifies primary emotions of the couple as she simultaneously creates safety and empathy between herself and the person. From a limbic perspective, this is a powerful combination that impacts physiology in the moment. Chapter 6 will examine these dynamics and provide guidelines for accessing the whole body during couple therapy.

In the field of affective neuroscience, Panksepp (2011) draws from animal and human brain scans to identify seven primal affective states. This summary is in Box 3.1. He uses capitalization to distinguish from common emotional states. These states of SEEKING, RAGE, FEAR, LUST, CARE, PANIC/GRIEF, and PLAY provide a framework for basic human needs that may be out of balance when health is compromised (Panksepp & Watt, 2011). For example, he explores the roots of ADHD in the context of PLAY (Davis & Panksepp, 2011). His work on RAGE also has important implications for aggression in humans, since SEEKING for food might be one form of aggression related to the cries of a newborn and RAGE in the face of confinement or bodily harm can be an entirely different from of aggression (Panksepp & Zellner, 2004). These distinctions can be helpful to family therapists who want to access primary emotions, such as EFT. They also provide a guide to the meaning and memory attached to certain behaviors (Panksepp & Bivin, 2012).

Memory is about history and pattern. There are several types of memory. *Explicit, or declarative memory* is about facts and events that can be verbalized (temporal lobe and hippocampus). *Implicit or non-declarative memory* includes skills and conditioned or emotional responses that specifically relate to survival (amygdala; LeDoux, 2003). It is the memory of the body as a toddler learns to walk. Once we consciously learn, we perform the operations automatically, without any conscious direction. The body learns by doing. The cortex directs it in the background of our conscious experience. In addition to movements, the body is also learning various chemical and cellular operations. These are

---

Box 3.1 Panksepp's seven affective states

SEEKING Wanting rewards, resources such as safety. Involves approach-exploratory behaviors, desires and aspirations. This is the basic control system of phenomenology of appetitive urges. It can link up with cognitive (secondary learning) and then with tertiary forms of awareness and appraisal.

RAGE Protects resources, activated by bodily restraint, no freedom of action. Threat that other life-supporting resources may be taken away. It is activated from aversive stimuli.

FEAR These are danger-escape and avoidance patterns such as freezing and flight. Mostly from learned experience, except smell of predators, loss of physical support or unprotected heights in humans.

LUST These capacities develop early during gestation, but are inactive until puberty. Female type desires can exist in male brains and vice versa (Pfaff, 1999).

CARE Maternal instinct in mammals and birds, needed for highly social species. Spontaneously activated by changes in estrogen, progesterone, prolactin, and oxytocin. More robust in adults.

PANIC When a child gets lost. Solidifies attachments. Feeling of sudden social loss.

GRIEF Crying out for care, separation distress, psychic pain. In adults, precipitates sadness and grief.

PLAY Explore diverse social possibilities in joyous ways, form friendships and alliances. Urge to play began deep in the mammalian brain. When neocortex is removed in animals, they still have the urge to play. If children aren't allowed enough play, there is more acting out and impulsivity, and they get labeled incorrectly as trouble-makers (ADHD). Drugs that treat ADHD reduce playfulness in animals. Laughter is a sign of engaged PLAY system (Panksepp, 2011).

---

happening, just like physical movement, automatically in the background without conscious attention. This is *activity-dependent learning* (Rossi, 2002), memory-learning systems that involve conscious and unconscious affect, meaning, memories, movements, skills, and molecular processes connected through circuits.

Schore (2005) suggests that implicit memory relates to the

non-conscious, non-verbal aspects of experience, including the attachment experience from the moment of birth. Developed before birth, implicit memory is what operates when newborns recognize music their mothers played during pregnancy. Fivush (2011) suggests that autobiographical memory is a cumulative life narrative that develops over time from subjective experience. It gives a sense of continuity to individual, gendered, familial, and cultural experiences that accumulate in a person's self-narrative. When mothers reminisce with their children, they develop more elaborate, coherent autobiographical memories.

As memories develop, they tie affect and meaning to an individual's perception of survival. Siegel (2012) suggests that memories consist of circuits, termed a "neural net profile." These profiles carry the probability of how past biology will affect future biology. The greater intensity of the electrochemical energy, the more likely there will be repetition. For example, Gottman's (1993) marital interaction research led him to note a physiological pattern of *flooding* that would occur in one or both partners during an angry conflict. The predictability of flooding suggests that this stress response was stored in the limbic region from similar experiences. In addition, analysis of oral histories identified elements of memory that strongly related to the likelihood of divorce (Buehlman et al., 1992). These memories clouded a couple's ability to see other options. Similar to infant cries, the flooding for marriage partners is the biological report that certain circuits sense threat. Over time, the repetition of this dysregulation leads to meaning and memory. Now, neuroscientists speak about "learned helplessness" and "learned safety" as two alternatives resulting from patterns of affect and response (Porges, in press; Seligman & Maier, 1967; Seligman et al., 1968). Regardless of the content of an argument, survival is still the dominant theme throughout the body. Without a feeling of safety, a sense of helplessness may lead to divorce.

PRINCIPLE TWO: THINK SURVIVAL

And what about the *ecology of survival*? One might wonder, "Does it all really come down to this?" Since human capacity involves higher level thinking, surely there should be consideration of our problem-solving capacities and the ingenuity of *Homo sapiens*. The response here is that when lower order functions are not working properly, all other operations are affected.

Thus, speaking the language of survival might be stating the obvious. Those who study human development usually learn the language of cognitive development, ages and stages, motor skills, psychosocial development, etc. However, the body responds in a limited number of ways, regardless of the theoretical construct. In order to address the heat of an argument, the sadness of isolation, or the chaos of a transition, stress hormones go to work sending messages throughout the body. Neurophysiology is a series of cycles and loops, not a straight line. The neurophysiology of *threat-survival* is the other consciousness in the room when people seek help.

THE LANGUAGE OF SURVIVAL

Learning the language of survival can be a multidisciplinary experience. Biology, evolutionary theory, and anthropology all have narratives about survival. Biology is most often the voice for Darwin's (1859) vision in *The Origin of Species*. However, if we are to fully grasp how threat and survival are biosocial processes for humans, there are interpretations and myths about Darwin's work on natural selection that are important to know. The term "survival of the fittest" meant something quite different in Darwin's day than how it is used today (Spencer, 1864). Those of Darwin's time saw survival of a species related to qualities of *adaptability*, given the environment. The migration metaphors in Chapter 2 are examples of adaptability. *Competition*, used in the context of limited resources, did not equate with might or dominance. In fact, to the contrary, a number of biologists point to *cooperation* between organisms as an important part of survival ecology. For example, in the animal world, small birds often perch on large animals and consume insects from their coats. Large, intimidating fish allow tiny shrimp to feed on microbes in their mouths.

Moving on to humans, Peter Kropotkin (1902), a Russian geographer and social activist, wrote about how survival narratives of civilizations contain central themes of cooperation. Anthropologists note the necessity of social networks for survival. Small (2011) suggests that marriage, family, and tribal bonds are the mechanisms of survival that protect against threat. For humans, survival of the fittest is actually survival of the <u>attached</u>. Epidemiologists and PNI researchers have produced years of data supporting this idea. In addition to the obvious benefit of family and tribe as protection from enemy attack, numerous studies with hundreds of participants show how social isolation predicts death rates in America (Berkman & Syme, 1979; Berkman & Glass, 2000). In these studies, there is a simple Social Network Index (SNI) that practitioners can use to inform treatment planning (see Box 3.2). The research version appears in the Appendix. Public health research tracks this information as part of disease-prevention efforts. In combination, these survival perspectives point to the biosocial ecology of threat-survival.

THE BIOSOCIAL ECOLOGY OF THREAT-SURVIVAL

Biologically, humans closely resemble other animals when it comes to physical defense and protective mechanisms. From immune systems and hunger pangs, to the formation of social bonds and societies, nature has provided defenses that protect the young and vulnerable at birth. The body is dominated by a number of abilities that protect a person from starvation, disease, and physical harm. At the same time, compared to

---

Box 3.2 Social network index (SNI)

1. How many *close friends* do you have, people that you feel at ease with, can talk to about private matters?
2. How many of these *close friends* do you see at least once a month?
3. How many *relatives* do you have, people that you feel at ease with, can talk to about private matters?
4. How many of these *relatives* do you see at least once a month?
5. Do you participate in any groups, such as a senior center, social or work group, religious-centered group, self-help group, or charity, public service, or community group?
   [ ] 0 No [ ] 1 Yes [ ] 9 Unknown
6. About how often do you go to religious meetings or services?
   [ ] 0 Never or almost never [ ] 1 Once or twice a year [ ] 2 Every few months
   [ ] 3 Once or twice a month [ ] 4 Once a week [ ] 5 More than once a week
   [ ] 9 Unknown
7. Is there someone available to you whom you can count on to listen to you when you need to talk? How many?
8. Is there someone available to give you good advice about a problem? How many?
9. Is there someone available to you who shows you love and affection? How many?
10. Can you count on anyone to provide you with emotional support (talking over problems or helping you make a difficult decision)? How many?
11. Do you have as much contact as you would like with someone you feel close to, someone in whom you can trust and confide? How many?

---

other animals, humans have a vexing capacity for higher order thought that leads past mere survival to endless possibilities that capture the human imagination. Visualizing future progress and asking "What else?" is uniquely human. Behind these possibilities, neurophysiology is backstage, alternating between basic survival needs, problem-solving strategies, intergenerational survival, and ultimately, rewarding sensations from collective human progress.

Despite this capacity for lofty, complex cognition, humans are the most dependent on caregivers for survival. This irony leads to the threat of social isolation at all ages. This social component carries with it the same cascade of chemicals as though the body is under physical attack. Experiences of emotional distress (activation) are chemical and electrical energy that lead to meaning, memory, and action. Whether the threat is biological or social, the body senses it through the felt sense and our five senses. They describe it to the amygdalae, hippocampus, OFC, and hypothalamus (Bechera et al., 2000, 2013). As the executive committee, this trio decides whether to take action, electrochemically and behaviorally. Oddly, the need for physical distance or emotional closeness can prompt the same flood of biology, if each comes from fear. This is why the body is no respecter of concepts! In marital therapy, the *pursuit-distance* dance is one that many couples do. In light of the transparent brain, each person may have very similar neurophysiology, but a personal set of meanings leads to different behaviors.

> **If activation is strong, threat can biologically trump reason.**

In addition to these ironic similarities within a dyad, there is another neurological component to their stuckness. If activation is strong, threat can biologically trump reason. Almighty adrenaline will shut down the cortex to provide the body with maximum resources for fight/flight. Repeating marital cycles can act like traumas in which the circuits are stronger from amygdala to PFC (we have a lot to fear!) then from PFC to amygdala (no, we don't . . .).

At times, the drama may turn to comedy, as we startle from something, then realize it's not serious. This is the OFC saying to the *amygdala*, "Chill out. It's not the way it seems." The amygdala must depend on the OFC to see what is lurking. At other times, messengers about high alert and life-threatening danger also send up a roadblock and detour around the PFC altogether. No dialogue now, just motor neurons . . . RUN!

This detour can be very problematic if signals get scrambled and the threat is actually mild. Our ability to assess threat develops through messages that range from low-level inconveniences to significant overloads. These overloads, unique to circumstances at the time, can send torrential chemical rains that cause electrical storms and blur our visibility during threat assessments from the OFC. Due to these conditions, many clients enter our offices on high alert. They desperately need biological empathy from a new stage manager who can orchestrate safety and calm. This can come about from speaking to the limbic region in order to break its cycle with the HPA axis.

Thus, during the heat of a marital battle, or the discouragement of parent-adolescent alienation, there is a biosocial stage behind an emotional drama that contains many entrances for therapeutic intervention. As true battles for survival, they beg these preliminary questions: Where in the body does it register with the felt sense? How much repetition is involved in the cycle? What type of threat is activated?

These questions prepare practitioners to develop pattern-breaking interventions and pinpoint biosocial release points. The logic of the body treats all threats as biological. Layers of social process influence the meaning and strength of each threat. Beyond physical threats, it is important to understand how the ecology of family relationships contains many highly charged threats.

PRINCIPLE THREE: THINK ATTACHMENT

Neurobiologists have found ample evidence that interpersonal/social process lies at the center of biological survival. Biologically, attachment has always been known as the primary survival process characterizing feeding reflexes such as sucking and rooting. However, many neuroscientists place interpersonal process at center stage in the threat-survival drama (Swain et al., 2007). These sensory capacities emerge in studies that investigate survival strategies of newborns. The process of *social engagement* is prominent in Porges' (2007) groundbreaking *polyvagal theory.* Tracking the function of each cranial nerve as it branches from the brainstem, he suggests that newborns achieve the finishing touches on their social engagement system, just weeks before birth. These nerves connect to eyes, ears, nose, and larynx for vocal communication and social engagement. These developments distinguish humans from lower animal forms and prepare the newborn for social engagement. Like stage hands before the curtain opens, these cranial nerves prepare babies for their grand entrance. There is a tiny stapedius muscle in the middle ear that helps an infant distinguish human voices from other background sounds (Porges, 2007).

In spite of humans' complete dependence on others at birth, we carry many sophisticated strategies that prepare us for success with interpersonal attachments. Polyvagal theory suggests a hierarchy of three pathways that encompass human response to threat. Porges' paradigm shift asserts that social engagement is really the first survival strategy, coming from the most advanced portions of our brains. Without social engagement, sucking or rooting do not occur. He challenges behavioral models based on instinct and behavioral observations (gross anatomy) and provides a window into the microscopic activity of the cranial nerves that branch off from the brain stem and wrap around sensory and visceral organs.

According to this theory, first, the social engagement system goes into action. Orienting and scanning the environment for familiar caregivers is not limited to infants. Most adults seek a sense of belonging that leads to mate selection and the hope of a safe haven. If the social engagement system fails to produce soothing, the second tier strategy is *fight/flight.* These are coupled in neuroscience literature because the HPA axis behaves the same, regardless of whether the person fights or flees. Similar to our animal neighbors, if the first two fail to get results, the last resort is *freeze.* The term polyvagal comes from the fact that each branch of the vagus controls either fight/flight or freeze, respectively. Most victims of child sexual abuse relate immediately to the notion of freeze. Biologically, freeze is the tragic option when social engagement becomes betrayal and fight/flight becomes impossible. The freeze response is an important focus in healing trauma-triggered, chronic, repetitive experiences. Interventions for traumatic conditions appear in Chapter 5.

These discoveries reach beyond child development research to show how anatomy and physiology of advanced abilities relate directly to survival. Porges (2001, 2011) suggests that we begin with our most advanced skill of social engagement. If that is not sufficient, we move to our less complex capacity, that of fight or flight. Third, if all else fails, we shut down or freeze. In the animal kingdom, a number of animals illustrate the use of freeze as a protective strategy. We will discuss these at length in Chapter 4. As the microscope turns to these interpersonal processes at the cellular level, family and relationship-centered therapists can say, with certainty, that relationship quality is a matter of life and death. Beyond infancy, studies in psychoneuro-immunology bear this out regarding marital discord, parent interactions, social isolation, and attachment (Kiecolt-Glaser, 2009; Kiecolt-Glaser et al., 1998; Kiecolt-Glaser & Newton, 2001; Kiecolt-Glaser et al., 2003; Kiecolt-Glaser et al., 2005; Parker-Pope, 2010). These cellular processes inform intervention strategies throughout the remainder of this book.

Other evidence about the *social brain* includes studies of brain structures. For example, the amygdala are larger when one's social network size is larger (Bickart et al., 2011). Currently, this is considered a chicken-egg relationship, with no conclusions about which has come first. Does the social network contain more stimuli in which babies' amygdala must be constantly assessing for threat? Does this increase the size and circuitry? Given that humans develop more social complexity than any other organism, scientists believe general brain size is related in some way to this complexity. Do humans have the largest brains because of their social networks or do these elaborate brains seek out larger networks? Whatever the answer, the interpersonally oriented landscape of the brain provides therapists with a prominent

> # Understand the interpersonal dramas and you will understand the person.

rule-of-thumb: Understand the interpersonal dramas and you will understand the person.

In mental health practices, mainstream family therapists have usually studied an array of approaches that provide analyses of family interaction. Many of these have great relevance to studies of neurocience. Although the pioneers of family therapy developed their own labels for a given set of interpersonal processes, many clinicians find that attachment theory provides an overarching framework for many family therapy practices (Johnson, 1996; Liddle & Schwartz, 2002; Hanna, 2009). In addition, attachment processes have become a prominent focus as a link between social sciences and neurophysiology (Cozalino, 2006; Porges, in press; Siegel, 2012). When anthropologist Gregory Bateson (1972, 1979) began discussing the relational and interactive aspects of consciousness, he may not have thought how the neuroscience of attachment would support his thinking, decades after his death.

ATTACHMENT

Attachment can be broadly defined as an emotional bond sought between people that has importance as a survival mechanism and endures over time (Ainsworth, 1989; Bretherton, 1992). It is a complex interpersonal process that underlies a sense of security. In children, secure attachment allows them to explore their environment without anxiety. Attachment researchers have spent decades examining the centrality of human attachment processes in mental health (Bowlby, 1969; Ainsworth et al., 1978; Main,

1995; Cassidy & Shaver, 1999). From infancy to old age, studies demonstrate the benefits of secure attachment and the liabilities of insecure attachment. These processes have been at the center of many studies by developmental neuroscientists, who connect these early attachment behaviors with mental health (Sroufe et al., 1999; Schore, 2005; Porges, 2007).

Once biological survival stabilizes for babies, attachment quality appears related to the emotional connections with caregivers who expand their responses to address the growing complexity of children's biosocial needs (*safe haven*). In turn, the fit between what parents offer and what children need influences self-esteem, social skills, and health throughout life (*attunement*; Siegel, 2012). Bowlby's (1944, 1969) work addresses *separation/ loss*, which is a topic of interest beyond the caregiving relationship. For example, Fisher's work in medical anthropology discusses love relationships and breakups as a condition similar to grief and loss that evokes the same neurochemicals (Fisher et al., 2010). Affective neuroscientists trace the neurobiology of addiction and withdrawal in similar terms (Zellner et al., 2011). Intuitively, many psychotherapists see the similarities in these experiences. Now, we see the biological realities that affirm these intuitions and the clinical strategies that attune to them.

During adolescence and adulthood, these attachment needs manifest continued importance for survival. Threat-survival experiences may look like psychological and emotional processes such as differentiation or pair-bonding. However, in an evolutionary sense, the body is responding to threats that have real importance for human progress. For example, research on teen brains explains how risk-taking behaviors paradoxically have survival value (Chein et al., 2011). When risk taking with peers, adolescents had high activation in reward-related brain regions (ventral striatum, OFC). This activation predicted future risk taking. Without a sense of risk taking that is higher than that of adults, adolescents might not leave home, thus threatening survival of the species.

With respect to love relationships, Fisher and colleagues illustrate how dopamine surges during infatuation and attraction encourage reproduction (Fisher et al., 2005; Fisher, 2009; Fisher et al., 2006). Dopamine leads to an increase of testosterone for both genders and this leads to increased libido. However, neurobiology suggests there is more to the love experience than sex hormones. The experience of love co-creates certain neural circuits based on the memory of prior experiences with attachment and intimacy. Such interactions with various brain structures has led some to suggest that lovers should actually be saying, "I love you with all my . . . brain" (Cohen et al., 2007).

Thus, popular notions about love and sex fail to account for the body's sense that physical extinction is a possibility. Fisher et al. (2002) suggest that in committed relationships, the "dopamine-drenched" state of being in love will wane, but neuropeptides such as oxytocin contribute to a nesting instinct that encourages bonding. For the species to survive, it is especially important for men to bond. The idea in anthropology is that Stone Age women had to be careful about choosing a partner because they and their children faced sizeable threats if the male failed to stay, defend their territory, and protect their offspring. However, as families bonded together, oxytocin may have been nature's way to promote survival of the species and lower the effects of stress chemicals. Oxytocin seems to stimulate empathy (Barraza & Zak, 2009).

With these chemical dynamics in mind, if practitioners are good detectives, like Sherlock Holmes, they can deconstruct coping strategies and attempts at attunement, recasting them in light of the interpersonal imperatives to be attached and the biological process that happens simultaneously. Studies of adolescent substance abuse treatment and marital therapy provide interventions that link these presenting problems to attachment barriers (Diamond & Liddle, 1996; Liddle & Schwartz, 2002; Johnson, 1996). As we will see in Chapters 6 and 7, these approaches to family therapy unravel the prehistoric entwined with the modern. With this multidimensional empathy setting the stage, the therapist coaches family members into new perspectives and behaviors that calm stress hormones and heighten the pleasure centers of the brain.

Belonging. In addition to the collection of attachment studies that have created an interdisciplinary subculture, there is work that links attachment processes to other interpersonal phenomena. Siegel (2012) explores how the experience of *belonging* relates to attachment. Hanna, Harper, and Nelson (2011) explore the interplay of belonging and individuality as elements of attachment that guide children as they gain a sense of identity in sibling roles. It seems that belonging happens as part of attachment in families, but also happens in social circles that do not endure over time. An interesting set of brain studies provides evidence for the importance of social rewards for adults outside the family. In one, volunteers played a game and received either money or praise as a reward. Using brain imaging techniques in real time, researchers found praise registered in reward centers just as forcefully as money. The strength of this social reward system led researchers to conclude that humans are "hard-wired" to belong (Izuma et al., 2008). Praise appears to be an indication of belonging, signaling the acceptability of the person in their social environment. Even without long-term bonds, the social self is a collection of biosocial processes that are linked to the experience of belonging (Hood, 2012).

For children in long-term foster care, one of their challenges in finding a safe haven is the difficulty in developing a sense of belonging. The power of "family belonging" remains strong for many foster children, despite many caregivers' hopes that they can transfer this longing. It may seem especially puzzling when the biological family failed to provide a safe haven. Even in some cases of incest, children may retain a sense of familial loyalty. However, if the concept of identity is added to the equation, then, even without the safe haven of secure attachment or a sense of belonging, survival may depend on one's sense of identity. The questions of this attachment-belonging-identity matrix may be,

"Who is there for me?" "With whom do I fit?" "Who am I to you?" "Who am I to me?" "To whom do I matter?"

Identity. Just as the drive to be attached is a central survival drama, humans also need to know that they matter. A suicidal man once stated to his mother, "Ever' body oughta have someone to love, Mama." Embedded in his poignant statement were a multitude of meanings that related to family of origin, larger social context, and definition of self. He went on to commit a murder-suicide, engulfed in a tragic melting pot of paranoid ideation, a compromised immune system, and failed mental health services. Clearly, he experienced his own identity as a matter of life and death. His was an interpersonal identity. As the old time song states, "You're nobody 'till somebody loves you."

The threat of being a nobody has some interesting elements tied to the actual word, "no-body." If we are not interpersonally recognized or validated as individuals, perhaps we fall prey to the neurochemistry of insignificance, a lack of sensation leading to a sense of no body. Just as the concept of *mind* has many definitions, so does the concept of identity. Used in philosophy and the social sciences, *identity* is the attribute of being recognizable and having a sense of individuality, a sense of self. Hood (2012) speaks for a number of sources who maintain that identity only exists in the context of relationships, that humans are highly responsive to their social environments, and thus, biosocially diverse contexts result in multiple identities for each individual (Mead, 1934; Rosenberg & Gara, 1983). He draws upon the concept of the *looking glass self* that came from Cooley (1902), who wrote about the *social self.* Insights from others suggest that *self-efficacy,* the successful results of an individual's actions, also impact identity (Gecas & Schwalbe, 1983). They argue that free will, not social influences alone, plays a part in identity.

Siegel (2012) integrates notions about the self with memory, consciousness, and neurobiology. This stream of thought draws from those who describe the autobiographical self that emerges from the memory of interpersonal experience (Schore, 2005; Jack et al., 2009; Fivush, 2011). Tracking the role of the hippocampus as it encodes memory, he reviews *working memory* as a collection of interactions between the PFC and other brain structures about present experience. This whole brain activity suggests that identity formation involves loops and cycles, including those between person and social environment. Some straightforward activities in family therapy are supported by memory research, such as the activity of having parent and child engage in conversations of past events. Jack et al. (2009) found that these conversations in childhood can influence adolescents' early memories. Thus, memories are influenced by parent-child conversations that "shape what we remember . . . how we remember and the very sense of self that remembers" (Siegel, 2012, p. 59). For this purpose, constructions of *family biographies* in therapy can help parents and children of all ages to shape new identities that emerge from collaborative reflections (Hanna, 1997, 2007, 2010; Suddaby & Landau, 1998).

Integrating these ideas, identity refers to the process of reward or safety that registers in the body from memories, narratives, and recognition. Part of the reward lies in a sense of individuality. Identities form in families and societies from either rewards or threats. Countless examples exist of *private dialogues* that individuals carry on with their families of origin (Hanna, 2007). These are unspoken statements about how a person intends to shape their identity. The dialogues may be about being the same as, or being different from family of origin. For example, those who grow up in poverty may resolve to overcome that disadvantage. Though their memories may include the stress of poverty, their identity lies with overcoming the trials of their parents. Others resolve to avoid the character traits of their parents or siblings. Experiences with an absent father may motivate a daughter to find a partner who values fatherhood. Many children of alcoholic parents resolve never to use substances. Neurobiologically, these experiences illustrate how memory and identity are tied to emotional intensity, whether pleasant or painful. Reward centers and stress hormones all play a role in shaping our identity.

The powerlessness that often attends children in stressful situations can propel them into desperate adult roles that carry the weight of survival. When hopelessness narratives relate to devaluation and misattunement (Hardy & Laszloffy, 2005), the survival mode might be fight/flight or freeze. One study highlights the impact of social acceptance on changes in brain waves when adolescents are excluded by peers during a game (White et al., 2012). Insecure-dismissing attachment related to the expectation of rejection, the under reporting of stress levels, and lower brain waves. The hypothesis here would be freeze mode. Those in the securely attached group manifest similar patterns of distress from exclusion, but did not have lower brain waves. Thus, identity may have its roots in primal attachment process that leads to varying patterns of affect. However, at any age, one's vulnerability to social isolation may seem a matter of life and death.

Rejection of a family's status quo may be a survival strategy for one who has yet to feel family-person attunement. By seeking attachment elsewhere, the rebellious may be the adaptable. In addition, the dramatic mood swings that are part of adolescent relationships have their roots in the tasks needed for survival of the species. Thus, the private dialogue may be, "I deserve to be loved and I'll look until I find it." Often, the term "deserve" is not verbalized. There are a number of family and cultural taboos against stating one's private sense of entitlement (Boszormenyi-Nagy & Krasner, 1986; Hargrave & Pfitzer, 2003, 2011). Chapters 6 and 7 explore therapeutic strategies that address this central issue. Because reproductive survival eventually depends on differentiation of children from families, Bowen (1978) was right. If reproduction is to be successful, humans must differentiate and attach outside the family of origin. This is where survival becomes complicated. In western societies, we develop an identity, first in the family of origin, then in a family or network of significant others outside the family, and also in larger systems defined by gender, race, class, work group, neighborhood, etc. Hood (2012) believes these multiple identities each have neurocircuits unique to them. In essence, identity is an interpersonal experience based on a variety of social circles.

In the formative years of the family therapy movement, Kantor and Lehr (1975) coined the term *psychopolitics of the family.* This is the interplay between family expectations and each person's needs for individuality. There is a need for balance between fitting in and being unique (Hanna et al., 2011). The salient questions are:

> Do I have a place here? What is my place? Is it a good place? Is support given or withheld? What are other members like? What is their style? What is my style? Am I alike or different from the rest of my family? If different, dare I show my difference? What alternatives to my family are there for me? Do I have a place somewhere else?
>
> (Kantor & Lehr, 1975, p. 180)

As central questions of identity in many private dialogues, these have tremendous relevance to physical survival. Lack of family-person attunement is the repetition of interpersonal cycles that co-create threat-survival responses in bloodstream and brain waves (Levine, 2010; Schore, 1994). Our bodies have layers of interpersonal circuits that form the biology of attachment, belonging, and identity. To date, there is no evidence of a single location that houses these experiences. Instead, their circuits fire away in webs of energy, connecting a panorama of locations, sights, sounds, and sensations for every significant event in our development. These circuits become templates for the detective work of brain-informed family therapists.

PRINCIPLE FOUR: THINK CIRCUITS

Our brains have networks of circuits, like cobwebs floating in a sea of fluid. They are thin layers, one on top of another. Since each neuron has as many as 10,000 possible dendritic connections, a circuit can zigzag through a number of layers, around a certain region, even detour to some unlikely dark alley. Throughout life, new neurons are rare, but dendrites and axons increase, becoming more dense or sparse, depending on the need and use of new functions. Brain researchers cite the "use it or lose it" rule when it comes to our circuitry. The possibility of developing new connections is nearly endless. Through activity-dependent learning, our circuits connect and reorganize according to patterns of experience. Synapses, even though they are mere nano spaces, strengthen their electrochemical charge with use. As in interpersonal relationships, perhaps familiarity between synapses creates a bond between neurons, like secure attachment. Thus, neuroscientists use Hebb's (1949) Law: "Neurons that fire together, wire together."

These exciting discoveries that began in the 1940s proved that Pavlov was right. Circuits of firing neurons chemically bind from repetitive sequences of sensation and interaction. We are all Pavlov's dogs. Circuits form from a variety of conditions that repeat in daily routines or from a single explosive moment of overload. After that, any one spot in the circuit can activate the others. For unwanted conditions, we might call it "guilt by association."

Associations

Chapter 2 illustrates the many parts, halves, and regions in brain anatomy. These become the multiple stages from which our dramas unfold. Circuits are not straight lines. As with Pavlov's dogs, the regions for salivation are different than those of hearing or seeing. With the vagus nerve extending to the bottom of our torso, stomach sensations, heart rate, even uterus, are all possible players in the cast of characters. In addition to the vagus nerve, we can visualize the transparent client with receptor molecules throughout the body, just waiting for the doorbell to ring. Thus, when strong emotion includes the limbic system in the script, neuropeptides and hormones become backstage messengers. They travel out to receptors who are like the director and producer sitting in the audience. They can "call the shots," even though they're not onstage. One experience can simultaneously involve circuits in the brain and the flow of chemicals to other locations.

In medicine, stroke patients have a number of treatments that help them regain functioning. One key is intensive use of the weak area. In one study, patients had a work program six hours per day for 10 days. Another key is focus. Directing the mind in certain ways can change the brain (Hubbard et al., 2012). For those who might have been paralyzed from a stroke, it can seem miraculous to have their competence return after a lapse of two years. In other cases, the right brain may compensate for a damaged left hemisphere and circuits work around the injured area. One interesting study found that people blind from birth have full activity in their occipital lobes. When? While they read braille. Their fingers become their "eyes" to read words and the process registers in the occipital lobe (Amedi et al., 2005).

It seems the brain can take advantage of any idle space. Like movie theaters with multiple screens, if one film isn't ready to play, let's schedule something to take its place! Thus, these regions are creative. If part of a brain does not receive a signal, it can recruit other signals to fill the space. Not only can the brain be transparent, we can view its versatility through the resilience of those who overcome injuries. These examples of resilience are key to helping our clients envision their transparent brains and what possibilities lie ahead.

> Not only can the brain be transparent, we can view its versatility through the resilience of those who overcome injuries.

Researchers are still trying to discover how certain circuits decide to develop. For instance, Italian scientists found groups of neurons firing off in monkeys when they observed some phenomenon in others. It seems that mere observation of others produced the same brain activity as though the monkey was actually performing the action (Rizzolatti & Craighero, 2004). Known as *mirror neurons*, they have sparked interest in the processes of imitation, empathy, theories of mind, and memory. In human studies, babies follow and imitate facial movements of caregivers. A number of studies examine the variety of brain locations that fire when humans engage in observation-action behaviors (Mukamel et al., 2010). There is emerging evidence that human mechanisms for imitation are more decentralized in the brain and involve more regions than what monkey research shows.

One study recorded evidence of empathy and emotional social cognition in humans (Schulte-Rüther et al., 2007). Another was able to track how learning and memory records information sequentially (Paz et al., 2010). This area of cognitive neuroscience is growing as more human research examines the ways in which our brains respond to social interaction. Those models of family therapy that emphasize therapist modeling of attunement may find that they are on the cutting edge of neuroscience. The power of observation-action, as the brain records it, has great potential to inform any profession that is interested in the social determinants of the change process in therapy. In Chapter 7 and 8, there is a discussion about how to engage the social network and community. When there are multiple role models in the natural environment, the probabilities for healing and growth increase.

In other instances, the associations are straightforward. Consider the following example: A moment of euphoria occurs for a man as he crosses the finish line of the ironman competition, an intensive challenge of endurance that includes running, swimming, and cycling. His wife and daughters are there to meet him, he can smell ribs cooking on a nearby barbeque, and there is a Beatles song playing in the background. His felt sense of exhaustion mingles with the exhilaration of success, positive family bonding, the smell of good food, and a song that will always remind him of this moment.

Each dimension becomes a web of circuits that begins with the five senses and felt sense as they deliver information to the thalamus. As a switchboard operator, the thalamus directs information to the appropriate location in the cortex. Is it an image of family? That might go to the hypothalamus (limbic system) so that dopamine receptors can register rewards, or to activate oxytocin during a congratulatory hug. Does sensory data contain sound? The announcer calling the time in the foreground and the Beatles song in the background. These data might go to the cortex for affirming thoughts about what this achievement means. Eventually, these regions may send their information on to the hippocampus. Then, the hippocampus will decide whether to store this in long-term memory.

When he hears the Beatles song on the radio, he can relive that moment, if all the stimuli flood with equal intensity. If not, at least bits and pieces will give him the gist of what he experienced and he will smile to himself. What may be less obvious is the private dialogue he is having about his father. He saw his father as a tragic figure who missed many opportunities for success. As he reached adulthood, he vowed not to be like his father. In that moment of euphoria, he was also affirming his identity as someone who lived life to its fullest. It may be this dimension that heightens his emotion and prompts the hippocampus to remember this forever. If so, he may intentionally savor (focus) the experience and let it sink deep into his bones. His worst fear is beaten back. "This is who I am. I won't end up like my Dad. I'll live life to the fullest!" These circuits and their electrochemical intensity can come back on stage for many curtain calls.

Triggers

Circuits are like videos of our lives, in living color and microscopic definition. Sometimes we decide what dimensions are the most relevant to record. At other times, we have no control over what invaders may enter the scene. When the video is threatening, circuits may go into overload and create havoc in unpredictable ways. Intrusive thoughts and puzzling adrenaline rushes may add a layer of shame to the identity. What's happening to me? Am I going crazy? Like a case of hiccups just at the moment of a public speech, circuits may fire away without warning at the most inconvenient times. These are *triggers*. Activate one part of the circuit and the entire circuit may fire. In the social brain, the whole body can activate from stimuli that are not even in the same room. As humans, we have only to imagine and our circuits will

> **Activate one part of the circuit and the entire circuit may fire.**

fire. Like a relationship duffle bag, our brain takes the images of relationships with us, wherever we go. Sometimes we say, "What was I thinking?" The answer, under stress, is, "Nothing." We only need to retrieve one image to activate an entire circuit. Take the case of April.

When April was 54, she was riding with a friend to an Avon party. On the way, her friend, having become quite close to April, innocently said, "Are you by any chance a victim of sexual abuse? I am, and I see something in you that makes me wonder if you are, too." With that one question, April's sense of identity came crashing down. She went into shock. When they arrived at the party, she immediately found an empty bedroom at the home and curled up in a fetal position. There she stayed until the party ended. The answer to the question was, "Yes." However, April spent 40 years working hard to expunge that part of herself. The men who abused her were her mother's boyfriends. They groomed her. Mother was emotionally distant. After her parents' divorce, she was starved for a father in her life. However, as she reached adulthood and married, she found great affirmation in a new church life, a husband who would protect her, beautiful daughters, and her artistic talent. Wouldn't this be enough to make all the bad go away?

It would take April 18 months to finally go to a therapist. In the meantime, angry rages tormented her. She changed into a fearful ghost of her usual self. Her husband responded to her distress with derision and critiques (primary emotion: panic). Her symptoms were circuits, triggered from an invitation to access her long-term memory. Her body still remembered. Unlike the ironman above, there was nothing to savor. Instead, her autobiographic memory was attacked by an invader. Unbeknownst to those around her, her new identity had been a matter of life and death, a lifeboat in the sea of a childless childhood. The truth, after all those years, threatened to sink her ship (circuits of identity). Our brains can be a built-in witness protection program when our social context doesn't provide safety for the testimony. The circuit that fired off that night was one that crossed the shame of those boundary violations with the security of her current identity. Like two live wires with no insulation, they literally scrambled her brain. The two circuits recorded completely different identities. One, a helpless child. The other, a caring wife, mother, and a prominent artist in her community. Each had its own location (stage) because they developed from experiences that contained different associations—sights, sounds, people, relationships, geography, etc. Each circuit regulated her emotions, memories, and behavior in separate worlds. Just as in espionage work, when an undercover agent is outed, the entire mission becomes compromised.

Ironically, the friend was the beginning of a safe haven for the telling of April's story. However, when the amygdala and PFC decided that she was an acceptable harbor, the hippocampus was caught off guard and didn't have the report organized. After all, it had been 50 years. Her trauma was not yet integrated into a coherent narrative. In addition to her childhood trauma, the invitation to address it also became a trauma. Now, at age 62, that has changed. She has spoken publicly about her experiences. Her adult children know and understand what happened to her. She integrated her identities and found peace and acceptance for the whole person. We will revisit April's case in Chapter 6 and examine why her marriage became the biggest casualty in her drama. Chapter 5 discusses her trauma work and how initial overloads like hers can be avoided.

Linking senses, affect, meaning, and memory together, circuits stretch their fireworks to different parts of the brain, reaching to every corner. If they are part of implicit (unconscious) memory, they are stored in the places of origin, such as the five senses, motor cortex, limbic regions. If they are part of explicit (conscious) memory, they may bounce back to the hippocampus before cortex regions decide whether to store them or let them fade. Like a racquetball that bounces lightening fast from side to side, back to front, and angled in corners, our circuits become snapshots of our experience and wait for the next event. With constant use, synapses became so strong that circuits fire off with no conscious effort (Konorski, 1948; Hebb, 1949). They loop through our brains under the electrochemical power of affect (Ferree & Cahill, 2009). This is why family therapy can be most effective when the process links multiple senses together. Family and social networks provide a rich array of ingredients for transformative social scripts and new brain circuits.

PRINCIPLE FIVE: THINK TRANSFORMATION

While *neuroplasticity* refers to the ability of the brain to change at any age, opportunity and caution lie within it (Jäncke, 2009; Doidge, 2007). Opportunity lies in how exception and repetition create new circuits. Caution lies in how novelty and surprise can hijack reward centers that are all too generous with dopamine release in the system. Conspiring with memory and learning centers of the brain, almost anything the body constructs as rewarding can become addicting, when other variables converge with meaning and expectation in the wake of chronic threat (Erickson, 2007). For example, some neuroscientists refer to the positive expectation that dopamine creates. They note how it may release just from the anticipation of a reward, including addictions (Erickson, 2007; Maté, 2010). Chapter 8 examines this neurobiology of addictions with implications for program development.

Thus, brain changes have pros and cons. A brain will register changes with any interpersonal experience. However, those changes may be superficial or even irrelevant. It is interesting how many clients cannot remember the name of a therapist they may have seen in previous years. Just as stroke patients can inch their way into functionality, so can those who seek new relationships and new identities. These are *transformations*, suggesting a change in structure or organization. Brain circuits change their form.

> Conspiring with memory and learning centers of the brain, almost anything the body constructs as rewarding can become addicting, when other variables converge with meaning and expectation in the wake of chronic threat (Erickson, 2007).

Under the right circumstances, what was once a small triangle might turn into a complex and beautiful hexagon with new sequences and neural activations in new regions.

Neuroplasticity

Previous exercises with the felt sense introduce the potential we have to connect our conscious minds to every inch of our bodies and create new circuits. Developing the felt sense is a mental skill just like crossword puzzles and arithmetic. The difference is that the felt sense engages the brainstem, not the cortex. A focus on internal sensations literally directs energy toward a specific area, like a mental laser beam. This process prepares the body for change. Chapter 5 illustrates how the felt sense becomes part of trauma treatment. In addition to using the felt sense, other forms of mental focus, such as mindfulness, bring about increased density in dendrites (Siegel, 2010; Kabat-Zin, 2006). One key to these useful tools is repetition. This is a critical aspect for clinicians to remember. Tapping into the reward system is a way to foster repetition. For example, when clinicians raise consciousness around the *hopes and dreams* of a couple or family, they tap into the reward system stimulated by expectancy. If they invite a few minutes in each session to sustain this focus on dreams, using their exact words, the ritual creates new circuits.

Reward Systems: Repetition, Novelty, Surprise, and Creativity

Activities that stimulate the brain's reward system and multiple other brain regions will have the strongest influence. Emotional, mental, tactile, kinesthetic, visual, and interpersonal circuits all contain great potential for rewards. Remember that praise is as good as money. Interpersonal rewards can create identity circuits that simultaneously activate multiple brain responses. For example, praise might involve positive identity (cortex), a sense of belonging (limbic), smiling (visual), and a hug (tactile). As children develop, repetitive patterns of family affirmation trigger the reward system. As part of a daily routine, their circuits may also involve lower heart variability as a measure of affect regulation (vagus nerve). These associations become even stronger when the affirmations come at unexpected times and in a variety of situations. This is also true of our clients. When we fail to live "up" to a negative expectation about therapists, they are "pleasantly surprised." These sensations are transformative in the body because one circuit goes inactive, while another circuit develops and strengthens. This becomes the biological affirmation for the common parenting prescription, catch children doing something right.

An example of the unexpected happened when Joy, a 16-year-old Caucasian female, began underage drinking during high school. Her mother sent her on a 30-day wilderness program that was sponsored by the local Sierra Club. Unlike therapeutic residential programs, she was surrounded by adults who had signed on for an experience in self-discovery. Despite being the youngest in the group, she was up to the task and met each challenge successfully, including a one-day solo survival experience. Upon her return, the other participants and wilderness leaders praised her performance and provided affirmation of her grown-up competence.

In fact, the burdens that she carried from her family of origin were more adult-like. Her drinking had been self-medication for the lack of fit between her precocious family role and her chronological age. She graduated from high school without incident and became a successful educator. Was this experience for Joy equivalent to stroke patients who work six hours a day for 10 days? Although there were no neurological data, we can hypothesize that it had all the right ingredients: reward, repetition, surprise, creativity, intensive activity, and focus. In contrast to programs that focus only on alcohol use, transformation should involve the engagement of many brain regions.

> Transformation involves the engagement of many brain regions.

With adults, neuroplasticity occurs every time they enrich their environment, learn something new, and perform a new activity. Transformation occurs when these new dimensions persist. Some scientists theorize that age-related losses are due partly to more restricted environments over time. Thus, for clients of every age, clinicians can stimulate brain functioning through encouraging new emotional, mental, and physical repetition across settings that involve nurturing people. An important way to reinforce any program is to involve the social network (Sluzki, 2008, 2010). There is a reason why many people find Alcoholics Anonymous, Weightwatchers, and other peer-support programs helpful. Social support is an important component of survival that can engage many senses in rituals, traditions, and daily routines.

Multiple Levels: Community, Family, Personal, Cellular

A good example of a therapeutic program that combines mental focus with repetition is McFarlane's (2002) multifamily psychoeducational groups for schizophrenia. In numerous clinical trials, these positive social networks promote convincing therapeutic gains with severe mental illness. Given the fact that schizophrenia often brings about individual and family isolation, McFarlane (2002) structures multifamily psychoeducational groups to benefit from *strength in numbers*. Besides the social bonds that form, an interesting problem-solving ritual occurs during each meeting. This structure seems to act as a type of "community frontal lobe," strengthening impaired cerebral functions that result from chemical and social imbalances. The clinical work is often low-key and systematic, producing gradual changes over 12 months. Brain physiology and attachment theory make the case for the importance of these interventions. They create the safe haven amid a traditional mental health service system in which some families and patients often feel mistreated (Woods et al., 2012).

With safety developing, a positive group environment fosters attachment and lowered *expressed emotion*, or criticism. Then, with safety established, brainstorming options, reviewing pros and cons—all the things a prefrontal cortex usually does—gives families and symptomatic members an opportunity to practice frontal lobe exercises. The pace, twice monthly, allows brains to develop new circuits. The repetition within this interpersonal environment creates circuits that strengthen the PFC. In addition, initial joining sessions provide novelty and safety for families who need time to test the waters.

In contrast to stroke patients who benefit from a fast pace and high intensity, those with schizophrenia benefit from a slower pace and lower intensity. Thus, repetition is a given for the formation of new brain circuits, but baseline symptoms related to affect regulation are an important consideration in brain-informed work. Some who have chronic conditions may need a slow, steady pace. Others who are in crisis may need frequent intensity. Chapter 4 provides guidelines for attuning to the pace of each client.

Numinosum

In many ways, these principles combine what we already know with the new language of neuroscience. Along the way, there are the mechanics of physiology that invite us to think more about the order of things. The body shapes the mind around survival priorities. Then, the mind connects these priorities to survival of the attached through circuits of belonging and identity. Once the basics are satisfied, it is supremely human to seek more. This is when transformation is possible. Rossi (2002) has elaborated on the concept of *numinosum* (Otto, 1950):

> the experience of fascination, mystery, and tremendousness that motivates our lives . . . a positive emotion of wonderment accompanying our sense of adventure in exploring the world, our creative endeavors in the arts and sciences, and our spiritual quest for the ultimate.
>
> (Rossi, 2002, pp. xvii–xviii)

Rossi continues by suggesting that when experiences evoke the novelty-numinosum-neurogenesis circuit, this transforms consciousness, relationships, and healing. Family therapists are in a unique position to address the basics of survival and then use those therapeutic gains to help clients orchestrate their own transformations.

In this regard, Perel (2007) offers some guidelines for sex therapy that use erotic fantasies as explorations of the emotional needs that couples bring to sexual experiences. She suggests that fantasies have themes related to problems in search of solutions. A person's emotional history leads to an "erotic blueprint." Her beginning conversations include these questions:

1. What does sex mean for you?
2. What do you seek in sex?
3. What do you want to experience in your encounters?
   (Perel, 2011, p. 9)

The answers to these questions form the quest for numinosum, as couples pursue the psychological safety they desire to overcome inhibitions and desires for intimacy. She relates these issues to a need for PLAY and helps each partner feel safe enough to adopt a sense of adventure. Enactments in sessions help people connect their attachment experiences with desires during sex. For example, having couples hold each other's face is an intimate experience that evokes primary emotions on both sides. The sense of play and imagination that emerges in her sessions becomes a transformation for couples layered with baggage that has had no voice.

THE NEXT STEPS

As we come to know our professional roots and traditions "for the first time," those who integrate neurobiology into their work can see that the relevance of couple and family has never been more relevant, even if one is not inclined to formally add layers of chemicals and nerves to the conversations of clinical sessions. Just like our physiology, these processes can run in the background, creating a greater consciousness about the whole therapist. As Chapter 4 illustrates, that is the best place to start. Then, as practitioners begin to "feel" it, new creative paths of integration will emerge from the right brain. Nevertheless, the five principles in this chapter outline a paradigm that illustrates how the bio becomes the social, and visa versa. Table 3.1 summarizes concepts of the five principles and their pathways into conversations with clients. These are suggestions to help practitioners dip their toe in the waters of the brain. There's nothing earth shattering or profound, here. The intent is to practice seeing how all the parts fit together. Questions from one section may

Table 3.1 Pathways of the five principles

Principle/Elements	Conversational Pathways
Whole Body	What are you feeling in your body right now?
Collective Intelligence	What is your gut feeling about it?
Felt Sense	As you're feeling that, where in your body do you sense
Affect	it? Can you stop and just take a few breaths to bring some
Meaning	calm into your body?
Memory	Can you trace these feelings back to another moment in
	time? Back then, what was happening?
	What would feel safe right now?
Survival	
Adaptability	Who are the people you most enjoy being with?
Cooperation/	When things get tough, who can you count on?
Teamwork	
Social Support	Do you have a favorite memory of a favorite relationship?
Biosocial Ecology	Have you had any life-threatening, or life-changing
Physical Harm	injuries or illnesses?
Isolation	When have you felt most alone?
Interpersonal	
Social Engagement	How do other people describe you?
Attachment	Who has most influenced on your self-esteem?
	Whose opinion matters to you the most?
Belonging, Identity	Who matters to you the most? Who do you matter to the most?
Psychopolitics	Growing up, how were you different than others in your
	family?
Circuits	Let me see if I can get a video image of what exactly
	happened?
Associations	Who said what to whom? What happened next? What
	exactly did you hear and see?
Triggers	What about you is most puzzling? Are there things you
	wish you understood better about yourself?
Transformation	What are your hopes and dreams for yourself and each other?
Neuroplasticity	What's the most significant change you've ever made in
	your life?
Rewards	What was happening when that happened?
Repetition	What was most surprising about it?
Novelty	How did it affect your family and social relationships?
Surprise	What was the predominant feeling in your body?
Creativity	Exhilaration or calm? Can your body still remember
Multiple Levels	how that felt? Where might you feel it now?
Community	What has been the greatest adventure you've ever been on?
Family	How did it affect the way you thought about yourself
Personal	and the world? Would you be interested in another
Cellular	adventure?

work as follow-ups to those in another section, without any particular order. Next, the parts come together in an exploration of the therapist-client relationship, the therapist-problem relationship, couple relationships, family relationships, and the community.

4

Soul Food
Neurobiology and the Therapeutic Relationship

When I was young, I did what I knew to do. When I knew better,
I did better.

Maya Angelou

In the United States, the term "soul food" has become synony-
mous with the tantalizing mix of flavors and textures that orig-
inally came from southern black cooks who were short on money
and long on creativity and innovation. At the heart of this "comfort
food" is the feeling of safety, knowing there are those who "have
your back," and a good feeling clear down to the bone. These resilient families didn't need brain science to tell them what they
needed to survive. Intuitively, a number of southern black traditions, such as the blues and jazz music, became mainstays in white
culture precisely because of their resonance. They felt good. They
fit. There is something brain-friendly that springs from the
survival strategies of those who are threatened with extinction.
Mainstream America may not have been in touch with the threatened part of the self, but the popularizing of soul food and
emotional music speaks to this unmistakable voice in everyone's
body. If therapeutic relationships provide nothing else, let them
bring to our clients these three elements: comfort, caring, and a
deep affirmation of self.

This chapter is about the dialogues and discourses that facilitate these elements. Psychotherapists have specialized conversations honed by generations of westernized mental health professionals as they evolved from Freud, to Rogers, to Bandura, to Satir, to Minuchin, to Erickson, to Beck, to de Shazer and Kim Berg, to White, to Gottman, to Johnson (Hanna, 2007). Yes, there are dozens more. With each one came a language that invited a mindset for a psychotherapist to use. In addition, various professions, with licenses and academic traditions, contributed more language to the culture of mental health services in America. These approaches and languages are also part of the therapist's personal story, even if education and training emphasized a few over the many.

Although our theoretical ancestors lacked access to the brain as we know it, we can recognize the value of their effort. While neuroscience has its own confusion with the glossary that appears in Chapter 1, it can still be a unifying framework for understanding the successes of many models. As a pioneer in clinical hypnosis, Milton Erickson used to say, "I invent a new theory for each client" (Rosen, 1988). He emphasized the importance of individualizing an approach for each person. Perhaps this is why the field of psychotherapy has become the "Tower of Babel" in the social sciences (Miller et al., 1997). The variety of approaches matches the variety of people who give help and need help. Yet, many of Erickson's protégés have described a number of central elements to his work (Zeig & Lankton, 1988; O'Hanlon, 1987). They show that, even though humans are complex, we still have many universal characteristics. It is between these two poles that neuroscience sits, able to provide a unifying framework to address individual differences.

Generally, current family therapy approaches may fall into one of three main categories. There are those that include 1) a theory of human development, or 2) a theory of how change occurs, or 3) an integration of the two. Brain-friendly therapy is largely integrative. In this view, development is cast in survival terms and transformation addresses our creative potential. Thus, the therapist-client relationship can be a developmentally appropriate tranformation for both parties. Here, we start with the therapist's development and how it can impact treatment.

THE SELF OF THE BRAIN-INFORMED THERAPIST

As Chapter 1 stated, one hope for readers is that they will step back and see themselves as part of a larger drama in the history of the world. That drama is about overall progress in the human condition, whether in our backyard or around the world. In our backyard, each practitioner has a story about how they decided to enter the helping professions. The story may feel like a drama or comedy; action film or love story. These range from the accidental to the providential; from an opportunity to a mission; from a scientific exploration to a personal quest for healing. Regardless of the story, chances are everyone's story has bits and pieces of these elements. The accidental student may have become smitten by altruism that fuels some personal quest. The person who feels called to the work may have migrated to an interest in outcomes and accountability. All these possibilities beg the question: Is my contribution what I want it to be? Am I getting the results that I desire? Is there anything I am missing? These are all uniquely human questions.

Beyond the backyard is a pluralistic society. Endless worldviews spring from more life stories and dramas. In brain language, we explore the amygdala, hippocampus, and reward centers to deconstruct the strength and repetitions of identity circuits. We can watch for signs of physiological activation. Does it flow, or does it get stuck in either "up" or "down?" Brain-informed therapists begin to notice this. What comes next depends on the therapist's self-development. Is the brain of the therapist transparent? Is the felt sense an anchor for the creativity that can spring from balancing the left and right brains? Does the first session with a new client have room for the body, mind, and relationships to unite? Or, will therapeutic discourse omit one or more dimensions?

Clinicians can take an inventory of their professional well-being by starting with their own survival narratives. The therapist's story is an important influence on the dialogues within each case. Cybernetic theory invites the awareness that relationships unfold through interpersonal loops, producing waves of brain circuitry. Each therapy session is an intersection of triggers from each person's development. Sensory loops survey the present relationship and compare it to previous experience that may or may not trigger certain circuits. Thus, stories preserved in the cortex and organized by the amygdala, hippocampus, and PFC will affect the emotional tone of our bodies during a session. In turn, this tone affects the language we choose to describe the presenting problem and the questions we ask.

The brain-informed therapist can model a *balanced nervous system* by doing an exploration of one's neural territory to identify intrusive thoughts, emotional distractions, and narrow thinking that may limit effectiveness in sessions. Are there fears, memories, or distractions that intrude on the anticipation of a new client? Does the client behavior affect the activation in our bodies? Once these are located in the body, their energy and repetitive circuits can be cleared away. Chapter 5 discusses the details of these processes as they apply to trauma, but they are also useful as a form of mindfulness in every day life. Neural explorations can be deep or surface, depending on the person. The following sequence of questions begins with the deepest reflections tied to explicit (conscious) long-term memory. However, a practitioner can begin the process at whatever level seems to fit.

Step 1: Decide on One Question as an Entry Point

The theme here is the importance of others in our threat-survival stories. Since our bodies are unaware that we live in the twenty-first century, our own survival story is an introduction to our conscious minds and explicit memory. Since survival is an interpersonal process for humans, significant others are part of every survival story. If someone, even a stranger, helped us survive in some way, they are tagged by the limbic system as significant. Thus, the "who" of survival is a very important association to make. Otherwise, an understanding of the circuit is incomplete.

As examples, one might use the following questions:

- What is my story of survival?
- Who is important in my history of survival?
- In childhood, who cared for my physical and emotional needs? Were they predictable?
- What are the stories of challenge, victory, or safety in how my caregivers provided for my needs?
- How did attachment occur? Growing up, who was there for me?
- What is my story of bonding, belonging, and identity? Whose voices are most prominent in the development of these self-perceptions?
- Is my identity a reaction to pain? Like the ironman in Chapter 3, must I be _____, in response to my perception of another's way?
- How does my identity come from physical, emotional, and interpersonal rewards that tell me I belong? Who gave me those rewards? How do I know I am important? To whom am I important?
- How is my behavior in a clinical session a survival strategy? How is my way of speaking tied to survival? Does it come from feeling safe or unsafe?
- In past clinical work, what have been some of my most "sparkling moments" (Epston & White, 1992)? When have I known I was making a difference?
- What clients are most difficult for me? Do they threaten bonding, belonging, or identity?

Step 2: Choose an Area of Activation

The theme here is how our bodies store our experiences. Since experience is stored somewhere in the body, these activations are a survival-attachment-body circuit. Clinicians can develop more left/right brain balance by tapping into this circuit. The grounding exercise in Chapter 3 can strengthen the positive by savoring that sensation and enjoying it. There might be words or an image that are pleasant. Before a session, this grounding activity can keep practitioners connected to their resources and keep their nervous system flexible (Ross, 2008).

- Which sensations in my body does this question activate?
- Which questions from Step 1 bring the strongest positive sensations in the body? The strongest negative?
- Is there a place of bodily activation that seems unrelated to any of the questions? (There may not be material from the conscious mind that is accessible, only the sensation.)
- What happens if I focus my mind on those uncomfortable sensations? Can I focus my mind on them and see what happens next?

Sometimes a focus on the place of activation will shift consciousness from the uncomfortable place to the comfortable place on its own, if time permits. If time does not permit, take your conscious mind back to the place of comfort, in preparation for your next session.

After a session, there may be a need to focus on a "hot" spot to clear the energy from it. The felt sense exercises from Chapters 2 and 3 introduce the yin and yang of clearing. There are places in the body that feel good and others that are less so. The good places are a resource and a fortress from which to explore tension or turmoil in another location. However, just as with clients, there is no mandated time for addressing turmoil. In fact, if trauma is folded into the cobwebs of our physiology, the

> When trauma is folded into the cobwebs of our physiology, the worst thing that can happen is premature exploration before a person senses their resources and safety.

worst thing that can happen is premature exploration before a person senses their resources and safety.

In Chapter 3, April's experience illustrates how profoundly a person can become disoriented when they suffer multiple, simultaneous threats without having a sense of safety. This sensing is not an event. Rather, it comes, just like secure attachment, from the therapist becoming attuned to the unspoken needs for safety that emanate from the other. In April's case, it was over a year before she felt safe enough to go to a therapist. Her friend, also a survivor of sexual abuse, was much further along in her recovery and was unaware of what resources April was lacking at the outset of her journey. Therapists are not immune from these threats of depleted resources. In fact, sometimes we are more vulnerable because of the social and emotional pressures that are part of our professional identity. This is why brain health is especially important for healthcare professionals.

Step 3: Practice Social Engagement

The theme here is how to minimize isolation and maintain connections to soothe the body. Psychotherapists may fall prey to a narrow set of interpersonal resources due to the characteristics of a practice setting or personal philosophy. From an evolutionary perspective, connection with family and tribe is the key to survival in our modern-day "concrete jungle." Humans are wired to use social engagement as the first strategy for survival. When this does not happen, fight/flight kick in. In practice, this may take the form of a therapist becoming too isolated and then having triggers of a fight/flight response in the session. It is no wonder that lonely, isolated, abandoned people have higher levels of emotional activation or freeze (Schore, 2003; Porges, 1995). Building on the questions from Step 2,

- What relationships will help me maintain a feeling of safety in that part of my body?

- What colleagues inspire me and help me do my best? How can I access them?
- Whose presence can I call into my mind to maintain that feeling of safety?
- What would these people say, if they were here?
- When my client arrives, how will I be transformed from that relationship? What adventure awaits me?

Are there areas of vulnerability that can guide the practitioner to reach out to sources of social support? In some cases, it is useful to rely on lists, pictures, and symbols to maintain the presence of our important relationships. Perhaps new connections with others can stimulate new social support. The result is more left/right brain balance, greater flexibility in body rhythms, a sense of safety, and most important, a wider range of options for helping the most challenging clients. Using the five principles from Chapter 3 can help clinicians identify survival-attachment-body circuits that are key to professional transformations. These transformations increase flexibility and promote successful therapeutic alliances.

THE BRAIN-INFORMED ALLIANCE

The first session in every case is a meeting of survival circuits between the total number of people in the room. There will be layers of threat, survival, and safety on the path to collaboration. Like a first date, the same questions loom large for all parties—"Will I be safe? Will you see me the way I want you to see me?" As clinicians identify tension, take deep breaths, call up the wisdom of mentors, and recall sparkling moments, it is time to provide soul food for others. Comfort brings tranquility, even in the face of danger. Caring brings hope in the face of discouragement. Deep affirmation brings safety and trust. As we have already learned from studies comparing praise and money, positive relationships are powerful rewards.

Tranquility vs. Mobilization: Speak to the Amygdala

Our interpersonal style matters. Griffith and Griffith (1994) speak of "psychotherapy as a biological phenomenon" (p. 37). Our interpersonal and theoretical style may soothe or activate. Neither of these is inherently bad. It is the timing and fit of these that impact the body. These authors suggest that language and emotional postures effect tranquility and mobilization. If certain vulnerabilities are not calmed, mobilization will lead to "no-shows." Addressing expectations and unspoken emotional needs is an important part of alliance-building. Allowing these to remain unspoken until the client feels safe is a critical aspect of creating tranquility. Since trust is a process and not an event, it behooves therapists to be patient with the developmental needs of their clients.

Thus, the art of psychotherapy should involve nonverbal communication with a client's unspoken needs. As the therapeutic dance begins, if there are too many unanswered questions, the amygdala and PFC may decide that the environment is not safe for candor. These two brain structures may take the client elsewhere. "This doesn't fit for us. Let's go." Table 4.1 outlines a number of unspoken needs and questions that relate to client comfort. It illustrates this dance by providing suggestions about clients' unspoken needs and how the therapist can indirectly respond to them. Just like a parent with a newborn, the initial stages of the relationship are a guessing game. However, the contribution of neuroscience to the therapist's dilemma is to explain why there may be these hidden vulnerabilities and why we should respect them. Just as attachment theory provides a map for parents with their infants, so can the theory help therapists respect the developmental level of their clients.

There is a context to the bias that appears in Table 4.1. Throughout the history of psychotherapy, there have been conflicting voices about how to address others' thoughts, emotions, and behaviors when a theory suggests they are unhealthy. Some

Table 4.1 Tranquility and hope

Client Need	Survival Need	Client Unspoken Messages	Therapist Response
Save face	Identity	Who am I to you? Don't humiliate me. Don't blame me. Respect my unspoken fears, shame, sadness, hurt. Help me put my best foot forward.	You have good intentions. You have a good heart. I respect you. I like you.
Therapist credibility	Attachment	Who are you to me? Can you do this? What can I expect from you? Don't expect me to always know what I want or how to get it. That is why I'm here.	This is what I know about your problem. This is what I can do. This is what I have to offer. Does it fit?
Order out of chaos	Attachment	What can you do to help me? You're the expert. How does this work? Don't ask me to be vulnerable until I feel safe. Be careful with me (if I've been through a trauma).	We can take this step by step. First, I want to know what fits for you. Different people need different things. Next, we can make a plan together. How does a win-win approach sound to you (if it's a couple)?
Possibilities	Identity	Who can I become? What do you think? I'm not sure I can do this. Is there hope for me?	I see strengths in you. The glass is half-full. Let's explore the possibilities together.
Connection	Belonging	Do you "get" me? Can you make sense out of my life? Can I trust you to have my back? Do you take me seriously?	Welcome. I want to understand you. Give me some time to learn all the important things about you. You matter.

say to confront with authenticity. Others say to educate. The addition of substance abuse treatment strategies within mental health services has also added to the maze of thought about how therapists should bring about change. As in a maze, there are many dead ends. These require us to retrace our steps and choose a direction that leads to the destination we desire. During the 1980s, a number of voices in the MFT community began to examine these dead ends. Some concerns related to the term *resistance*, and how therapists could lapse into spoken and unspoken criticism when they interpreted clients' behaviors in this way. Some gravitated to Milton Erickson's suggestion that resistance is the expression of the client's uniqueness. Ericksonian therapists find numerous ways to use a client's uniqueness, rather than challenge it (Erickson & Rossi, 1979; O'Hanlon, 1987).

As these analyses lead to changes in language, many family therapists also sought a greater sense of collaboration with their clients (White, 1986; Berg & Dolan, 2001, McFarlane, 2002; Cunningham & Henggeler, 1999). It would be nearly thirty years before addictions researchers would develop a collection of interventions that would resonate with the practices of family therapists from earlier decades. An example of these is *motivational interviewing*. It is a strategic method that attends to micro interactions between therapist and client to address ambivalence and enhance motivation for change (see Chapter 5). Now, there is scientific recognition by the federal government that these collaborative approaches are an important component of successful treatment (Miller & Rollnick, 2013). Neuroscience explains how confrontation can lead to a therapeutic dead end and why the following micro processes are so important. Many people are fearful, even when they do not appear to be. Chapter 8 provides recommendations for how to provide nuturing in brain-friendly programs.

Save face. Everyone has a need to save face, including professionals. The amygdala, hippocampus, and PFC decide who I want you to think I am. This need is tied to our identity and to who we hope we are to others. Saving face is a biological process that calms. Humiliation and shaming are interpersonal assaults that reach deeply into our attachment-identity-belonging circuits. Although most therapists approach the first session with an intent toward empathy, clients may exhibit behavior that triggers fear circuits in clinicians. Perhaps they emote intense anger, sadness, agitation, or blaming. Chances are, their amygdala is already speaking about some type of humiliation. These are the clients who most need calm. Once therapists diffuse their own anxiety, their calm speaks to the amygdala, not to the overt speech or behavior that is governed by the PFC. The following example illustrates this point.

A client once brought me a postcard that read, "If you could only hear what I cannot say." This was his amygdala reporting that it was locking him down into the freeze mode. I didn't know about neuroscience then, but I understand why my intuitions got results. Nearly mute in the first 10 sessions, he was able to write to me in between sessions. Deliberately following his lead, I responded to his writing each week when he returned. Those exchanges enabled me to communicate in a way that gave him comfort, and demonstrated my caring. As I learned about common family interactions and conversational patterns in his family, I was able to provide systemic empathy for his particular influences, emotions, and dilemmas. This reached into his hippo-campus, where memories were not letting down their guard until they knew whether I would be like his family (negative expecta-tions). When I recognized these, we evolved into a relaxed mode. Now, amygdala, hippocampus, and PFC were lined up and calm. Like a stranger at someone else's Thanksgiving dinner, I had to show that I could fit in. Not too critical of family, not too accepting of them . . . Just right! My nonverbal behavior allowed him to save face. I didn't require more than his anxious amygdala and hippo-campus could give. In time, we "dodged the bullets" of the almighty adrenaline. Saving face in the presence of fear and threat provide a solid foundation for therapists to establish their credi-bility (Cunningham & Henggeler, 1999).

Therapist credibility. Clients have the right to question and receive evidence of a therapist's credentials. However, credibility is more about getting results. In the face of intense anger, sadness, agitation, or blaming, the client might be saying, "Can you handle me?" Stereotypes of therapy may come from sensational media portrayals of psychotherapy that do not fit a practitioner's values or philosophy. Do clients expect social judgement in which participants brace for criticism, like television reality programs, or have they heard from a friend that therapists are nonjudgmental listening ears and sounding boards? A typical scenario between spouses involves use of the phrase "You need therapy" as though it was diagnosis, punishment, or criticism. When one partner comes in alone and states that the other is unwilling to attend, the therapist can immediately deconstruct the <u>language</u> of their conversation and discover that reluctance is merely a refusal to attend an ambush. Once the therapist is able to speak to that reluctant spouse, the threat-survival circuits can be calmed.

Ignoring these preconceived notions leaves out the influence of the hippocampus and amygdala, where memory is stored and anxiety is the file clerk of experience: "Should we retain this memory? We might need it if she ever seeks counseling." When new clients come for the first time, the hippocampus and the PFC need information to dispel stereotypes or to distinguish this from a previous unsuccessful experience with psychotherapy. Once they have the information, they can calm the amygdala, who is just waiting to see you make the same mistakes. Practitioners can calm these structures and avoid activation of a fight/flight mode.

An example of this from my clinical work involved the parents of a boy I saw in a residential facility. There had been a tragic death of an older brother in the family. When I explored the unpleasant characteristics of a previous therapy experience, the family described the exact direction that I was about to pursue! "Hmmm. What now?" I said to myself. The first thing to do was to learn why that direction was uncomfortable. Parents said it made them too sad to discuss the details. I thanked them for the valuable information. I made a vow to them that I would not take that same approach. Although I felt disadvantaged by my biases, the experience became an adventure in flexibility. Now, I knew what <u>not</u> to do. There were plenty of here-and-now issues related to their survival. Thirty years later, I see their wisdom in avoiding experiences of high activation at a time when they wanted to attend to the immediate welfare of their other son. Similar to the Hollywood film *Ordinary People*, the threat of losing control of emotions can be terrifying and an assault to one's identity. At the time, many theories suggested that the death was central to the younger brother's acting out. The contribution of neuroscience to this debate introduces the logic of the whole body and the physiology of timing and emotional regulation. In the film, the brother's activation was more from his perceptions of relationships with his parents.

The issue was not whether to address the death, but how to address the <u>effects</u> of the death. Levine's (2010) approach to healing trauma achieves excellent results without the need of re-experiencing. Chapter 5 reviews details of the gentle and resourceful way he taps into body signals to help rebalance the nervous system. His first step is to build resources by sensing positive sensations present in the body. However, since I had no knowledge of these new developments, I maintained my vow and we worked on the son's truant behavior. I could speak to their nonverbal grief by helping them develop a plan that would increase communication in a safe way. For example, education on individual coping styles sent an unspoken message that I accepted individual differences. This led to discussions of their son's coping style and what he might need that is different from either parent. We could talk about each person's behavior and the messages implied in the behavior. Then, we were able to develop a plan of communication that would help parents attune to their son's mental states. The message that he missed his brother could be sent in a simple signal of sadness. When he's sad, what would he like to have happen? He wanted to hear that it wasn't his fault, or that it was OK for him to have some fun, even though he missed his brother. He also wanted his parents' acceptance: messages about attachment and belonging. He wanted reassurance that his parents would be alright.

Without ever discussing details of the death or analyzing its context and meaning, we moved into the future. Without calling it grief therapy, we accomplished all the same tasks such as emotional attunement, forgiveness, and reassurance. Rather than discussing what happened, we discussed how to survive now. As the clinician, I learned that I didn't have to embark on a crusade to fix everything according to my best theories. Instead, I could take one small part, dictated by the threat-survival system of the family. This enabled the family to feel tranquility, a pre-requisite for making order out of chaos.

Order out of chaos. Making order out of chaos involves the therapist's attunement to the family's need for structure. Most families don't know they can ask for a plan. How many therapists offer a plan at the end of the first session? Sometimes, a client only needs a rationale for what the therapist plans as the next step. For others, they want to look farther down the road. These differences in information-processing relate to preferred modes of self-soothing. Over time, different people calm themselves in different ways. Some want logic, some want the big picture. Thus, a therapist can address multiple cognitive styles by describing general stages of a counseling experience with a rationale for each stage.

Explore, clarify, analyze, educate, experiment, discuss, brainstorm, decide, commit, plan, revise, question, answer, communicate, celebrate

The politics of collaboration can acknowledge different styles and place equal weight on what works for all parties. There is usually an unspoken dilemma around clients' assumption that therapists know best. They may know what they need to feel more secure, but don't know whether it's appropriate to ask for it. In the face of a power differential, they usually need permission. Therapists can describe how they usually work and provide options within that frame. Then, clients can brainstorm their preferences. For example, at the end of the first session, like a first date, do we kiss or go home and think about it? When therapists merely conclude the session by asking, "Would you like to return?" The question is like asking, "May I have a kiss?" The wisdom of the elders used to say, "If you have to ask, then don't!" This is an excellent metaphor for the dance of attunement. If the therapist has read the nuances up to this point, a better question might be, "Now, have I missed anything? Are there some other questions you would like to have answered? Some people like to go home and think about it. Others have some suggestions to add to the process, and some are interested in scheduling the next appointment. What works for you?" If I sense that someone wants more time, but is hesitant to assert himself, I'll suggest that they take a little time to think about it and call me back. They invariably call back.

The microprocesses at the end of a first session will involve a number of gut feelings. Do we fit? Does the client's body language suggest a fit? I begin the first session by saying that the purpose of the session is to explore whether we fit, since the quality of the therapeutic relationship predicts the best results. "If you tell me what you'd like help with, I'll tell you how I would normally address a situation like that. We can put our heads together to see if that fits, and if you need something else, I'm happy to provide a referral to someone who might be a better fit." This establishes a spirit of exploration in which the therapist is not assuming too much. Also, the dance of engagement allows options and freedom to go elsewhere. When the therapist communicates these implicit possibilities, it is a signal to the client that they don't have to worry about offending the therapist, if there isn't a fit.

From the beginning, I allow for the possibility of lack of fit. This keeps the conversation flexible, with many options. At the same time, I have a plan. This provides structure. Some amygdalas want options, some want structure. As leaders of the first session, therapists can attune to clients by acknowledging the variety of experience and preference that may exist within a family. This conveys an implicit awareness of psychopolitics within the family. Chapter 6 discusses how men's and women's brains differ and how clinical process can become attuned to those differences.

Regardless of client preferences, a generic proposal that provides logic and order to the process will engage the PFC and empower it to tame the amygdala. Then therapists can encourage clients to respond, revise, and counter propose. By taking the lead, the therapist also establishes the order of therapy—organize the process first, then address the details. Table 4.2 provides suggestions for elements of a preliminary plan. What verbs describe clinical behaviors? Explore, clarify, analyze, educate, experiment, discuss, brainstorm, decide, commit, plan, revise, question, answer, communicate, celebrate? Griffith and Griffith (1994) suggest that the language of tranquility can include reflecting, listening, wondering, creating, musing, fantasizing, day-dreaming. Brain-friendly therapists can use a combination of these verbs, propose a certain order, and ask the client to revise it.

An example of this was with Ellen, who came to explore a conflict with her family of origin. I asked to meet her husband

Table 4.2 Elements of structure for a plan

Element	Possibilities
Problem Definition	Start with their words, try on expanded language to include body, threat, relationships. See if they fit. Be tentative
Client Preferences	Structure, vision, options, appreciation, advocacy, insight
Process Options	Explore, clarify, analyze, educate, experiment, discuss, brainstorm, decide, commit, plan, revise, question, answer, communicate, celebrate, reflect, listen, wonder, create, muse, fantasize, day-dream
Motivation	Hopes and dreams, possibilities, justice, safety, relief from pain, crisis

during the first session to hear his observations about her situation and to explore any needs that he had for their relationship. With a stable marriage and shared perceptions of her family, he agreed to be available if she needed his support during the process. By mutual agreement, he did not attend any further sessions. I explained to Ellen that I could respond in a few different ways. Would she prefer to invite a family member in to discuss her feelings, or have homework and experiment with behavioral strategies, or more analysis of her family, in which she would take time in between sessions to reflect on different ideas that we discuss. She chose the latter.

> reflecting,
> listening,
> wondering,
> creating,
> musing,
> fantasizing,
> day-dreaming

Providing these choices is meant as an exercise to connect the mental states of therapists with mental states of clients, not a formal treatment plan set in stone. Because language can be a stimulant, these procedural considerations can provide positive activations in the body as a person reviews the options. The therapist is conveying that she can be flexible and that the problem is solvable through any of these strategies. These activations are often dopamine secretions that come from hope.

Hope: The Dopamine Rush

The most reluctant client has a sense of what they wish could happen, even if it is only to be able to leave. If we fail to tap this in the first session, we miss an opportunity to awaken the reward system of the brain. Miller and Rollnick (2013) note that everyone is motivated for something. It is the therapist's responsibility to discover the client's strongest motivations. Dopamine is released at the mere expectation of something rewarding. Some approaches ask clients in the first session about their "hopes and dreams" (Liddle, 2000). After many years as a solution-oriented therapist,

Bill O'Hanlon evolved his therapy to one called "possibility therapy" (O'Hanlon & O'Hanlon, 1999). His approach looks realistically at the depth of some pain and suffering, acknowledging those limitations, but still exploring all possibilities for healing. As a sexual abuse survivor, he suggests that therapists co-construct possibilities with clients through language (O'Hanlon, 1999).

Possibilities. Some language keeps possibilities open and some closes them down. For example, a student recently shared some educational material intended for survivors of sexual abuse. The first draft stated, "Although you can never fully heal from this abuse, it is possible to cope better." He was trying to acknowledge the depth and seriousness of pain that emerges from sexual abuse. However, it is important to use language that leaves all possibilities on the table. Eventually, the pamphlet read, "Everyone is different. There are a number of new treatments that can help you individualize your healing process. It is always possible to feel better than you do today. The key is finding the right fit for you."

There is ample research on placebo effects that reminds us how positive expectations and hope can have powerful, healing effects on the body. In addition, motivational interviewing studies suggest that a number of people are ambivalent about change because they lack the confidence that they will succeed (Miller & Rollnick, 2013). The language of possibility acknowledges existing strengths and instills hope for a better day. This is why Pavlov's dogs salivated, even when there was no food. The language of possibility primes the dopamine pump that sits in the reward system of the brain.

Connection. In attachment theory, Siegel (2012) suggests that attunement is the ability of one to read others' signals and to respond to their state of mind. This leads to a sense of "feeling felt." Secure attachments will form for infants who come to expect attunement from repeated communications. For clients, a growing connection develops from a therapist's attunement. Feeling understood and important touches the belonging circuit, just like praise. Attunement suggests a resonance of mind and heart that affirms basic human needs while clients find their voices.

One lesson from McFarlane's (2002) multifamily groups is that new group members will return when they feel welcome, even though they may not feel safe yet. The training manual for these groups teaches facilitators to assume the roles of *host and hostess*, as though it is a social club. This unorthodox approach stimulates a sense of belonging as facilitators roll out the welcome mat for timid and weary parents who may feel blamed for the schizophrenia of their son or daughter. Feeling welcome allows the participant to return and test the waters. These repetitions are vital to changing brain circuits. When feeling welcome advances to feeling felt, this creates the beginning of secure attachment.

> When feeling welcome advances to feeling felt, this creates the beginning of secure attachment.

Studies show that when infants feel securely attached, they feel free to explore their world (Ainsworth et al., 1978). On the way to secure attachment, adults and children need to know that therapists understand what they cannot say. Often, they have no language for family psychopolitics and interpersonal dilemmas that deserve affirmation. Identifying unspeakable dilemmas is the deepest form of empathy, felt right down to the bone (Griffith & Griffith, 1994).

Deep Affirmation: Unspeakable Dilemmas

The content, process, and substance of family therapy converge in threat-survival circuits that are backstage during every conversation in new territory. In the body, content is about threat, process is about attachment, and substance is about protection and defense. Circuits are loops of firing neurons that light up pathways to create the mind. Thus, how a person balances personal needs versus those of the couple or family creates a complex set of politics that is unique to them. Biological processes reflect how comfortable the person is with the perceived balance of family psychopolitics. When something seems out of balance, dilemmas arise from relationships, memory, identity, and attachment (Friel & Friel, 2012). When interpersonal conflict is understood in the larger picture of competing interests, this is *systemic empathy* (Hanna, 1995).

Cognitive neuroscientists suggest that memories and learning create our identity within a variety of social contexts (Hood, 2012). At six months, babies learn that they are separate from others. Our explicit memory begins sometime after year two. As children develop, the reward system of the brain remembers positive messages that come from others. In groundbreaking research with infants, Hamlin, Wynn and Bloom (2010) document a baby's ability to favor a puppet that demonstrates pro-social behavior over one that does not. This only reinforces how sensitive the brain is to social process. Around age four, young children begin to have a *theory of mind*, in which they become aware of others' thinking (Siegel, 2012). This is when the *looking glass self* emerges. They begin to interpret how they think others think about them.

Hood (2012) provides an extensive review of research that suggests identity is socially constructed, even when our conscious thoughts tell us that we are autonomous and independent thinkers. He suggests that *implicit memory* has a hand in hiding some of the unconscious social processes that are important for everyday functions. For example, most people have learned to tie their shoes. However, the memory of this may now be implicit or unconscious, unless there is a strong emotion that resides in the same circuit. Interpersonally, there are webs and networks of family process that reside in the brain, but we may not have much consciousness about how our behavior first emerged from these stimuli. Hood suggests that we are largely unaware of the implicit politics in relationships that lead to our sense of self. He also suggests that because we are sensitive to each social context we enter, we have multiple selves. These selves can be at the heart of some unspeakable dilemmas, because they may be largely part of implicit memory until a therapist decides to explore them.

Whatever the final formula, family interactions stir the pot with emotional spice that sticks to each memory. Each memory differs in intensity and importance. Social learning takes the form of dopamine surges during the good times and cortisol surges during the bad times. The private dialogue for each child in a family is, "Who am I? How do I fit? How am I different or the same from others? Will I still belong, if I am different?" Practitioners can also use the questions at the beginning of this chapter. The important tasks are to enter the client's world, understand its complexity, and celebrate existing survival skills and strengths. The advantage of using attachment theory as a framework is that it normalizes basic, universal, human needs and validates any painful chapters that warrant special attention. Basic needs become dilemmas when the balancing act of fitting in and being unique becomes stalemated.

Identity. During the Vietnam war, when Glen, 17, went to his mother for permission to join the Army, he was humiliated when she exclaimed, "Why, you're still just a boy!" His five younger sisters, overhearing the conversation, teased and taunted him by imitating their mother. In a nanosecond, his flash of humiliation turned to anger and resolve. He would show them. His journey to Vietnam became a vendetta to prove his manhood. As a helicopter gunner, one of the most risky of all assignments, he survived and became a sargeant. Hanging halfway out of a helicopter, firing at the enemy, his adrenaline, coupled with his declarations of manhood, must have been exhilarating.

Looking back, he describes himself as tough, fearless in the face of death, and stoic as he responded to traumatized soldiers who had just lost a comrade. His job was to keep them "on their feet" and combat ready. There was no place for weakness or vulner-ability in his world. Years later, he would say that the death of others was never traumatic for him. He brushed it off as just "a fact of life." For Glen, that split second of humiliation was as close to death as anything he had experienced. Under fire, he had no fear of physical death because proving his manhood was the only survival that mattered. When he returned from the war, he spent 30 years in near isolation, prospecting for gold. Out in the gold fields, isolation was his safety. He didn't have to worry about humiliation. Survival in that setting didn't involve the complications of relationship dilemmas.

> **The important tasks are to enter the client's world, understand its complexity, and celebrate existing survival skills and strengths.**

Ultimately, the body becomes a collection of identity narratives that we selectively and subjectively send to the hippocampus and temporal lobe (autobiographical memory). These unique stories are more like a "compost heap" (Hood, 2012, p. 82) than a file cabinet. Over time, the circular influence of one story on another leads to a sense of self that is a portrait, distilled from the mutual influences of our stories. Family therapists can "walk the walk" of systemic empathy by identifying attachment dilemmas that arise from the dualism of individuality and belonging needs in the family. For Glen, the dilemma was how to belong in a female-dominated household in which he felt devalued as a man. The "enemy" was more formidable than Vietnam. However, he knew his anger kept him off balance. It would be forty years before he began selective relationships with the sisters he could trust. Fight/flight responses begin with an instantaneous exchange, but they can last a lifetime when the potential loss involves identity.

Roles. If identity is socially constructed, the roles that emerge in different settings contribute to our identity. Family roles are a special category because of lifelong attachment processes. Some siblings are conscious and others unconscious of what role they play in their families. When asked about their role, individuals may respond by describing functions within the family (I was the peacemaker) or personal characteristics (I take more risks) (Hanna et al., 2011). Dilemmas of role develop when children assume responsibility for certain functions in family life, but do not receive credit for their contribution (Boszormenji-Nagy & Krasner, 1986). These are often unspeakable dilemmas when roles are unconscious assignments and thus, there is no language for their unique lived experience. One rule of thumb with adolescents is: Those that look the most irresponsible are often those who feel the greatest burden. Family communication patterns can acknowledge or stifle each member's life story. Although few practice environments consider autobiographical memory as an important component to the traditional psychosocial history, it is an important component that includes a discussion of roles and the dilemmas that emerge from them. Such discussions access and integrate both types of memory, the explicit and the implicit. This, in turn, balances right and left hemispheres.

Communication: speaking the dilemma. Therapeutic conversations have the potential to resolve unspeakable dilemmas in a number of ways. First, by using the client's language, we acknowledge that we are a visitor in their world. If dilemmas have suppressed life narratives, it is important to make space for new language to tell the story. Engaging multiple senses can facilitate the emergence of deep conversations about attachment, identity, and belonging. Music, journaling, visual timelines of nodal events, and wall-sized genograms provide visual and auditory stimulation that can activate new circuits and emotional states. Verbal narratives may emerge from the images that other senses provide. Photos and art engage parts of a memory circuit that is usually not accessed from traditional introspection. Story-telling is important work that can acknowledge dilemmas, give credit and identify areas in the body that need healing (Stanton, 1992).

Developmentally, systemic dilemmas are unspeakable because they often involve hidden agendas or organizational needs of the family that are outside verbal discourse. For example, families that lack a strong leader may contain a vacuum filled by a child who takes charge in certain situations. Assuming the role is not in itself a dilemma. What matters is whether a person's experience in the role is devalued or suppressed. Then, is the role developmentally appropriate? When the role is not openly valued, or it is a psychic and interpersonal burden, this is when biology takes its toll. Here is a transcript between a therapist and a foster child, Ben, about his transition of roles in his foster home. He was the oldest of four siblings taken from their mother's home. Her prostitution left the four, ages 9–2, alone for long hours each day.

Therapist:	It sounds like you really did a great job holding things together for your brothers and sister. When there was no one else, you cared for your siblings the best you could, changing diapers, finding food for them to eat. You were really there for them.
Ben:	(Nods) Yeah.
Therapist:	I'm just wondering about something . . . even though you've said it's nice not to be left alone anymore, after being the one that everyone depended on, did you feel any loss when your job was taken away? When the kids no longer looked to you for help?
Ben:	(Tears streaming down his face, shakes his head "no").
Therapist:	O.K. So . . . what are your tears saying? Are they comfortable or uncomfortable?
Ben:	Relieved! (more tears).
Therapist:	Ah. Very good! So, there's relief.
Ben:	Yeah. I don't have to do that anymore (still tears).
Therapist:	Good, Ben! That's good that you can feel that relief with your tears! Just take a minute and feel all that relief . . . That's great that you can let your tears discharge all that pressure. Just feel how good relief feels.
Ben:	(Smiles; foster mother puts her arm around him.)
Therapist:	Yes! You don't have to do that anymore. Wonderful.

The stress of being left alone for long hours full of uncertainty would be biological and implicit. The spontaneous tears came from the body feeling that transition, discharging the energy. Accessing the explicit memory and verbalizing the implicit memory (systemic empathy) allowed Ben to integrate both memories into a more coherent narrative. Although his PFC knew that he "didn't have to do that anymore," now, his body knew it, too. The new narrative integrated what his body felt in the old dilemma, but he had no words for it. The language of the therapist is very intentional to celebrate the sensations and savor the moment, staying with his exact words. Ben was also given an award for being the "pillar" of the family and he placed this in a binder that stored his achievements and his biography. Table 4.3 contains a number of examples for exploring unspeakable dilemmas.

Griffith & Griffith (1994) describe numerous examples of medical symptoms that abate when clients find a voice for their experiences of dissonance. Speaking the dilemma leads to strategies that free them from it. Wolin & Wolin (1993) have stated, "To name the damage is to conquer it" (p. 22). Since cortisol and adrenaline cannot distinguish between a bear attack and an identity attack, the body becomes polluted when there is no physical release for the fight/flight or freeze energy. If there is no focus on the primary affect connected to the energy release, there is less probability that memory will be adjusted. Thus, dilemmas begin as mini biological dramas that can turn into life-threatening emergencies. Table 4.3 lists examples of situations that can lead to unspeakable dilemmas. Accessing implicit memory may require the therapist to help as narrator while clients find their voices. There are some suggestions in the table for encouraging clients to claim their experience and create a more complete narrative.

For example, in Glen's life, he discharged a lot of energy hanging out of his helicopter. However, he was shooting the wrong enemy, since it was his mother and sisters that shamed him. What he needed was a way to discharge the humiliation

Table 4.3 Deep affirmation: unspeakable dilemmas

Issue	Dilemma	Therapist Response
Power differential with the therapist.	What's acceptable in therapy? What are my rights? How does this process work? What if we don't fit?	Travel guide. Here's how it usually goes ... This is how I work ... I want to make sure you get the right fit. We have options.
Identity	Humiliation	Sympathy. That must have been terrible. What do you wish you could have said back then?
	Multiple selves	Validation. Our world is so complex now. It's hard to juggle all the competing demands. Let's map out all the different worlds you're in.
	Psychopolitics	That took a lot of courage for you to stand up for yourself. What do you say to yourself about it? What would you like to have happen now?
Role	Boundary distortions/ violations	You were powerless. It wasn't fair. You have a right to be angry.
	Entitlements	You deserve credit for what you did. Have you ever thought of yourself as being deserving?
Attunement	Parental lack of attunement	There was a mismatch there. It's not your fault. What's the most painful part for you?
	Spouse/peer lack of attunement	Let's clarify the issues and work toward a new process so you can get that connection.

stored in his body and develop emotional defensive mechanisms he could use to work around the psychopolitics of his sisters. For him, therapy consisted of the eastern religion he adopted while in Vietnam. He began to investigate the ways he could change through meditation. However, since he could not resolve his humiliation through social engagement, he likely stayed stuck in the fight/flight mode. The energy release that can come from felt sense exercises, focusing, and mindfulness lowers stress hormone levels. Although it still took him thirty years for his avoidance to abate, his story illustrates how the elements converge in the whole body to develop identity. Isolation became his tranquilizer (flight mode) when it came to relationships with his family. He developed other selves in other worlds that made positive contributions to his identity. Brain friendly therapy could have helped him deactivate his circuits of shame and helplessness. Then, he would be in a position to navigate safety and threat without cutting off his family.

SOUL FOOD AND THE ART OF RELATIONSHIP

In this chapter, we reviewed our own survival stories and scanned our bodies for areas of activation that might tighten their grip on our creativity and authenticity. We also revisited our interpersonal resources, the important ingredients in our lives that nourish and calm us. Before we cook up a meal for someone else, we give ourselves some comfort and caring. We get centered so our own starvation won't intrude on what might be the best cuisine for someone else. What fits for them? There are individual and universal elements here. Just like some good soul food, it has to be just right. Some want mac and cheese. Others have got to have greens. Not too sweet, but get those ham hocks in there! Some want chitlins. Others pass on by and go right for the chicken. Rich in the amino acid, tryptophan, chicken is a natural antidepressant!

When we are centered and flexible, it isn't hard work to negotiate all these preferences. Our right brains pick up on the nuances and we plan for these unique features to emerge. As they do, we work from a menu that informs our diners of their choices and explores their preferences. However, there is more to our meal than just matters of taste. What is their developmental level? Do they need soft food or can they handle a steak knife? How about food allergies? These biological and psychological considerations are more than metaphor. The question of fit must allow dialogues that do not force feed anyone. To the contrary, a gracious chef will allow diners to sample the wine. Choice and preference allow the right fit to evolve.

In most cases, therapist and client can come together in a brain-informed alliance that is a mix of the ingredients in this chapter. In some special cases, additional accommodations become necessary. If we were rescuing someone from starvation, famine, or serious wounds, first aid requires a different type of nourishment. In these cases, intravenous fluids and small portions of special foods are administered for bodies and souls that are especially vulnerable. This is the work of trauma therapists. In the next chapter, we become acquainted with the basics of these extreme conditions.

5

The Brain Interrupted
Trauma-Informed Family Therapy

"What does *tamed* mean?"

"It's something that's been too often neglected. It means, 'to create ties' . . ."

"What do I have to do?" asked the little prince.

"You have to be very patient," the fox answered. "First you'll sit down a little ways away from me, over there, in the grass. I'll watch you out of the corner of my eye, and you won't say anything. Language is the source of misunderstandings. But day by day, you'll be able to sit a little closer . . ."

(Saint-Exuprey, 2000, pp. 59–60)

Throughout this book, there has been a focus on threat and survival as main operations that occupy the whole body. In general, we survive a myriad of milestones and challenges. Our bodies develop *learned safety*, which is a set of expectations that regulates our nervous system, based on predictable daily routines and patterns (Porges, in press). However, there are a number of experiences that interfere with the electrochemical flow in the body and these can reach a level of trauma. A great deal of what we know about the brain has come about because of trauma science. In this chapter, the emphasis moves from normative threat-survival responses to those that reach the level of injury and wounding. Trauma is often a ghost that haunts important relationships.

The following ideas are possibilities for becoming more trauma-focused and body-focused. Ultimately, the average practitioner sees a range of people for which some of these suggestions may be relevant. However, Chapter 4 reminds us that there is a careful dance that is part of being brain-friendly. Even when trauma is the presenting problem, tolerance for affective arousal greatly varies. As a reminder from Table 4.1, some clients will non-verbally say, "Don't ask me to be vulnerable until I feel safe. Be careful with me." For good reason, there is a need for all therapists to take a step back and consider the strengths and limits of traditional mental health services. Sometimes our traditions block us from recognizing trauma behavior and then knowing what to do about it.

The decade of the brain and the decade of attachment theory followed previous decades in which American consciousness began to embrace the personal impact of war, sexual abuse, and mass murder. Add to these, disruptions of community in the form of divorce, racism, gang violence, and an epidemic of child neglect. The result is overwhelmed social programs that yield poor outcomes, crowded prisons that are modern-day insane asylums, and mental health providers whose clients have complex symptoms that challenge the limits of "talk therapy."

> **Trauma is often a ghost that haunts important relationships.**

This chapter introduces readers to the exciting and inspiring world of trauma healing in the twenty-first century. While there are many causes for the social ills that beset us, the body has predictable responses to a range of unfortunate suffering. However, the human spirit is rising to great heights, through the resilience individuals display each day as they live with trauma symptoms and in the creative treatment strategies that are destined to revolutionize mental health treatment as we know it today. With eastern healing traditions meeting western science, humans are proving they can solve the complex problems they make. This global integration brings together the brain's left and right hemispheres. If ever there was a need for relationship specialists to facilitate networks of healing, the time is now for family therapists to seize these opportunities and support innovative trauma healing for individuals, couples, and families. From attachment injuries in marriage to combat stress symptoms that wreak havoc in military families, trauma experiences drain the life from family relationships, our most important tool for survival.

WHAT IS TRAUMA?

Trauma includes a wide range of experiences. These all share a common physiological outcome: disruption of the nervous system. Whether an experience is traumatic at a given moment depends on the variety of bodily states that lead to mental and emotional turmoil for a person. The nature, timing, and frequency of events become a unique internal ecology that determines whether a traumatic event leaves a lasting effect. Currently, studies have found that attachment injuries have the same physiological effects as physical injuries (Hood, 2012). There is also evidence that younger children and adolescents have fewer resources to resolve complex developmental trauma naturally. Thus, electro-chemical energy may linger when they are too young to know how to discharge it (adrenaline, cortisol, shock, overwhelm, etc.). This is part of the memory of the body. In addition, youth may need guided interactions with parents or caring adults who can help them rebalance their bodies after a stressful event.

Thus, trauma is not an event. It is any overload that leaves a person powerless. It is a response to one or more experiences that overwhelm the capacity of the nervous system to adapt at any given moment. The experience may have the effect of a "straw that breaks the camel's back." In these cases, an experience becomes part of a larger circuit that has points in the hippo-campus and amygdala related to other events or environmental factors. The entire circuit now becomes the "straw" and trauma symptoms develop. For example, injuries to the body from an auto accident may combine with the untimely death of a loved one in the auto accident. Add to these a family squabble with the loved one on the night before the accident. The overall meaning of the squabble might be minor or major for some people. Bodily injuries may be minor or major. Medical procedures for these injuries differ. In some cases, experience(s) may involve a shock that overwhelms nervous system response at that moment. With all these possible permutations, it is easy to understand why trauma symptoms form a unique blueprint. This complexity also explains how parents and others might overlook trauma symptoms when they see them.

The case of Damien illustrates the more subtle process of how a buildup of experiences leads to trauma. One day, while attending his Headstart program, he erupted in the cafeteria and hurled the tray of a nearby boy across the room. Predictably, such a shocking display of force mobilized adults to intervene and regain control of the group. Damien received disciplinary measures and his grandparents sought help for him. His mother visited with him sporadically when her drug use would permit. Father was unknown. After a few sessions, an art therapist learned what Damien's experience was that day. Leading up to the incident, he had begun to develop his social sense at age five. As we age, survival gets complicated as identity and belonging become life or death issues in peer groups. He began to see that his family was different from other families. He was sad when his mother would fail to show for visits with him. These attachment experiences were resonating with his sense of identity and belonging when the boy in the line turned and began to tease him, stating that he didn't have a mother or a father. Damien's use of force is a common example of how stress chemicals respond to threat as part of fight/flight behaviors. However, in most settings, observing adults are not fully prepared to understand how to prevent the buildup of tensions and the breakdown of resources. A number of practitioners suggest precautions and practices that can often prevent trauma symptoms for youth (Ross, 2008; Levine & Kline, 2008).

A prominent debate within the trauma treatment community is whether the best approach should involve reliving the experience versus working with natural cycles in the body to restore nervous system balance going forward. For example, there is convincing evidence

> ... trauma is not an event. It is a response to one or more experiences that overwhelm the capacity of the nervous system to adapt at a given moment.

that many trauma debriefing protocols have a negative effect on survivors, compared to involvement in activities of social support and resilience (James et al., 2011; Rose et al., 2002). There are also thousands of clients experiencing trauma symptoms who want to recover from their injuries, but prefer not to discuss the experiences. After receiving training in both approaches, the bias I present is toward working with the whole body and recapturing the resilience that lies deep within our tissues. This approach has four advantages. First, accessing the whole body enables practitioners to individualize experiences and symptoms. Second, naturalistic approaches can depathologize and normalize the body's response to overwhelming circumstances. Third, leading trauma researchers note the significance of affective physiology on memory and meaning (Porges, 1997; van der Kolk, 2003; Schore, 2003). Whole body approaches integrate these three elements. Fourth, there are many survivors who cannot tolerate re-living the experience. Why subject them to needless distress, due to a lack of skill in the professional community? Numerous approaches exist that do not require survivors to re-live traumatic events (Levine, 2010; Rothschild, 2010; Ross, 2008; Heller & La Pierre, 2012). Since whole body approaches integrate affect, memory and meaning, the body tells its story first. Thereafter, the person can decide what other parts of the story are important to tell.

This chapter provides guidelines for becoming more trauma-informed, with an emphasis on how family therapists can integrate a whole perspective. Some of this work should be conducted in individual sessions. However, many trauma specialists overlook the benefits of including supportive family members in certain interventions. For example, one man reported the benefits of including his wife in his sessions of eye movement desensitization and reprocessing (EMDR). He explained to his therapist that he didn't want to go home and try to capture all the nuances of the process so that his wife could understand. With hesitation, the therapist consented. They developed ground rules for the sessions, since she was there as an observer. His wife was a positive support and the couple increased their intimacy as a result. A careful assessment of significant relationships identifies these important resources. Family and social network can have a significant impact on all types of trauma recovery.

In addition, there is a focus here on healing and recovery, not treatment and cure. Moving away from western medicine toward eastern paradigms of growth and transformation is a trend that trauma scientists embrace (van der Kolk, 2000; Siegel, 2010). Because right and left brain integration is central to this work, trauma specialists adopt language that mirrors the processes of healing. This language suggests that an injury or wound has occurred and it is possible to heal. Thus, there is no mention of mental illness or disease that would stigmatize or threaten someone's identity.

TYPES OF TRAUMA

In the trauma treatment community, there is a consensus around a number of distinctions. First, childhood and adolescent traumas have particular developmental considerations. The Complex Trauma task force of the National Child Traumatic Stress Network emphasizes the need for a separate diagnosis for children who have sustained chronic, repeated trauma, *developmental trauma disorder* (van der Kolk, 2009). Studies have shown that there are clearly delineated patterns of dysregulation in childhood and convincing susceptibility to chronic disturbances in adulthood (Schore, 2001; van der Kolk, 2009; Siegel, 2012). Second, multiple episodes complicate symptoms and recovery. Third, interpersonal traumas have multiple layers of symptoms. Fourth, the range of biological disruption reaches from localized to pervasive throughout the body (van der Kolk, 1994, 2009; Schore, 2001). Ironically, none of these elements appear in the category of post-traumatic stress disorder in the DSM-IV.

In addition to complex developmental traumas, children and adults experience a range of other single incidents that breach available resources in the body and generate considerable energy that lingers in the body. Some of these may be extraordinary and others from ordinary life events. The variety of experience that exists in trauma science is too expansive to cover here. However, Table 5.1 outlines general categories and their examples.

Table 5.1 Traumatic experiences

Category of Experiences	Examples That May Lead to Symptoms
Extraordinary	war, racism, cultural wounding, persecutions, gender and class discrimination, natural disasters, incarceration, homicides, assaults, immigration
Ordinary	auto accidents, falls, medical procedures, life-threatening illnesses, chronic pain, losses, drowning, suffocation
Complex	childhood abuse & neglect, foster placements, sexual abuse, domestic violence, rape
Child/adolescent	bullying, being lost, animal attacks, failure to meet others' expectations, death of important family member, teacher/ school relationships, peer or romantic rejection, internet violence & exploitation
Shock (can be part of any experience)	high impact, inescapable attack, physical injury

Adapted from Ross (2008)

Of particular note are attacks of race, culture, gender, class, and sexual orientation. Most education on cultural competence falls short of discussing physiology or the biological empathy that is critical to understanding these potential traumas. Just as van der Kolk et al. (2005) argue for expanded designations in the DSM-IV for complex trauma, a number of voices in communities of color identify symptoms of trauma that fall outside descriptions for PTSD, even though there are clusters of shared experience (Pieterse et al., 2010; Butts, 2002; Franklin et al., 2006).

> **Most education on cultural competence falls short of discussing physiology or the biological empathy that is critical to understanding these potential traumas.**

For example, trauma exposure is high for African Americans who live in stressful urban environments (Woods et al., 2012). In a study where 96 percent of participants were African-Americans, Alim et al. (2006) found that the rate of PTSD exceeded that of the general population. Pieterse, Carter, Evans & Walther (2010) found that symptoms of racial or ethnic discrimination challenge current criteria for PTSD. In discussions of race and ethnicity as sources of psychological trauma, it is important to understand that these traumas are cumulative in nature, much like developmental complex trauma. To illustrate, the psychosocial needs of Native American women include the importance of recognizing ongoing intergenerational trauma associated with loss of land, identity, and rights (Walters et al., 2002; Shepard et al., 2006). For people of African descent, there is a need to understand discrimination and historical legacies such as slavery, colonization, and share-cropping (Bryant-Davis, 2007; Bulhan, 1985). While younger generations may not have as much consciousness about these, the risk of intergenerational trauma is great, as with those who survive a holocaust. Chapter 7 describes how transitional family therapy can involve extended family and social networks in the healing of these secondary traumas.

Thus, traumas such as those coming from race, culture, gender, sexual orientation, and class may be cumulative, recurring, and intergenerational in nature (Bryant-Davis, 2007; Cross, 1998; Ford, 2008). Franklin and Boyd-Franklin (2000) found that psychological responses to discrimination were predicted by number of prior experiences. As a coping strategy, some Black men develop a sense of vigilance and anticipate racial hostility. Additionally, emotional reactivity (e.g., anger, hostility) in some Black men can be a type of defense in anticipation of racial discrimination. The role of the amygdala in the face of ongoing threats is clear. These behaviors are consistent with common responses to trauma, including avoidance, identity confusion, difficulties in interpersonal relationships, and feelings of guilt and shame (Carlson, 1997). For biological empathy to occur, therapists must become familiar with trauma symptoms. For systemic empathy to occur, therapists must become familiar with the unspeakable social dilemmas that occur for vulnerable groups.

TRAUMA SYMPTOMS

Until the advent of neuroscience, the most puzzling aspect of recognizing trauma symptoms has been the range of symptoms and stark contrasts from one survivor to the next. One common thread of symptoms is coping strategies taken to the extreme. They may be depressive-looking or aggressive-looking, but the common denominator is the intensity. Whether stuck in fight, flight, or freeze, there will be a rigid or extreme quality to it. When the body is in defensive or protective mode, there is no room for relaxation. Safety is a luxury. The body has learned danger, injury, and near destruction from either repeated interactions or a single blow of epic proportions to the body, identity, or attachment bond. As examples, in the face of a physical assault during war, social harassment at school, or humiliation within the family, "the body keeps the score" (van der Kolk, 1994; van der Volk et al., 2005). It is impossible to review all possible trauma symptoms, but practitioners can become more brain-friendly by understanding the internal experience that accompanies some of the most challenging behavior.

Given the range of problems that lead clients to seek therapy, it is easy to see lower levels of activation present in all of us. Talk therapy is often successful with these lower levels because the PFC is still online, even during symptoms, and it is possible to have dialogues based in cognition. It is when activation is extreme that the PFC goes offline. Yes, even healthy people may have times when their PFC goes offline. Take political discourse as an example. Many attempted conversations between the best of friends may deteriorate because political consciousness is part of a circuit attached to many media-related messages that are threatening to family and identity. These may take our PFC offline, but the symptoms do not interfere with overall functioning. This is not the case with those who have suffered significant trauma. Small successes in family, job, and school are often heroic, given the psychic burdens they carry. Clinicians can celebrate these examples of determination and courage with clients. Thus, the extremes of triggers and their resulting behaviors become hallmarks of most troublesome trauma symptoms.

Unsung Heroes

With heightened vigilance and calculation, survivors hope to navigate the emotional ups and downs that form the landscape of the body. They are heroic. Rather than walking a regular sidewalk, their path is more like the loop de loops of extreme sports. An instructive resource is van der Kolk's (1994, p. 3) extensive mapping of those who have suffered childhood abuse and neglect.

> many triggers not directly related to the traumatic experience may precipitate extreme reactions. Thus, people with PTSD suffer both from generalized hyperarousal and from physiological emergency

reactions to specific reminders . . . The loss of affective modulation that is so central in PTSD may help explain the observation that traumatized people lose the capacity to utilize affect states as signals . . . Thus, they are prone to go immediately from stimulus to response without making the necessary psychological assessment of the meaning of what is going on. This makes them prone to freeze, or, alternatively, to overreact and intimidate others in response to minor provocations.

These quick, generalized responses make it hard to put memories in their broader perspective and this may lead to a tendency to continuously relive the past, a process that has physiological components related to a repeated startle response in sensory circuits in the brain. Stress chemicals also lead to gaps in memory storage and the reliving may be an attempt to fill in the gaps (de Quervain et al., 2000). For example, oxytocin has a role in certain types of amnesia. Van der Kolk (1994) notes that childbirth is rarely remembered in a traumatic way, despite all the stressors that attend it. He suggests that oxytocin may lead to gaps in stressful memories for those with PTSD, leading to distortions that have a cascading effect on the next cycle of triggered memories and behaviors. Layered distortions are a tough act to follow.

Add to these amnesias the complex balance between pain-motivated behaviors and defensive behaviors. During defense, natural stress chemicals include opioids to block pain. In animals, licking a wound can signal vulnerability and attract predators. Opioids lower the urge for attention to wounds during attack. During World War II, some observed that strong emotion seemed to lessen physical pain, based on the low number of wounded on the front line who requested morphine. The interplay of these systems in the body lead to hyper defense on the one hand, and blunted response to pain on the other. This can seem like a nervous system "spasm," given that humans can experience emotional and bodily pain in the same physiological way.

In addition, the overload results in something called "speechless terror" that makes it difficult to explain the experience with words or symbols (van der Kolk, 1994). This is another reason to focus on body sensations, rather than words. Even in children as young as two, the process of bi-lateral scribbling without form can be an outlet for victims of auto accidents. Art therapists who work with the trauma of a child's body can provide the narrative of what happened, while the child chooses a color and organically uses the motion of the scribble to represent affect in the body (Chapman, 2012, 2013). This body-based activity moves the experience from right brain implicit memory to left brain explicit memory. This helps them create a coherent narrative that also involves a physical discharge of energy in the process. These coherent narratives for all trauma survivors expand aspects of the experience from a snapshot to a video, moving through the entire event to safety. Triggers are physiological boomerangs that travel the experiential circuits of a traumatic event and limit the narratives about safety.

Triggers

Continuing from our review in Chapter 2, trauma triggers are possibly the most puzzling of symptoms. Moving from sights, sounds, and smells to tension and acute arousal in the body, they are electrochemical surges in the body that send flashes through the conscious mind and become emotional quicksand in the heart. During a traumatic event, the five senses take a snapshot of the environment. The vagus nerve takes a snapshot of the body. These have their own unique mix with other experiences already stored in memory. As an example, consider an experience of deep humiliation that happens in a social setting with adolescent boys sparing and jockeying for position at a pizza party. Then, things turn ugly. Perhaps someone was taking a dare. Perhaps the victim already suffered trauma from parent abandonment at home. No matter how unintentional the act, if a person's resources are already on the brink, the humiliation may turn from horseplay to quicksand. If there is sadism as part of the act, this becomes an added layer of complexity.

Afterward, it may only take the smell of pizza to trigger the shame, anger, sadness, and fear that surged underneath the superficial tendency to save face. Alienation begins to set in. Maybe the smell of pizza is in a grocery store line, in which tears, flushed face, and racing heart are not only embarrassing, but frightening. This creates a layer of alienation away from the original site. Licking the wounds would only attract more predators. Alienation continues. We can only imagine how much destruction may have already come from commonplace jousting in which one is more vulnerable than others. The famed Oklahoma City bomber, Timothy McVeigh, was small for his age in elementary school when boys assaulted him and stuck his head down a toilet.

> Whew! Take a few deep breaths to avert some secondary trauma. You may need to stop and digest life with trauma. Exploring trauma can be a trauma in itself. If this discussion triggers some stressful sensations for you, take a moment and get grounded again. Respect what your body tells you. If your body needs some resourcing, take time to allow that next step. These are small, but powerful ways for us to connect to our bodies as messengers of the survival process, and what we might need to restore a relaxed flow of energy. In a clinical session, there is healing power in breaking up a story into small segments separated by grounding and resourcing.

Then, let's return to the grocery store line. Triggers lead to a person's internal dialogues that ache for a witness and some biological empathy. "What's happening to me? Am I going crazy? Are others noticing? What can I do?" If the person is lucky, they have these words. However, speechless terror can happen in nanoseconds over the most ordinary events when vulnerabilities run high. Add to this the frequency and strength of triggers. Yes, we all have triggers. We can recall words that hurt and scenes that still activate our nervous system. However, we may be lucky enough to have low frequencies and manageable intensity.

Thus, trauma symptoms bring their own set of dilemmas. Fight, flight, and freeze in the body compete with a desire for social bonding, saving face, and identities full of hope and promise. At any age, these dilemmas begin as unspeakable, but they cry out for a voice. Recovery is the liberation of the body from trauma symptoms and of the spirit from unspeakable dilemmas. Family therapists have the privilege of participating in this liberation by assessing trauma and attuning to a client's *tolerance for affective arousal.* This relates to the internal intensity of their arousal. They may prefer to avoid certain discussions because the intensity of affect may be embarrassing or frightening. As one client said, "I can't think about that, Doc. Every time I do, it just makes me want to go out and kill someone." In other cases, crying, sobbing, or panic may be too much to manage. Later in this chapter, there is a discussion about this intensity.

TRAUMA ASSESSMENT

Regardless of how the mental health establishment addresses these issues, as we can see, the body does not lie. Jackson, Knight, and Rafferty (2010) report a longitudinal, positive relationship between stressors and chronic health conditions in over 2,000 African American and White respondents. It is important to know a client's history with the experiences in Table 5.1 and to assess the degree of trauma physiology that may interfere with individual, couple, and parental functioning. For example, Johnson (2002) suggests that emotionally focused couple therapy (EFT) is contraindicated until a trauma survivor has integrated their trauma. The steps toward integration include acknowledging the abuse (remember the case of April?), informing others about the abuse, understanding how it has affected their life (psychoeducation), and working on symptom management (felt sense, trigger relief, etc.). Certainly, couple therapy is important from the outset of any trauma treatment plan. Chapter 6 describes how to organize this process. The first step can be to help a couple identify and integrate the trauma. Then, they can benefit more from EFT as a second stage of treatment. The same is true for children and adolescents who arrive for therapy without integration of the trauma within their family. Family psychoeducation may be the first step. Then, treatment for symptoms and triggers can occur more effectively. Chapter 7 summarizes the structure and process of MFGs that are relevant for use with trauma.

Thus, a trauma screening should occur in every case, regardless of the presenting problem. This can be accomplished with a few surveys during intake. For those who desire their practices to be evidence-based, asking for this data during intake becomes a pretest. These assess the occurrence of various experiences, symptoms, and their severity. They help clinicians make the distinction between trauma and chronic stress that may affect relationships, but not overall functioning (school, work, friends, etc.). The Appendix contains four surveys: The SNI is from Chapter 3. The Checklist of Experiences (CE) is Table 5.1 formatted as a checklist. The Post-traumatic Checklist (PCL), civilian version, follows DSM-IV criteria and allows clinicians to scan the severity of clients' symptom distress. The Relational Ethics Scale (RES) assesses attachment quality in family of origin and couple (trust, loyalty, justice, entitlement).

These are provided as options, representing a range of intensity. For example, one might screen with the CE. Then, if there were a number of experiences that led to a need to know about intensity of symptoms, the PCL might be informative. The RES can be divided. The first half assesses family of origin. The second half relates to a current adult/peer relationship. For clinicians who prefer less formal information gathering, the content of each survey might simply structure conversations, without any formal administration.

With couples and families, these instruments obtain an overview of perceptions from others. A comparison of scores alerts practitioners to differences in perceptions within the social network. For example, partner reports of men's health is often more consistent with medical evidence than the man's report. Spouses often play a critical role in providing a fuller picture of psychopolitics and physical vulnerabilities. Children and parents may differ in their perceptions of each other. The surveys provide a safe way for the clinician to learn about those differences before addressing them openly. However, since the same experience may have a different effect on different people, it is important to consider these assessments as merely an overview of possible trauma triggers. Ultimately, clients provide confirmation as to their relevance in a recovery plan.

While these may seem unnecessary to some, it may be important to consider van der Kolk's admonition:

> Research has shown that traumatic childhood experiences are not only extremely common; they also have a profound impact on many different areas of functioning. For example, children exposed to alcoholic parents or domestic violence rarely have secure childhoods; their symptomatology tends to be pervasive and multifaceted, and is likely to include depression, various medical illnesses, as well as a variety of impulsive and self destructive behaviors. Approaching each of these problems piecemeal, rather than as expressions of a vast system of internal disorganization, runs the risk of losing sight of the forest in favor of one tree.
> (van der Kolk, 2005, p. 402)

Discussion: Yes or No

It is important to follow a client's comfort level regarding a discussion of survey responses. Each response contains a story. However, for some, these may be too upsetting for discussion. The clinician's options may include no discussion at all, or extensive discussion, depending on client preference. The following is a description of possibilities for both options. To choose an option, begin with the following questions.

1. Is the description of the presenting problem trauma or no trauma?
2. Do surveys contain high, low, or medium scores?
3. Do clients manifest high or low tolerance for affect arousal?

The therapist's zeal for this work should take the form of self-mastery, rather than overreaching with a client. It is better to plant seeds of thought, rather than pull weeds. When a client seeks help for trauma, explain the options for helping them heal. Reassure the client that it is possible to recover from these challenges without ever discussing details of the story (Levine, 2010; Rothschild, 2010; Heller and La Pierre, 2012; Ross, 2008). Thank them for providing the information and help them become affectively grounded through the exercise in the next section with the felt sense.

When the presenting problem is not voiced as trauma, but the therapist sees some items with high scores, the first session can be a bridge between these two worlds. Exploratory, noncommital questions are a useful way to plant seeds of thought and assess tolerance for affect.

1. Do you think there might be any connection between (the presenting problem or client goal) and stress?
2. Have you ever thought that stress might play a role in this?
3. Would you be interested in a work plan that includes stress management as part of our work together?
4. Are you interested in discussing these surveys or is there something more pressing right now?

The more severe the trauma, the more frozen survivors may be. Respect this with a relaxed, slow, and indirect approach. Follow their lead. Use the presenting problem as an avenue to gain trust, create safety, and plant seeds. Do not imply that you need to discuss the surveys.

Remember Glen, the Vietnam vet? He might have healed his family-of-origin wounds sooner if he could have come into counseling for something else first. This is why screening is important. He married shortly after returning from the war. He mentioned that his wife became best friends with his sisters. Shaking his head, he said, "That just wasn't going to work out for me!" This was an unspeakable dilemma. He needed his wife to understand the painful divide that lay beneath the surface. How could he speak it when he needed to prove that he was a MAN. Had they sought marital therapy, a simple geno-gram with some relational questions about growing up in a family of sisters could have been the starting point. Then, a brain-friendly, trauma-informed therapist could have recognized this as a trauma. They could have explored the issues in the ways that Chapter

> **Reassure the client that it is possible to recover from these challenges without ever discussing details of the story.**

7 describes. Instead of thirty years out in the desert, he could have been a present husband and father for his two children.

From working with military personnel, it is clear that these survivors of trauma need language that is de-stigmatizing and de-pathologizing. Issues of identity and belonging are intense for service members who define themselves as patriots, protectors, and fighters. There are all types of survivors, even those who are unaware that they have survived extreme circumstances (possibly due to dissociation). Introducing brain basics around common-place activities is a way to plant the seeds of recovery. In my practice, there are cases in which the client is ready and able to explore survey responses. In other cases, survey follow-up occurred after eight sessions. It provided direction and focus for the middle stage of therapy. With others, it never fit, therefore, the work proceeded with the language of the presenting problem, sugges-tions about stress management, and ultimately, action-oriented experiments that helped clients to discharge energy. Even in these cases, survey information was always invaluable for me as I worked to be attuned to the client.

<u>When the presenting problem is about trauma and survey scores are high</u>, there is still an important need to assess clients' tolerance for affective arousal because triggers can quickly lead to no-shows in a therapist's schedule. In this case, erring on the side of caution can provide safety. As a starting point, I usually give clients a choice between discussion of their distress or trauma

education. If they choose education as a place to start, this can signal their need for greater safety. As with the multifamily groups for schizophrenia, psychoeducation is a low risk, high yield activity because it keeps the PFC engaged and empowers individuals with information. There is a great

The more severe the trauma, the more frozen survivors may be. Respect this with a relaxed, slow, and indirect approach.

need for family therapists to provide relevant psychoeducation to clients, spouses, parents, and friends about trauma. This information can give voice to dilemmas in an emotionally controlled way.

Contrary to other forms of psychotherapy, there are times when clients need the therapist to do more of the talking when there is a need for education. This allows them to scan their environment for signs of safety in the therapist's body language and words. Psychoeducation is also an important opportunity for the therapist to send nonverbal messages that can be sent and received more safely. These can indirectly address stigma, dilemmas, and psychopolitics without blame or criticism. Client friendly diagrams and language in Chapter 2 can provide visuals of the process. When practitioners describe trauma process in the body, clients can compare and contrast this information with their internal experience. As they find their own words and adjust the narrative to fit their experience, a *coherent narrative* can emerge about what happened (content), how others reacted to it (process), and their biological experience (substance).

When the client would like to discuss the trauma, ask permission to discuss survey information by using the felt sense exercise in Box 5.1. This is a script that uses the felt sense as part of the survey discussion. In early stages of therapy, the focus must stay on safety and comfort. In the script, note the emphasis upon moving away from uncomfortable sensations. This helps to lower affective arousal. Two important activities are *grounding* and *resourcing* (Ross, 2008; Heller & La Pierre, 2012; Levine, 2010). These follow the logic of the body as it seeks stability and safety. As basic survival tools, the sensations that accompany grounding and resourcing provide physical security at the earliest point in the discussion. Introducing these positive felt sense exercises helps to grow tolerance for later affective arousal during other recovery activities. Just as Table 4.1 provides a dialogue for addressing interpersonal safety, these address affective safety in the moment.

Box 5.1 Felt sense assessment

Grounding: If you feel comfortable doing this, close your eyes (or not, if they prefer eyes open) and take the deepest, longest, slowest breath possible. Inhale and exhale slowly. Besides your heartbeat, can you feel the slightest vibration in different locations? This is more than just oxygen flowing through your arteries and capillaries. We are electrical and chemical beings. Notice your relationship to the ground: your feet on the floor, your seat in the chair, your back to the chair. Take a few minutes to focus on the safety in these.

Resourcing: Next, where are the <u>positive</u> energy states in your body? Allow yourself a few minutes to review these. Once awareness emerges, locate and focus on one spot. Stay with it for a few more minutes. Savor it. What is your experience? Does it "say" anything? Notice your breaths as they relax you. Focus on what is pleasurable about the spot and how you feel. Take a few minutes for this before we move on.

Survey responses: Now, consider one survey. Here are the items that have the strongest answers. Which two do you think are the most relevant right now?

- Do you register a strong sensation to either of these right now?
- If so, which ones? Let's take one with the smallest reaction. Where in your body do you feel it? Is it pleasant or unpleasant? If it's pleasant, stay with it or, if it is unpleasant, take a moment to go back to the previous place in your body that feels comfortable. Let yourself focus on the comfortable place. Notice your breaths as they relax you. Take as long as you need to feel relaxed again. If there is any difficulty, you

might want to move away from your body and look around the room. Pick out some interesting objects.
- Next, is there a story that goes with this survey item? Some people prefer not to share these stories, others would like to. What fits for you? It's completely up to you because we can effectively work on your goals either way.

Explain that the exercise helps people to take the process slowly. This provides a "backwards" way of discussing trauma. It begins with strengths and resources in the body, then moves to a discussion of the effects and symptoms (items on the surveys). Last, it moves to what the survivor wants the therapist to know. The exercise can be adapted to use grounding and resourcing during any part of a session in which there are signs of distress. The repetition of this exercise over time can help the body return to a state of normal ebbs and flows of affect, without getting stuck. In addition, as part of a trauma assessment, it is helpful to know

1. Number of experiences, frequency, pace
2. Age at the time
3. Type of injury: physical, developmental, interpersonal, intergenerational
4. Others harmed? How?
5. Social Environment at the time
6. "Pile-up" (accumulating stressors)
7. Others' responses: caring, concerned, nurturing, dismissing, disapproving, laissez-faire.

Discussions of Trauma

As a record to help with treatment planning, Table 5.2 is a worksheet to note some of the issues that come up during discussions of survey responses. This form would begin where Box 5.1 ends, with a discussion of the story behind the responses. It is possible to show the worksheet to the client and collaborate on filling in the blanks. This keeps the PFC online. Because this is an

Table 5.2 Survey stories

Survey	Item #	Item Content	Story Summary	Survival and Attachment Affect	Dilemma?
CL				☐ fear ☐ anger ☐ distress ☐ disgust ☐ surprise ☐ joy ☐ other _____ ☐ other _____	☐ Belonging ☐ Identity ☐ Boundaries ☐ Psychopolitics ☐ Roles
				☐ fear ☐ anger ☐ distress ☐ disgust ☐ surprise ☐ joy ☐ other _____ ☐ other _____	☐ Belonging ☐ Identity ☐ Boundaries ☐ Psychopolitics ☐ Roles
PCL				☐ fear ☐ anger ☐ distress ☐ disgust ☐ surprise ☐ joy ☐ other _____ ☐ other _____	☐ Belonging ☐ Identity ☐ Boundaries ☐ Psychopolitics ☐ Roles
				☐ fear ☐ anger ☐ distress ☐ disgust ☐ surprise ☐ joy ☐ other _____ ☐ other _____	☐ Belonging ☐ Identity ☐ Boundaries ☐ Psychopolitics ☐ Roles
RES				☐ fear ☐ anger ☐ distress ☐ disgust ☐ surprise ☐ joy ☐ other _____ ☐ other _____	☐ Belonging ☐ Identity ☐ Boundaries ☐ Psychopolitics ☐ Roles
				☐ fear ☐ anger ☐ distress ☐ disgust ☐ surprise ☐ joy ☐ other _____ ☐ other _____	☐ Belonging ☐ Identity ☐ Boundaries ☐ Psychopolitics ☐ Roles
Other Stories				☐ fear ☐ anger ☐ distress ☐ disgust ☐ surprise ☐ joy ☐ other _____ ☐ other _____	☐ Belonging ☐ Identity ☐ Boundaries ☐ Psychopolitics ☐ Roles

assessment, client discomfort with any part of the process is important information that should guide the therapist toward or away from certain territory. If the client seems uncomfortable, drop this exercise entirely. Unlike talk therapy with other cases, it is not helpful to stay focused on negative affect. Clients may even try to please the therapist and then fail to return for a second session. Be sure to thank the client for expressing their preferences, since trauma survivors have been robbed of control through violations, shocks, and invasions. Control equals safety for many people. In cases of trauma, it carries life or death importance.

With those who find it empowering to tell the stories of their challenges, it is possible to judge whether their story contains *survivor's pride* by listening to their affective stance and reflecting on primary emotions that are attached to the story (Wolin & Wolin, 1993; see a later section of this chapter on resilience). If there is a story of survival, celebrate this achievement with them. If there is residual fear, sadness, anger, or shame in their voices, look for the unspeakable dilemma in the story and provide sympathy in the moment. Later, these may inform a *recovery plan* (not treatment plan) and become concrete goals.

It is possible that a person's resources provided resilience and there is no need for trauma treatment. Many people experience an event with a nervous system impact, yet balance it at the time through their own intuition, resources, and social support. If children have a single episode experience, but have attuned social support and a sense of empowerment that enabled them to discharge energy, they may have avoided development of trauma symptoms. For example, children might be in an auto accident or get lost for a period of time without injury. In these instances, they need to be held and to have the feeling of safety reenter their body and conscious mind through reassurances. Sometimes, there is so much chaos and panic that parents are distracted and do not realize how simple the process can be. However, when it works well, there is a sense of breathing that comes back into a child's body and an involuntary sigh that signals a re-balancing of the nervous system (discharge).

On the other hand, if an adult still remembers a negative aspect of a childhood experience and can feel a change in physiology (e.g., heart rate, tension), there is likely undischarged energy from a thwarted fight/flight response. Thus, awareness with restraint is an important balance when assessing trauma because of these individual differences. Combining surveys with felt sense explorations can help practitioners and clients determine whether there is trauma with current activation. The client's body language can also be an indicator.

Body language. Most people assume physical positions and use gestures that carry a level of affect with it. During the first few sessions, it is possible to use the lens of survival to learn how these behaviors may be appropriate defensive measures for a trauma survivor. Err on the side of observing without discussing. Instead, use these as a way to develop biological empathy. Never call attention to these unless the client is already comfortable discussing traumatic situations. At that point, following or tracking nonverbals can explore the message they may convey. For example, "That must have been terrible at the time. It's almost as if your hands are saying, 'get away from me!' Does that fit, or are your hands saying something else?" When clients acknowledge their symbolic gestures of defense, attack, or protection, be sure to celebrate them. "Good for you! That's right! You have the right to _____!" This type of intensity may be unusual for some therapists, however, affect is the energy that drives memory and change. The body is affect. The art of trauma recovery work is knowing when to be calm and when to celebrate. There is also calm celebration. As in the fairy tale about Goldilocks, "Not too hot, not too cold. Juuuust right!"

TRAUMA ASSESSMENT GUIDELINES

1. Ask for survey information, but be prepared to avoid discussion of it.
2. Observation is more important than discussion.

3. Keep somatic explorations focused on the comfortable and positive.
4. Plant seeds rather than pull weeds.
5. Celebrate defense and protection. These are how we survive.
6. It is not necessary to discuss the details. This is solely the prerogative of the survivor.
7. Remember that many people recover from trauma without any help.

TRAUMA RECOVERY

Recovery is the journey from threat to survival to transformation. The location of the journey traverses interpersonal-body circuits that develop, grow, and change through experiences measured in nanoseconds. The most common elements of trauma recovery are the overlapping realms of relationship, body, mind, and spirit. This order favors Porges' (2007) polyvagal theory, one that suggests social engagement is the first survival strategy humans use. If this strategy fails, we resort to fight/flight strategies. After this, freeze takes over in the face of shock or inescapable conditions. For those tormented by war, the possibility of death may have flashed through their brain. Taken to its ultimate conclusion, freeze leads to death. In animals, feigning death is a survival instinct. In humans, it may appear as dissociation or silence. Thus, relationships, body, mind, and spirit are the elements of personal experience that lead to survival. They are also the road to transformation and visionary progress, the most human trait of all. However, because of their interlocking nature, injury to one can compromise functioning of all. This great discovery is one way that east and west came together in the journey to the center of the brain.

Family therapists are familiar with variations of these concepts. A number of cutting-edge practices in the field are brain-friendly because they instinctively honor survival, attachment, and physical needs. Later chapters outline these advantages. However, the missing piece in family therapy education and other professional training programs is an understanding of trauma process and a conscious awareness of what is trauma-informed. This section provides guidelines that organize matters of relationship, body, mind, and spirit into trauma recovery.

Relationships: Friends and Foes

The roles of the therapist change as recovery becomes a journey of transformation. They begin as protector, then mediator, tour guide and facilitator. In trauma work, the therapist adopts the role of protector. Protection on many levels is highly valued by trauma survivors. This sounds like it would run counter to notions of self-determination and self-efficacy, but it matches the developmental trajectory that often accompanies the resolution of trauma symptoms. Once infants feel a secure attachment, they feel more able to explore their boundaries. Thus, by going slow, the therapist becomes the keeper of the overwhelming affect that is a survivor's nemesis. Once the therapist-client relationship feels safe, clinicians can become mediators between the overwhelming affect and our protagonist. See details of this work in the body section.

With respect to trauma recovery work, references about drama attune to the experience of trauma survivors. Especially when survivors may have social environments that belittle their affective arousal, it is important for therapists to attune to the drama. As recovery continues, clients transform these realities into their own creative stories. However, in the initial stages of trauma work, they are literal. The threat of destruction is a life-changing event for body, mind, spirit, and relationships.

As protectors, family therapists can survey the family and social network for "friend and foe." Genograms that are visually large on an easel keep the PFC engaged and the limbic system contained (Hanna, 2007). "Friends" in family and social network have an important role to play in trauma recovery. Even the "foes" might transform, depending on each situation. However, the involvement of those who care and those who are safe is an important component of this work. Sometimes a person is a foe, but has important information about individual and family history. Creating ground rules for safety in advance can allow therapists to benefit from extended family knowledge without compromising the well-being of survivors. In extreme cases, I ask permission to gather information by telephone. In addition, genogram sessions alone and with other family members allow therapists to assess the potential for unspeakable dilemmas that might be lurking in trauma symptomology.

Griffith & Griffith (1994) detail cases in which medical family therapy either helped symptoms diminish or abate entirely. Inviting clients to tell their stories in a medical setting was rare for the time. However, stories told of secrets, shame, or fear of abandonment that became dilemmas to attack immune systems, digestive tracts, and lungs. In all cases, there was a feeling of entrapment and isolation for clients. Clients' life experiences were too dangerous to speak, as dictated by perceptions of binding narratives in family, culture, or society. These interpersonal dilemmas are often about attachment and identity as clients navigate the balance of psychopolitics within their families.

One case is particularly striking. The authors tell how Frances, an adult woman, planned to kill herself through bulimia in order to send a message to her family that the ongoing sexual abuse of herself, and now, the younger generation had to stop. She insisted she could not tell her mother. She would not be able to handle it. Surprisingly, even her siblings agreed that she must not tell her mother. They expressed understanding as to why she might have to die. Frances prepared for her death by writing a letter for her mother to read posthumously. However, as life goes, she indicated one day, "God can do a lot more with me than you can ... the truth, not death can set me free" (Griffith & Griffith, 1994, p. 52). And with this, she changed her letter to a living one that forgave her mother, but asked her to acknowledge all the years of abuse. Mission accomplished! She and her mother began a new chapter that allowed her to overcome her bulimia. The politics of attachment, identity, and belonging literally became life and death issues. Ultimately, her identity as a woman of faith came to the rescue.

Because social engagement is so vital to human survival, expanded social functioning and intimacy is the true measure of success when survival becomes transformative (Heller & La Pierre, 2012). Plant these seeds and explore how they might fit for each client. Some will be like the man who wanted his wife to attend his EMDR sessions. "Bring 'em on!" Others may have attachment injuries that require a safe period of gestation. "No way!" Still others just need the suggestion, a rationale for how others can help, and a plan that allows the novelty of the idea to fit within their current mindset. "Hmm, I can see what you mean."

> Because social engagement is so vital to human survival, expanded social functioning and intimacy is the true measure of success . . .

When the recovery process proceeds in stages, therapists can propose a plan for how to involve significant others. Woods et al. (2012) found that many family members want to be involved in helping and they have secondary trauma from survivors' symptoms. At the outset, psychoeducation can be the great equalizer to lower conflict in a living situation. Once conflict is contained, the interpersonal field may be calm enough to begin body work. This leads to changes in memory and meaning that may improve significant relationships. Memory and meaning have a way of sounding off in the body.

Body: Where Do You Feel It?

Although working with body sensations is a key element in trauma healing, there are direct and indirect ways to do so. Some clients come with enough education and orientation to the mind-body movement that they welcome this approach. Others may come from environments that are highly traumatizing, leading to high distrust of therapists or mental health facilities. However, regardless of a client's level of preparation for whole body work, there are approaches that educate and motivate by using the client's motivational set. Hesitance is just a signal that the therapist needs to learn more about the client.

The assessment process creates a space to simultaneously gather information and plant seeds. The felt sense exercise during assessment provides a brief interaction that consists of a dialogue between the body and the conscious mind. Grounding and resourcing are protective. The body is in touch with the ground and the chair. When a person feels protected, these can be a ritual at the beginning of each session. Use this as a safe way to bring awareness of the body into traditional talk therapy or during a few more assessment sessions. As part of psychoeducation, grounding and resourcing with members of the support network can plant seeds about the importance of knowing the body. These exercises create a calm and safe atmosphere.

In the event that someone feels uncomfortable sensations during any part of the exercise, ask them to open their eyes. Closed eyes may be intolerable for those with high amounts of fear and vigilance. They may be able to tolerate the exercise with eyes open. When someone cannot tolerate grounding or resourcing, indirect approaches provide body-oriented healing without engaging the conscious mind. The therapist can drop the felt sense exercise altogether and explore general experiences of calm and satisfaction. Then ask where they feel these in the body, etc. Notice that the emphasis is on body sensations, not emotion. There is no need for content at this stage, unless something spontaneously pops into the mind. The primary goal is to establish comfort somewhere in the body. When there is chronic pain from health conditions such as fibromyalgia, there is usually still some place, no matter how obscure, that feels neutral or positive.

A number of trauma practitioners use techniques that Gendlin (1996) developed as part of his body-oriented psychotherapy in the 1980s. These direct approaches educate clients about the physiology of trauma and how those are related to trauma symptoms. They explain how body-oriented techniques can help reorganize the nervous system. Over the past 40 years, Peter Levine (2010) developed Somatic Experiencing® (SE). This approach brings his vast knowledge of animal physiology, medical biophysics, and psychology to the work. His explanations of fight, flight, and freeze in the animal world bring a deep understanding of essential survival processes and why animals in the wild never develop trauma symptoms, but humans do.

Inspired by Levine, I will explain this using the example of my dog, Leo, a golden cocker spaniel. When I give him a bath, clean his ears, or put drops in his eyes, what does he do afterward? He shakes. Not just a slight twitch. He really shakes. Animals can shake in the most elegant of ways. Oh, that humans had this gift! Actually, we have a similar ability, but it is usually buried beneath social convention, peer group expectations, and lack of awareness. Animals' shakes are nature's way of allowing them to rebalance their nervous system after a threat, shock, or invasion (I suppose this is why my dog still loves me!). It is also a metabolic transition state that helps them move from freeze, during an inescapable threat, to fight or flight, where they can regain equilibrium. During primitive times, *Homo sapiens* had places to run when under attack. In today's concrete jungles, there is little room in social circles, crowded trains, or even homes to allow ourselves the proper discharge of unused defensive energy after a threat. Adrenaline is already pumping, but we have nowhere to go.

In SE, clients learn about their own energy through the felt sense and how to discharge stuck energy from states of fight/flight or freeze. As a cousin to the practices of mindful meditation (Kabot-Zinn, 2006) and focusing (Gendlin, 1996), SE is trauma-focused and needed for clients who have retractable symptoms. Levine (2010) emphasizes use of the felt sense to help clients tune in to their own sensations. He also developed a process called *titration* that refers to the smallest steps possible when directly connecting to trauma sensations. Because direct approaches focus on affective sensations, discussing small segments of a story prevents retraumatizing the person, especially when the therapist begins at the end of the event—"When did you first feel safe?"

One way to envision this process is to think of a story in written form. In the story, the therapist would titrate at the end of each "paragraph" by asking the person to stop and track their body to see what they feel. When the focus alternates between comfortable and activated places in the body, tension stays contained. The script in Box 5.1 is an example of an alternating sequence.

Therapists who are trained in SE go beyond these basics, and provide corrective experiences by separating fear from helplessness and encouraging the active, empowered, defensive responses that were thwarted at the time of the event. However, for those without training, refocusing on a comfortable location is a safe, helpful way to begin a whole body orientation.

SE basics:
1. **ground**
2. **resource**
3. **track sensations**
4. **resource**
5. **ground**

Ross (2008) describes her use of these SE basics with couples and families. Just by slowing down difficult discussions and teaching all in attendance to track, ground, and resource, the process changes to include the body as a player in the transaction. Anxious amygdala can relax and this prevents almighty adrenaline from dominating the next eighteen minutes of the session. In the early stages of Gottman & Levenson's (1985) marital research, they began asking couples to take their pulse and slow their heart rate. He was on to something. We just lacked a coherent frame for how to sustain that bodily state until it reorganizes brain circuits.

If clients become aware of what they wish they could have done, physically, at the time, symbolically, the same muscle groups can move, such as shaking the fist, moving legs up and down, or pressing against a hard surface to engage the defensive muscles in the arms. Movements can change from fast to slow, until those muscles go at slow motion while there is breathing and focusing on that part of the body. Using the felt sense during each slow-motion defensive response will allow a reorganization of the body with calmness after the discharge of energy. Ross suggests some additional questions to explore a place of activation:

> If the tightness could speak, what would it say?
> What do you notice right now?
> What would help (take away the image, like fire, black hole, etc.)?
> If the slightest movement in your body could happen right now, what would that be?
>
> (Ross, 2008, pp. 99, 226)

In body-centered work, the body's resilience is the primary force for recovery. Symptoms are the result of natural survival processes that have no outlet. The outlet can take many forms, such as movements to complete fight/flight responses, imagining those responses and focusing on how the body feels, or focusing on the activated part of the body until the tension leaves on its own. When the later happens, there is often a sigh, yawn, tingling, or other pleasant sensation that the client reports.

Mind: Speaking to the Right Person

Some approaches respect the fact that clients may be in bodies that are one chronological age when their affective-memory circuits may be a younger age, without benefit of information from the PFC. Van der Kolk notes that those with developmental trauma may have lived for decades with ongoing misattunements, injuries, and isolation. On the way to adulthood, these children may have coped with the micropolitics of various professional settings.

> When professionals are unaware of children's need to adjust to traumatizing environments and expect that children should behave in accordance with adult standards of self-determination and autonomous, rational choices, these maladaptive behaviors tend to inspire revulsion and rejection. Ignorance of this fact is

likely to lead to labeling and stigmatizing children for behaviors that are meant to insure survival.

(van de Kolk, 2005, p. 404)

The cumulative effects of labeling and stigmatizing become a tangled web of circuits tucked into the compost heap of the mind. Those who are trained in social constructionist approaches often affirm the expertise of the client while being careful to keep their expectations attuned to the affective availability of clients. This is accomplished through careful attention to language.

Clean questions. The work of the late David Grove (1988), a New Zealand psychotherapist of Maori and European ancestry, developed *clean language* to work with victims of sexual abuse. Box 5.2 compares a few common questions with clean questions. Grove's work began in the 1980s on the cusp of the decade of the brain. He examined minute aspects of language for their value in eliciting a survivor's own experience and strengths, free from biases, assumptions, and mindsets of the therapist. Clean language avoids assumption, suggestion, and interpretation. The model suggests that this enables access to subjective experience with minimal interference. One of the advantages of clean language is that it attunes to children's experience. For adults stuck in symptoms from childhood, the questions stay with primary and basic experience, not those from the PFC of adults.

Box 5.2 Clean questions

Common Questions	Clean Questions
What can I do for you?	And what do you want to have happen?
How can I help you?	And what would be helpful?
What seems to be the matter?	And what do you want?
What is your problem?	And what would you like?
How do you feel?	And what is happening?
How did you feel about that?	And when that happened, what was that like?

Motivational interviewing. Miller & Rollnick's (2013) study of language and communication patterns that promote change. These authors provide research evidence for therapeutic dialogues that are most likely to stimulate motivation. They suggest that stimulating motivation can be the therapist's first task because everyone is motivated for something. Two of their most important findings are 1) <u>ambivalence</u> is a natural part of the change process, and 2) many people may behave as though they do not want to change because they do not <u>think</u> they will be successful.

These two principles are particularly helpful to adopt when working with survivors. Ambivalence becomes an opportunity for the therapist to embrace and explore a dilemma, rather than taking a position. When clients respond with "Yes, but . . ." this is a sign that the therapist is out of attunement with a client's internal experience. The development of mind is a mix of circuits that include the PFC <u>and</u> centers of affect and memory. Brain-friendly practices such as motivational interviewing explore all realms of brain functioning, not just reason alone. Conversations that lead to the resolution of ambivalence are those that affirm, reflect, and summarize. For survivors who are struggling to find their voices, these interactional styles allow the space for new associations to develop. When individuals do not have to defend their autonomy, paradoxically, this safety promotes more flexibility.

Survivors may also be prone to shame and self-criticism. These set the stage for a lack of confidence about most changes. Immense and exhausting effort goes into managing trauma symptoms. It is important to see a refusal to change as a lack of confidence. For example, Gail, 25, a survivor of bullying, attended an initial session with her parents. After years of emotional tirades and hopeless debates with her parents, she had developed coping strategies that were her best attempt at functioning, isolation and music. Her mother would say, "You can change if you want to." With self-criticism about her academic performance and discouragement from her parents' lectures, she adamantly stated that she was not going to change. Both sides of the argument were caught up in a battle of wills. The therapist suggested that Gail could attend without making any commitment for change. They all agreed something changed in middle school and she had been charming, outgoing, and precocious prior to age 12. Her PCL scores were in the range for clinical PTSD.

Gail agreed to come and participate in her parents' genograms and in reviewing her life story. The therapist used this to build a directory of family and individual strengths. She learned about traumas that plagued her grandparents. She disclosed three episodes of "horrific" bullying and humiliation that had remained private all those years. After initial family sessions, she asked to see the therapist for individual sessions and trauma work began. With psychoeducation about trauma symptoms, the old battles between Gail and her parents transformed into opportunities for her parents to think through the needs of an 11-year-old girl and how they could now be there for her as she reclaimed her rightful identity. She was highly motivated for relief from her trauma symptoms and reclaimed a confidence in her own abilities. The battle of minds and wills can dissolve when autonomy for a survivor is protected and parents learn the truth about their children. Gail began to believe in herself again.

In the case of April, from Chapter 3, her reluctance to seek therapy ended when her emotional rages continued to escalate and she exhausted her own insight as to what was happening to her. In hindsight, she described her therapist as

> low key and very permissive. She let me talk as much as I wanted and didn't press me for things I didn't want to discuss. If I became frustrated with something, like the fact that I couldn't remember who the third man was that abused me, she'd just say something like, "Well, maybe it's not necessary for you to remember. Sometimes, our minds only need certain things in order to heal." Then, I would relax and not worry about it.

Outside of therapy, April also discovered a technique she found on the internet, writing with the non-dominant hand (Capacchione,

2001). She began to express herself through sessions in which she would pose questions to herself and then begin writing any words that came into mind. She indicated that her non-dominant writing seemed to be from her as a child. She wrote regularly for herself in this way over the next two years. With her calm and present therapist and these exercises that brought left and right brain together, April reported a healing process for herself that brought acceptance, integration, and a new sense of self-respect as part of her coherent narrative. As Levine (1997) has said, trauma may be a fact of life, but it is not a "life sentence."

As a reminder, in addition to accessing the strengths of each hemisphere, it is possible to balance them. The *corpus collosum* is a band of tissue that joins right and left, by carrying information between them. It is thought that writing with the non-dominant hand engages both hemispheres equally. This is particularly stimulating as a personal growth exercise for therapists, couples, and clients who are interested in accessing deeper wisdom to solve some problem (Nelson, 2010). When people have little access to their primary emotions, these exercises can help them discover what their emotional system "thinks." The process begins with an explanation about left and right brains. The therapist encouraged clients to avoid penmanship, coherence, and grammar. Just let the words flow out and write them. Typically, a question or topic initiates the process. It can be therapist or client-generated. Provide a rationale that connects the exercise with the presenting problem. Is the goal greater insight, disclosure to the therapist, or developing a sense of direction that is comes from intuition? The person writes the question or topic with the non-dominant hand, then allows the writing to continue with any words that come up. April reported a sense of spiritual connection with herself that was new and healing.

Spirit: Expanding the Universe

Amen (2002) suggests that one's spirituality, such as the qualities of love, compassion, empathy for others, etc., develop from a healthy PFC. Given trauma's dysregulation of the limbic-PFC circuits and imbalances in the right hemisphere, these invasions are ultimately violations of the spirit. Thus, practitioners may find it important to think of recovery with an eye on transformation. Tapping into the human potential for transformation brings together wisdom of the ancients with new support in the present.

Safety first. A turning point in the stories of many survivors can be the instant in which they realized they were safe or had survived. As mentioned previously, an important question to ask is, "When did you first feel safe (or know that you survived)?" The language is adapted for a given situation. This is the first point of transformation, but it may have been brief, fleeting, even unconscious until hearing the question. For example, a woman who survived a life-threatening auto accident, but sustained many head injuries, paused when she heard this question.

Therapist: After the accident, when did you first realize you were going to make it?

Woman: (Pause . . .) (she was searching her conscious mind for this small instant in the wake of blood, ambulance, sirens, hospital gurneys, etc.) Oh! (with a smile), it was when they were wheeling me down the hall in the hospital. I saw the lights and all the people around me . . . (chuckling), I must have felt safe then because I seemed to snap back to myself and started asking them all kinds of questions about my condition, what did my face look like . . . telling them where it hurt . . .

Therapist: So, take some time and notice where you feel that safety in your body as you remember the lights and the people surrounding you. Take it in and let your body feel that chuckle. Where do you feel it now? Take some time to focus on it now (resourcing).

In another instance, the survivor went for years in fear before feeling safe. The father who abused her continued to stalk her mother and siblings. They moved frequently to avoid him. They were never sure when he might appear to harm them again. After fifteen years, she said she discovered him on the internet—in prison. As the therapist discovered this experience, they celebrated together and allowed her body to take in the sensation of safe. Many people have lost the ability to celebrate. Resourcing is a way to teach the body how to celebrate again. When survivors cannot pinpoint a time of safety, therapists can use the present moment to focus on feelings of safety. Then, they may want to imagine a protector who can keep them safe. They can focus on this ally, sense where in the body they feel the support, and savor the sensation (resource).

Resilience. Wolin & Wolin's (1993) work on resilience came from pioneering research on families and children who coped with alcoholism (Steinglass et al., 1987). They interviewed 25 adults whose childhoods included poverty, racism, violence, substance abuse, and family disruptions. They observed an attribute they called survivor's pride. It is the feeling of accomplishment from overcoming adversity. Composed of pain and triumph, some express it openly and others only hint at it. Working with at-risk youth, they could detect and celebrate survivor's pride as part of their overall strength-based approach to healing. Noting this transcendence and connecting it to body and mind is transformative and empowering. Including others in celebrating this work can also strengthen these circuits.

"How did you do it?" This seminal question was the center of their research. It balanced the stereotype that children at-risk were only damaged. They note that there is a mixture of both, damage and survival. Box 5.3 lists the seven resiliencies employed by participants in their interviews. They note that traumatized children are neither completely damaged or completely invulnerable. Brain-friendly practices can help trauma survivors identify what strategies worked for them and incorporate them into their survival-transformation narratives. They found that when survivors could identify the damage and the resiliencies, they could overcome it.

Box 5.3 The seven resiliencies

Insight	Asking tough questions and giving honest answers.
Independence	Distancing emotionally and physically from sources of trouble in one's life.
Relationships	Making fulfilling connections to other people.
Initiative	Taking charge of problems.
Creativity	Using imagination and expressing oneself in art forms.
Humor	Finding the comic in the tragic.
Morality	Acting on the basis of an informed conscience.

(adapted from Wolin & Wolin, 1993)

TRAUMA RECOVERY GUIDELINES

As an introduction to the vast world of trauma treatment, this chapter provides basic principles for those who hope to integrate biosocial processes into their work. In general, one can think of the process as a healing circle around the outer edges of affective intensity, allowing experiences of grounding and safety to connect body and conscious mind. As these provide calm, the circle can become a gradual spiral into the center of symptoms. As the safety and calm continue to grow, when we reach the center, we find the intensity has gradually drained away during these earlier stages. There may be little intensity left. If some remains, now there is safety and strength in addressing other body sensations. Since we're not talking about the event, whatever the body continues to bring up becomes the agenda. These are the effects. As a starting place, the following guidelines summarize this section on recovery. Other examples of trauma work appear in the next chapters as developmental issues, losses, and other types of trauma emerge in the work of couples and family.

1. Consider how trauma work can improve relationships and how relationships can improve trauma symptoms.

Whenever the social network is involved in any of the above processes, new circuits become even stronger.

2. Develop a rhythm that alternates between comfort and discomfort in the body.

3. Remember that it is not necessary to re-live upsetting experiences. Focus on the effects of the trauma and work on overcoming those.

4. Use a knowledge of child development to help clients and families envision steps of progress as a person grows into the present.

5. Celebrate safety. Celebrate resilience. Celebrate creativity. Celebrate the future.

6

The Brain in Marriage, Love, and Sex

Eat your soup and let the lady talk.

L.L. Cool J.

The decade of the brain was not lost on advances in couples' therapy. Marital attachment and conflict are neurobehavioral processes that either help or hurt intimate relationships. In her extensive body of research, Kiecolt-Glaser has shown that marital quality is also a major variable in heath and illness (Kiecolt-Glaser, 2009; Kiecolt-Glaser et al., 1998; Kiecolt-Glaser & Newton, 2001; Kiecolt-Glaser et al., 2003; Kiecolt-Glaser et al., 2005; Parker-Pope, 2010). As an extension of communication theory, we might say, all behavior is communication, and all communication is physiological. Perhaps nowhere do body, mind, and spirit come together as powerfully as they do in love and sexual relationships.

In recent years, mate selection and marriage have received unprecedented attention from an interdisciplinary cadre of scientists who are trying to connect the dots to form a whole body perspective on these important relationships. From medical anthropologists to social endocrinologists, there is a wealth of information along the entire spectrum of human functioning. An unlikely body of research is dubbed *neuroeconomics* (Zak, 2008). It might seem unrelated to couple therapy, except some of this work examines oxytocin and trust. What could be more relevant for couples than trust? In other fields, a look at the endocrine system reveals that women need testosterone, too. The last section of this chapter reviews three excellent models that address neurobiology, either directly or indirectly. These approaches are the new wave of how art and science go hand in hand when it comes to obtaining deeper, longer lasting intimate relationships. These give guidance for some common factors that couples' therapists can integrate into their practices. To begin this chapter, some brief reminders from disciplines that can inform couples' therapy. Anthropologists often take us back to the ancestors. So do neuroscientists. In our neurobiological drama, this scene features dopamine and a number of chemical colleagues that give us new life, euphoria, and a lifetime of rewards. If only we can master the basics . . .

SURVIVAL OF THE TRIBE

There are a growing number of scientists who invite us to examine the myths that spring from dominant discourses. For example, much of this book examines the body's experience of threat and connections to the circuits of fight/flight or freeze. Taylor (2006) suggests that humans are biologically programmed to nurture. Her research on the neuropeptide, oxytocin, suggests that it is a stress reliever and may motivate a "tend and befriend" pattern during stress, not only fight/flight (Taylor et al., 2000). This matches Porges' (2007) work that suggests humans use social engagement as our first survival strategy. Her findings regarding oxytocin's altruism and cooperation link these interpersonal strategies to survival of the species. In addition, Zak, Stanton and Ahmadi (2007) have found oxytocin levels related to increased empathy during a research task.

With respect to mating, Small (2011) believes that the cultural institution of marriage comes from the need for elaborate social networks that increase safety and survival. She thinks of marriage as a survival strategy of the species characterized by cooperation. Her observations do not see monogamy as a necessity for civilization, but rather, alliances and connections. Human need for cooperative ventures is what keeps marriage alive. Thus, the challenges that come to contemporary couples may be due to *constraints*. Instead of what causes the problems, what keeps the better side of humans from emerging?

What keeps men and women from privileging their true nature? From accessing the cooperative, prosocial part of their nature? Social constructionists in family therapy recognize these questions immediately (Bateson, 1972; White, 1986; Jenkins, 1991). Michael White (1986) based his narrative family therapy on a theory of restraint. His central question was, "How can we liberate people from their restraints?" Neurobiology as couple education frames a couple's behavior and desires as a normal part of being human. A knowledge of physiology and culture helps them overcome their restraints. In the face of an externalized, no-fault perspective, they can forgive each other. As one couple announced at the beginning of a session, "We've decided to grant each other amnesty." This normalizing process uses neurobiology to paint an interesting picture of women's and men's brains.

MALE AND FEMALE: HEMISPHERE OR ATMOSPHERE?

Since the advent of feminist movements in the U.S. and around the world, there has been an important need to deconstruct women's limitations as cultural rather than biological. The movement toward women's equality has had to challenge a number of cultural myths. Thus, most neuroscientists emphasize that their findings do not promote a certain stereotype or gap in women's functioning (Taylor et al., 2002). To the contrary, current knowledge from neuroscience suggests the survival value of differences between female and male brains, casting our ancestors in cooperative roles that challenge contemporary stereotypes. Both genders participated in acquiring food. This activity was not limited to male hunting. In fact, some believe that women acquired proportionally more of the family's food each week than men. However, overall brain differences in regional activity and areas of density provide an interesting look at why teamwork and cooperation should be the hallmark of a good marriage. Studies compare physiology during specific activities and relate these to evolutionary needs. As Tannen (1994) has maintained, both responses are important. The key is to understand them and incorporate them into a model of teamwork.

Many express concern about the disparity between young males and females regarding certain conditions. Studies document pronounced differences between genders (Cahill, 2006). McCarthy, Arnold, Ball, Blaustein, & De Vries (2012) report that dyslexia and stuttering occur three to four times more in boys. Attention deficit hyperactivity disorder occurs ten times more often in boys. They are also four times more at risk for autism spectrum disorders. The same rates are true for early onset schizophrenia. In adulthood, major depressive disorder, anxiety, and panic disorders are twice as common in women. Anorexia bulimia occurs three times more often; anorexia nervosa is thirteen times more frequent in women. These disturbing numbers suggest vulnerability for males with developmental onset disorders, and for females, adult onset disorders.

As preparation to fully appreciate the biosocial hemispheres and atmospheres of each gender, these public health statistics should give pause to every couples therapist. Regardless of presenting problem or how partners may appear as adults, hetero-sexual couples come from different worlds with different vulner-abilities. As cutting edge models of couple therapy will illustrate, it is critical for clinicians to understand childhood affective devel-opment and attachment threats that may influence emotion and behavior in marriage. This is true, whether gay or straight. Thus, a review of brain differences under various conditions provides a degree of transparency to the hidden worlds that men and women bring into an intimate relationship. First, a look at circuits of activity will provide descriptions of gendered hemispheres. Then, social endocrinology will describe the reciprocal dance between hormones, behavior, and environment.

The Brain at Work: Connectivity and Reactivity

Many studies examine young brains as children and adolescents develop. Girls seem to have a larger corpus callosum near the back part of the brain that represents language. There also seem to be greater density (more connections) in the back temporal lobe. On average, girls have earlier speech, more ability with phonics, and greater verbal fluency. There is also data about how boys' PFCs, the sites for judgment and planning, mature at a slower rate than girls'. Witelson (2007) suggests this may lead to more risk-taking during adolescence. Chapter 7 discusses interventions that can redirect aggression during adolescence.

A number of studies examine sex differences during stress. Here, the anxious amygdala and almighty adrenaline return to center stage. In one study, male amygdalae communicated more strongly to motor parts of the brain. Thus, behavior may be directed to the external environment. In women, the amygdala connected more strongly to the hypothalamus, which regulates internal body environment such as breathing, heart rate, etc. (Witelson et al., 1995). Wang et al. (2012) found that male and female brains were different in gray matter density notably in the occipital lobe and the cerebellum. Men showed higher connectivity in their right hemispheres, women in their left hemispheres. For some tasks, women had more visual focus and men more activity related to movement. In an interesting review of research to date, Andreano and Cahill (2009) found evidence that sex differences sometimes emerge during stress, with interactions between stress and sex hormones.

Other studies found greater activity for men between the right amygdala and memory when viewing emotional films (Cahill et al., 2004a; Cahill et al., 2001; Cahill et al., 2004b). For women activity was greater between the left amygdala and memory for the same task. For these hemispheric processes, right relates to global/central aspects of the situation, left to local/fine detail. This may mean that men see the forest, women see the trees. For both genders, emotion, that fluid state within the amygdala, has a significant influence on memory. This may be one reason why DNA exoneration cases are finding that eyewitness identification was the strongest contributing factor in the conviction of innocent people (Wells & Olson, 2003). Thus, marriage education curricula could include the neurobiology of memory and help couples embrace their experience without embracing their memories.

Although it is common to mention differences in brain size between men and women, proportionally, men's brains are in proportion to their bodies. However, to eliminate the need to focus on size, recent studies now control for this. Luders et al. (2009) used male and female brains that were the same size. They found that women had greater density in right and left caudate, adjacent regions of the basal ganglia, left orbito-frontal region, left superior temporal gyrus, and left superior frontal gyrus. Consistent with these previous findings, Gong and Yong Evans (2011) found that men were more efficient in right hemisphere, women in left.

From child development research, Baron-Cohen (2002) suggests that these differences translate for males as *systemizing*, and for females, *empathizing*. Systemizing is the drive to analyze and identify the underlying rules that govern a system. A system is any process that has an input and output. Empathizing is the ability to understand the mental states of others and to respond to their affect. He cites research on 16 variables for females and 13 for males that provide evidence of these central tendencies. What both types share is the need to understand and predict behavior.

His work provides a framework for assessing brain type, since most people are a combination of these due to culture and environment. He argues that autism may be an extreme male type and points to infant research that reports day-old boys stare longer at a mechanical mobile than at a face. On a personal note, there was a time when I would have found his ideas to be far-fetched. However, Porges' (2007) polyvagal theory now suggests that a weak muscle in the middle ear might be preventing autistic children from distinguishing human voice from other sounds. This could compound a male's focus on mechanical (system), rather than human stimuli (empathy). He is currently testing this hypothesis through auditory tones that strengthen that muscle. In preliminary reports, families report more social engagement from their children. Thus, Baron-Cohen's ideas have a platform provided by a range of neuroscience studies that bring them down to earth. In the next section, a discussion of testosterone helps to make Baron-Cohen's theory even more plausible.

A final set of studies examines menstrual cycle as an influence on brain structures. Goldstein et al. (2010) scanned healthy women twice, during the early follicular phase (day 1 of period, all hormones low) and late follicular–midcycle (day 14, estrogen peaked, progesterone still low). They found that men's and women's brains responded to stress stimuli similarly when women were at day 1. Compared to women at day 14, men exhibited stronger stress reactions. The strongest differences were in the PFC and orbito-frontal cortex (behind the eyes). Thus, women's hormones help regulate stress during these points in the cycle. The authors suggest possible functions of these differences:

> From an evolutionary point of view, it is important for the female during midcycle to have a heightened cortical capacity, unencumbered by excessive arousal, to optimally judge whether a potentially threatening stimulus, such as an approaching male, is an opportunity for successful mating or for fight or flight. Thus, females have been endowed with a natural hormonal capacity to regulate the stress response that differs from males. This mechanism may have been maladaptive or unnecessary from an evolutionary point of view for the male, who had primary responsibility for protection of the species, thus necessitating a constant fight-or-flight behavioral response.
>
> (Goldstein et al., 2010, p. 437)

Andreano & Cahill (2010) also studied the influence of menstrual hormone levels by comparing fMRIs of women at approximately day 1 and day 21 of their cycles. For both groups, negatively arousing pictures produced significantly increased activity in the amygdala and hippocampus, compared to neutral pictures. These differences were larger for the group at day 21, when progesterone is elevated. At day 1, estrogen and progesterone are at low levels. Thus, the brain's arousal system varies over the course of the menstrual cycle, and higher arousal appears to relate to higher circulating progesterone levels. These studies provide a picture of activity for women and men that factor hormones into the equation. Although the most common references in popular culture relate to women's emotional reactivity due to pre-menstrual syndrome (PMS), here, there is room to expand the picture of women to include cycles when they are less reactive than men. These cycles illustrate how important it is to educate men and women about the timing and differences in reactivity. Education about variability can bring greater predictability into a marriage. A summary of these differences appears in Table 6.1. This lessens the temptation to minimize one or the other during the heat of a disagreement. A knowledge of these variations also comes from some interesting studies in the field of social endocrinology.

> **Education about variability can bring greater predictability into a marriage.**

Social Endocrinology

This field is emerging as an interdisciplinary group that studies the interaction between hormones and behavior. A number of their projects examine testosterone (T), cortisol (CORT), and oxytocin (OT). Mehta & Josephs (2010) identified baseline T as a marker of chronic status-seeking motivation in both men and women. Different stages of their work reveal how T and behavior have mutual influence. Taken as a whole, their research identifies

Table 6.1 Female and male brain differences

Female	Male
Verbal ability—corpus collosum larger by verbal areas	Visual-spatial—more testosterone
	More density in right hemisphere
More density in left hemisphere	PFC development slower—more risks, less planning, judgement in adolescence
More PFC development by age 11	
Amygdala connects more to hypothalamus (internal)	Amygdala connects more to motor areas (external)
Sees the trees (for certain tasks)	Sees the forest (for certain tasks)
Empathizer	Systemizer
More eating disorders, depression, anxiety, panic attacks	More dyslexia, stuttering, ADHD, autism, early onset schizophrenia
More reactivity than men during periods of elevated progesterone	More reactivity than women during cycles of low progesterone for women

chronic status-seeking motivation, and short-term status-seeking motivation. These are analogous to personality versus mood (Mehta et al., 2008).

Mehta & Josephs (2010) note the following results from their research.

1. T is negatively associated with affiliation and social bonding.
2. Married men have lower T levels than unmarried men.
3. Unmarried men in romantic partnerships have lower T levels than single men.
4. T levels are lower in new fathers.
5. Divorced men dropped in T when they remarried.
6. Partnered women have lower T levels than single women.
7. Polygamous women have higher T levels than single and partnered women.

In a cyclical way, interpersonal bonding leads to lower T, which leads to more bonding and cooperation (Zak et al., 2009). These researchers wonder if those who are low in basal T are more likely to develop and maintain committed, romantic relationships. While their studies do not include couple data during various experimental conditions, the variety of their individual data includes men and women performing in math, leadership, and competition. Eight studies yielded the following results:

1. Low T men and women performed well in a cooperation setting.
2. High T men and women performed poorly in the cooperation condition.

Because the field of social endocrinology is new, scientists caution against overgeneralizing these results. However, they also cite clusters of studies that achieve similar results. Thus, lower T is associated with social bonding and lower status-seeking motivation.

With respect to stress, social approach and aggression, some studies include CORT, secreted from adrenal glands as part of the HPA axis. It interacts with T in some interesting ways.

1. Elevated CORT relates to social avoidance, inhibition, anxiety, defensiveness, and internalizing behaviors.
2. Low basal CORT relates to social approach, aggression, extroversion, and memory for happy faces.

A study of men in dominance contests found that when defeat and victory were experimentally manipulated, neither T nor CORT predicted responses to defeat. Only the T-CORT interaction reached significance, presumably because defeat involves status (identity) and coping (threat). T relates to the drive for status, CORT relates to social distance. The same interaction emerged in a study of leadership.

1. High status-seeking motivation (high T) and social approach (low CORT) lead to good leadership.
2. High status-seeking motivation (high T) and social inhibition (high CORT) lead to poorer leadership.
3. High T-High CORT individuals respond to social stress with negative affect, compared to High T-Low CORT individuals. They may experience a social stressor as a threat, whereas the latter may see it as a challenge.

Again, although these studies are preliminary, the discussions in Chapters 3 and 4 about identity, threat, and survival come to bear on these results. Carre & Mehta (2011) strongly urge researchers to include the interaction effects of CORT whenever studying T, as this combination relates more to aggression than either alone. The research of Gottman and colleagues with men and domestic violence has particular relevance as an interdisciplinary connection to social endocrinology. In that study, a group of men showed a drop in physiology during conflict (Gottman et al., 1995). They also had more adverse experiences in childhood. Although neither T or CORT was part of that study, it is possible that these observations are part of a freeze response in the moment that eventually leads to outbursts of violence. Feelings of helplessness in one area can trigger over-compensation in another. Certainly, high CORT is already implicated as a factor in the undischarged energy of overwhelm during trauma. In addition, given the fact that Mehta & Josephs (2010) find similar results in women, practitioners would be wise to drop stereotypes of "male testosterone" in favor of an evolutionary perspective that continues to find no fault in a given tendency, but instead, links it with overall survival. This frame can redirect time and energy into cooperative problem-solving strategies.

In this same vein, OT is no longer considered only relevant to women. A number of studies illustrate how OT affects affiliation and bonding in both sexes (Zak et al., 2005). Social support and OT interact to lower a stress response. Social support alone was not as effective as the combination with OT. Recursively, OT exists in the face of social gaps and leads to affiliation. It is also the result of social contact. Studies have performed before/after designs that show changes in OT levels in a variety of sequences, leading to the belief that there is behavior-hormone circularity. Thus, raising awareness of conscious-unconscious physiology as part of a relationship dance can bring a coherent narrative that includes content, process, and substance.

These loops provide therapists with a number of possibilities for fine-tuning interventions based on what hormone is associated with which desired behavior. Taylor's (2006) important work on OT has lead to her respected "tend-and-befriend" theory. She demonstrates that, in women, stress promotes social contact through greater access to oxytocin. Rather than fight/flight alone, she warns that a male dominance model of stress response can lead to a research and social bias that ignores the important qualities of bonding, affiliation, and cooperation that are available to men and women.

In fact, one study found that OT leads to empathy, an increased ability to recognize emotions and infer mental states in others for both genders, although it was stronger for women (Barraza & Zak, 2009). In addition, studies administer OT through a nasal spray and document increased trust scores for men in an economic investment game (Zak, 2008). Heinrichs and Domes (2008) found similar results with OT and provide some early evidence for the other neuropeptide, arginine vasopressin (AVP), that has been linked to monogamy in mammals. The explosion of these studies in the science community has already led to marketing opportunities. Acevedo and colleagues (2012a, 2012b) have dubbed OT the "cuddle chemical" and AVP the "monogamy molecule." At this writing, there is extensive evidence for OT's nickname, but only emerging evidence for AVP.

If the reader needs a break from this technical review, go to your favorite internet browser and search for "oxytocin perfume." Already popular culture is rushing to judgment as though OT will be enough to combat infidelity because of its effects on empathy and trust. Is it possible that this will surpass the marketing frenzy for drugs that enhance erections? Should we laugh or cry? All kidding aside, there are numerous possibilities as to how couples therapists may use this emergent body of research. As we continue to examine the content, process, and substance of family life, this research provides a good deal of validation for a number of clinical observations that therapists have had for decades.

The quest for equality between men and women will also benefit from understanding the similarities and differences that exist in the world of hormones. Adding to this work on social endocrinology in general, Fisher (2004c, 2009) has conducted pioneering research on human brains and the hormones and neuropeptides that become active during dating, courtship, marriage, and break ups.

Chemical Messengers in Love and Loss

Fisher (2009) studies our ancestors and examines how romantic love is mediated through the body. Working with neuroscientists who perform fMRIs on people dating, courting, and married, she would say we are hardwired for lust, attraction, and attachment. Testosterone gets everyone out on the dance floor by stimulating sexual desire. Dopamine, goal oriented and motivational, helps everyone focus their energy on a suitable mate. When the body builds tolerance to dopamine highs and they diminish, oxytocin settles us and makes it possible to tend the nest and raise children (Frank, 2001). According to Fisher,

> We Americans are especially hooked on the second stage of romantic love. As a culture, we're a little leery of lust, and attachment seems to bore us to death, but we love love.
>
> (Fisher, 2009, p. 87)

The brain in love. To date, Fisher has studied collections of fMRIs for groups in each of these stages. The second stage, being in love, reveals women's brains that show increased activity in the areas of attention, emotion, and memory recall. Men's brains light up in the areas of visual stimuli and sexual arousal (Fisher, 2004c; Acevedo et al., 2012a). As a survival strategy, some might say that women evolved the use of attention, emotion, and memory to assess whether a man showed signs of being a suitable mate that would protect, provide, and lessen her vulnerability during childbearing and child rearing. Repetition and pattern registered with her. Men have been hardwired to rely on visual cues to assess safety and sexual arousal to assure reproduction. They noticed immediate visual cues. When each partner perceived these attributes in the other, boom! A "dopamine-drenched" state of intoxication ensues. In this stage, the PFC becomes focused on one goal. This may be one reason why pre-marital counseling can often be perfunctory. Few couples really have sufficient rational focus to benefit from the education. However, it can still be a valuable way to plant seeds for future prevention work, once the dopamine state has waned. From this progression of chemicals, it would seem more advantageous for young adults to receive premarital education before they begin seeking committed partnerships.

In passionate lovers, the fMRIs showed increased activity in the ventral tegmental area (VTA), where dopamine is produced and in the caudate nucleus, where dopamine is processed. Dopamine and the caudate nucleus play key roles in motivation, goals, and rewards. Activity here was greatest among subjects who scored high on the Passionate Love Scale. Fisher (2004c, p. 83) observes,

> We are coming to some understanding of the drive to love—and what an elegant design it is! This passion emanates from the motor of the mind, the caudate nucleus, and it is fueled by at least one of nature's most powerful stimulants, dopamine. When passion is returned, the brain tacks on positive emotions, such as elation and hope. And all the while, regions of the prefrontal cortex monitor the pursuit—planning tactics, calculating gains and losses, and registering one's progress toward the goal: emotional, physical, even spiritual union with the beloved. Nature has produced a powerful mechanism to focus our precious courtship energy on a special other—an evolutionary miracle designed to produce more humans.

Once lust and attraction turn to attachment, sexual satisfaction will continue the floods of dopamine, plus contribute to well-being in some studies (Brody, 2007). Fisher also suggests that oxytocin plays a role in stability (Acevedo et al., 2012b). It's possible that Taylor's tend and befriend concept applies here, although it is more pronounced in women. For men, it is possible that home and family represent safe havens for their amygdalas, as they scan the environment for danger. However, despite this new-found knowledge on the brain during arousal, attraction, and attachment, many studies and most clinicians attest to the fact that maintaining the attachment and reconciling the physiology of gender contain many complexities that still baffle science.

The brain rejected. When rejection occurs, the brain scans of those who reported "still feeling in love" show how love and anger circuits are closely related and how it is possible to love and hate someone simultaneously (Fisher et al., 2010). In addition to dopamine centers continuing to be active (goal seeking), the stress system also activates. This brings on a complicated mix of motivation and the fight/flight response. Fisher (2004a; Fisher et al., 2010) notes some interesting dynamics that could explain how stalkers and those who kill spouses during divorce can escalate. The dopamine centers are implicated in addictions, especially to cocaine. When expectation for reward activates dopamine, but the reward fails to appear, the rage circuits become active. Some speculate that it is the anger that enables someone to finally move on, rather than stay in a dead-end relationship.

Eventually, depression sets in. Fisher (2004c) notes that in the tribe, depression serves a clear evolutionary purpose. It becomes a cry for help so that the community rallies around the wounded person and provides help and resources until they recover and can begin the search for new companionship, reproduction, and survival. In addition, there are parallels with infants who manifest separation anxiety when sensing abandonment. The depression of rejected lovers may be the freeze stage of survival, once fight/flight prove unsuccessful.

This chemical activity, coupled with attachment narratives about identity and belonging, may also generate some thoughts about how attachment-meaning-loss circuits interact with emotional memory and autobiographical memory. These can provide an individualized template to explain the dopamine-stress connections. Other researchers examine these hormones under different conditions.

The brain and sex. Low sexual desire in both sexes is difficult to study because it is multidetermined (Yarber & Sayad, 2013) and there is a delicate balance of hormones that is little understood. Bos, Terburg, & van Honk (2010) found that testosterone administered to 24 women in a research condition decreased trust. In another study, van Anders & Dunn (2009) found T linked to men's desire and women's positive orgasm experience. Estradiol (E) linked to women's desire. Hiller (2004) reports that during sexual activity, oxytocin was related to arousal and orgasm in both sexes. In another case, oxytocin resolved a case of ejaculatory difficulties (Ishak et al., 2008). Diamond's (2004) reviews evidence that women tend to connect love and sexual desire, something that may be influenced by the greater availability of OT. Thus, T and OT are linked to various aspects of sexual experience for both sexes.

Couples therapists might wonder if those who seek sex therapy are at the extremes of a continuum whereby differences in sexual desire may stem from a man's high status seeking needs and low ability to bond, thus creating a combination of high T and low OT. Conversely, women who feel a gap in social bonding may have more OT and low T. Since T encourages libido for men, these contrasts in extreme cases would also lead to low libido in women and higher libido in men. Since the data from social endocrinology documents the reciprocal nature hormones and behavior, there is every reason to believe that sex therapy could facilitate the production of either more T for women or more OT for men (without using the perfume!). Neuroscience may be helpful by providing new language for old problems. Since there is convincing evidence that tend and befriend is necessary for survival, lower stress response, connection, bonding, trust and empathy, male status seeking could be cast with these characteristics, rather than the victory/defeat or fight/flight paradigms. Contemporary competitive sports also provides encouragement for teamwork rather than dominance alone. "Teamwork" may be the male counterpart to tend and befriend. Perhaps it could become the name of a new aftershave!

Marital teamwork. Thus, the language of survival provides a way to use hormonal narratives as evolutionary strengths during conflict resolution. Most couples therapists have heard the common complaint by men that women make mountains out of molehills. For women, the complaint is that men have a "fix it" mentality or they minimize the seriousness of a woman's complaint. When viewed through these evolutionary lenses, women focus on behavioral patterns over time (thus, a series of molehills becomes a mountain). Men focus on only the present molehill in real time (what they see is what they get). The discrepancy of pattern vs. event leads to repeating arguments over competing realities. However, each reality made sense for the ancestors. When couples have a no-fault explanation for generations of strategy, the differences can be redirected toward better outcomes. Women can learn how to negotiate in the present moment (something a man understands) rather than waiting for the pattern to emerge. Men can take a step back and review the big picture for implications that go beyond the present moment (something a woman appreciates). The no-fault atmosphere enables brain transformations that respond to novelty as a challenge, rather than a threat.

About men. Notions of teamwork and survival can also be helpful in the therapeutic atmosphere. Brooks (1998, 2012) has outlined why so many "traditional" men are reluctant to seek therapy. Addressing gender scripts, he compares the culture of men with the culture of therapy. With the former, there are issues of competition and hierarchy. Many men don't see how a therapy hour will help them in their "dog eat dog" world. With the latter, emotional expression, equity, and vulnerability are the very things that men are taught to avoid. Consequently, they are aware that they will have trouble being the ideal therapy client.

Brooks encourages therapists to recognize the irony for male clients, in light of the way women were silenced prior to feminist critiques of mental health treatment. Essentially, mental health was dominated by men who were condescending to women. Now, he suggests, the primary consumers of psychotherapy are women. The tables have turned and the process is now female friendly with more female practitioners and an interactional style that is more attuned to the socialization of women. He advocates adapting interpersonal styles that adapt to the culture of men. Those include more skill-building, having a goal orientation, outlining roles, and defining tasks.

In addition, Brehm (1985; as cited by Brooks, 1998) describes women's preference for communication as "face-to-face" whereas men prefer "side-by-side." In family therapy, a simple acommodation to these gender attunements is the use of diagrams. Like a "chalk talk" during half-time at a football game, when genograms, timelines, and relationships are illustrated visually on an easel, the atmosphere in the session lowers anxiety and constructs a side-by-side style where everyone focuses on the diagram, rather than face-to-face (Stahmann & Hiebert, 1998; see Figure 6.1). Elsewhere, I have explained how this format also facilitates an informal trance during the initial stage of therapy (Hanna, 2007).

Clark (2000) outlines these issues in a biosocial way. He notes the relationship between T, the PFC, and the amygdala for men under relationship stress (van Wingen et al., 2010). Men tend to react more strongly to lower levels of partner negativity than women (amydgala). This leads to flooding, the creation of circuits that involve emotional memory. Once these circuits form, adrenaline flows more quickly from even lower levels of negativity and keeps the PFC offline. Once flooded, physiological recovery takes longer in men than women. He suggests that the stonewalling behavior found in Gottman's research may actually be a defense against flooding (Buehlman et al., 1992). However, then stonewalling may lead to more partner criticism, which leads to more stonewalling, etc. Also, others have noted that CORT inhibits

Figure 6.1 Use of visual maps.

sexual response (Uckert et al., 2003). Thus, sexual dissatisfaction may be a private dialogue that becomes an unspoken dilemma for men who come from a high T upbringing. In an evolutionary sense, if they voice vulnerability, they may lose status. In the animal world, animals hide their pain so as not to attract a predator. Thus, attuning to the amygdala first can create the safety needed to become vulnerable. In working with traditional men, Clark (2000, pp. 26–29) cautions against the following:

1. a cool, disappointingly-appropriate therapist
2. jargon
3. trying to control the client's behavior
4. blaming the client for resisting participation
5. emphasizing right-brained efforts (symbols, metaphors, intuition, dreaming, emotions)
6. demands that feelings always be verbalized
7. failing to attend to the aggressions of the male's partner.

As the substance of neurobiology continues to inform the work of family therapists and psychotherapists, guidelines and common factors emerge to provide a brain-informed framework for clinical decisions. A number of couples therapists tie their work to this emerging knowledge.

THE NEW WAVE: COUPLE THERAPY AT THE CUTTING EDGE

Toward the end of the decade of the brain, family therapists began to dip a toe in the water of neuroscience (Atkinson, 2005). As the evidence mounted for the centrality of relationships in the neurobiology of attachment, family therapists began to see how the entire field could be validated by neuroscience (Sluzki, 2007; Fishbane, 2007, 2008; Hanna, 2010). These streams of thought converge in narratives of attachment, emotional reactivity, and love. The holy grail of therapy for love, sex, and family is within reach as a critical mass of family therapists emerge with an awareness of how brain processes provide a stage for difficulties and how brain processes also provide a map to help people out of their pain. The future of family therapy, as a modality and as a profession, is greatly enhanced by the results that a new generation of brain-informed clinicians can document.

Restoration Therapy (RT)

For decades, practitioners of marital therapy have discussed marital distress from dozens of perspectives. Hargrave & Pfitzer (2011) finally dare to speak about love and trustworthiness as central desires along the road of human endeavor. This is their language for the secure base of attachment. They are on a mission to restore love and trustworthiness to the mosaic of human connection. Building on their long-standing work in contextual family therapy (Boszormenyi-Nagy & Krasner, 1986; Hargrave, 1994; Hargrave & Pfitzer, 2003), they expand the concepts of *trust, justice, loyalty, and entitlement* to include a definition of love that ties these four dimensions to three types of love: *companionate, romantic* and *altruistic*. If Fisher (2002) can deconstruct the biology of love, the time seems right to explore the restoration of love, the most central of all survival processes. Along the way, restoration therapy helps therapists learn the art and experience of being a healer.

Just as eastern traditions bring together body and soul, RT is a western version of hope and healing that touches energy in the heart and recovers lost parts of human connection. This model promotes a set of values that brings about enlightenment and transformation through channels similar to zen, the art of using paradox to by-pass rational thought. While not explicitly para-doxical in the ways of earlier family therapy models, the paradox in this model comes when clients hear narratives that are opposite their conscious experience, but have a deep ring of truth. Intuitively, they know there is something right about these new constructions of identity. The seeds of transformation are sown in the narratives that suggest a person is worthy of love and safety. They deserve fairness. Their intentions are inherently good. Hargrave & Pfitzer (2011, pp. 121–122) provide this example:

Man:	She (his mother) probably just felt like I was another potential thing that could get out of control. She laid low with me. It sure didn't do me any good.
Therapist:	No, it didn't, and it hurt you because you never were really sure if she loved you and was willing to make sacrifices for you. Instead, she expected you to lay low also and make it easier or more controlled for her.
Man:	That's absolutely true. I always felt like if I wasn't worth something to my mother that I really must be worthless. It was more important to keep her fragile life together than protect me from her husband.
Therapist:	[Long pause.] You think your mother's actions were about you being worthless.
Man:	[Long pause.] Not really. I mean, that is my knee-jerk reaction to feel like I was unloved. But I think deep

	down my mother loves me . . . I love my kids. I don't show them because I'm so tied up with my own feelings, but I really do care for them.
Therapist:	[Long pause] So, if you lay low and really do love your kids, you believe that your mother also loved you even though she laid low.
Man:	I think so. It had more to do with her stuff than it did with not loving me. [Long pause.] The same is true with my kids. They probably feel like they are not important to me. Actually, they are everything to me. I just don't show them.
Therapist:	The reason you don't show them . . .
Man:	Too tied up in my own stuff—just like my mom.
Therapist:	So, if it is true that your mother just got too tied up with her own fear to take up for you and show you love, what does that mean about this feeling of unworthiness that you carry around?
Man:	It means that I am no more unlovable and unworthy than my children.
Therapist:	Can you say that you are lovable and worthy?
Man:	I am lovable and worthy. Easy to say but hard to believe.
Therapist:	Say it again.
Man:	[Slower and tears up.] I am lovable and worthy.
Therapist:	[Long pause.] If you were able to hold that for just a little, what difference would it make for you?
Man:	[Long pause.] It would free me up some. I could be more loving to my wife and kids.

Hargrave & Pfitzer (2011) provide a map that travels through three-generational terrain, over the hills of hope and the valleys of despair. By giving words to parent-child wounds that have become anchored in the adult mind, the healing of injuries starts with education and empathy directed at the PFC. As trust develops in the therapeutic relationship, the therapist creates a narrative that provides validation for the client's long-standing but unspoken pain. Siegel (2012) would call this process feeling felt, something that registers in the limbic region. The client sees that the therapist "gets it."

The limbic system will often process primary emotions that trigger self and other blame, but are rarely spoken out loud. When an infant feels abandoned, the first expressions of PANIC may be crying that looks like anger, but is really an expression of grief. Blaming is really about helplessness. Expressing primary emotions without fear of criticism can strengthen limbic system-PFC circuits in preparation for new behaviors to emerge. The therapist directs the dialogue into speaking the truth about one's worthiness during the self-healing process. Reflecting on the traditional men who are uncomfortable with therapy, the second stage comes after systemic empathy and understanding create an empowering frame, "I am worthy of love and safety." Like a Zen master's chant, clients receive an invitation to repeat this during a couples' session when each partner is lapsing back into old circuits. In fact, the steps toward entitlement and truth about the self can effectively soothe a sense of dominance/hierarchy because of the empowerment that comes from such validation. For example, a high T man with high CORT will likely feel a drop in his stress

> **I am worthy of love and safety.**

level and the attending CORT levels in his body. As social endocrinology studies show, high T and low CORT seem to go with those who make good leaders. The self-healing process is a good match as goal-oriented and skill-building activities appeal to men who may prefer concrete process.

In addition, there are no models of family therapy besides contextual family therapy and RT that speak so centrally about entitlements. What does someone deserve? This powerful set of dialogues penetrates deeply into memory-affect-PFC circuits. The dominant discourse in the U.S. is often about overriding childhood injustices. Unspeakable dilemmas develop in the wake of such phrases as "The past is past. You have to move on." or "Life isn't fair. You just have to deal with it." In fact, those are often spoken by others who have felt injustices, but had no framework for how to right the wrongs. These are messages about helplessness as they have lived it. As Hargrave (1994) has suggested, the past gets "buried alive" in the absence of healing. The dialogues in RT become healing emotional experiences for those who have been injured and wounded by the lack of love and trustworthiness of others. Self-healing is framed as something clients deserve. This affirmation of entitlement can be felt in the body and used for grounding and resourcing (see Chapter 5).

RT is guided by an intergenerational theory about unexplained pain that comes from lack of love and safety during the attachment process. Hargrave & Pfitzer (2011, p. 119) some brain-informed assumptions:

1. All humans have intrinsic value.
2. All humans deserve love and safety.
3. Victimizers do not have to be monsters and victims do not have to be unworthy.
4. Self-reactivity is not a cognitive choice, but comes from the limbic system registering lack of love and safety.
5. Justice is an intrinsic human value.

This last assumption has some interesting validation found in breakthrough studies of infants. Hamlin, Wynn & Bloom (2007, 2010) have developed ways to study the social cognition of infants as young as three months. They measure length of time infants watch or reach for something in experimental choice situations. The design involves watching puppets or computerized shapes who engage in two types of activities. One is prosocial and behaves in a helpful way. The other is aggressive and behaves in a hurtful way. Controlling for various extraneous variables, researchers bring both images forward and provide an opportunity for the babies to interact. Reaching and staring are measured and quantified. Three-month-old babies reliably stare at the prosocial figure. Six-month-old babies reliably reach for the helpful figure.

Most neuroscientists use infant behavior to assess what is hardwired for humans. When Hargrave & Pfitzer (2011) speak about justice as an intrinsic human value, these babies satisfy most voices in neuroscience today. Thus, to the dismay of many a parent who goes on the defense when their children cry, "That's not fair!" RT would say that discussions of fairness and entitlement are important opportunities in which to explore a child's developing world view. Humans have a universal sense of fairness, but no one dares speak of it in most family therapy approaches. The lack of discussion leads to private dialogues and unspeakable dilemmas that risk becoming fuel for the fire of *destructive entitlement*, that sense of injustice that explodes into rage or self-harm. Chapter 7 contains a discussion on how the issues of justice can trigger rage during adolescence.

The primary interventions of RT include:

1. Begin the self-healing process through understanding and identifying the *truth about self*, that sense that one is lovable and worthy.
2. Relational interventions align messages and needs within the appropriate level of relationship, such as which issues are really family of origin, which issues are marital, and how can children be afforded what they deserve.
3. For marital issues, map separate cycles of pain and peace. These create an awareness of contrasting patterns that set the stage for a transition into intimacy. Each cycle has specific circuits of memory and learning. In order to consolidate changes in the brain, both partners engage in an exercise with four steps:

   1. Say what you feel.
   2. Say what you normally do.
   3. Say the truth.
   4. Make a different behavioral choice.

4. Intergenerational interventions include

1. Provide opportunities for compensation.
2. Develop protection from future harm.
3. Assess possibilities for forgiveness.

Victimizers are understood within their context and this prevents a dilemma of loyalty, whereby the person would have to defend the parent if the therapist became judgmental or critical. Instead, in marital and intergenerational relationships, the balancing of responsibilities and entitlements maintains the opportunity for justice and fairness.

RT has great relevance for April's case. Although she healed from her childhood abuses, her marriage to Karl was a casualty in the process. At the time they married, the underlying marital dynamics related to Karl being her savior and April believing that she needed a savior. In most social settings, their behavior appeared quite the opposite. April's gregarious nature and Karl's quiet, retiring, manner belied their implicit marital needs. When April began to heal, Karl became angry, distant, and derisive. At one point he disclosed, "I just want my little girl back." The marital therapy they sought failed to grapple with the developmental issues that emerged as April's identity became more coherent and her sense of empowerment grew.

RT has the potential to address the deep issues that April's growth triggered for Karl. Her trauma therapy addressed many of these issues for her, but there was no context available that would help Karl address his entitlements, the losses of love in his family of origin, his sense of unworthiness, and their cycles together. Given their personalities, the calm steady flow of RT, with its attention to childhood issues and marital cycles could have saved April's marriage.

Emotionally Focused Couple Therapy (EFT)

Anderson (2000) once observed about the field of marriage and family therapy, "we have set out on a vast and troubled ocean in a very small theoretical boat." That would soon change as the decade of attachment theory lay before her. Emotionally focused couple therapy (EFT) converged with the decade of attachment, and together, they've sailed into the waters of marital therapy with a transcontinental ocean liner full of couples therapists who want to apply attachment theory to marital therapy. Today, EFT is the most researched of any model of marital therapy, all without losing sight of the art and soul of clinical experience. Johnson's (1986) dissertation compared experiential with problem-solving interventions in marital therapy. During the next 25 years, EFT became wedded to attachment theory. It brings together a set of stages and strategies that combine art and science to help couples identify and transform emotion stemming from attachment injuries. As neuroscience began to nudge practitioners into a whole body perspective, the EFT community also examined the biology of emotion (Johnson, 2012).

In EFT, the emotions of attachment are like hostages in a drama that wait for others to free them so they can be reunited with their loved ones. Often masquerading as anger or resentment, the fear, betrayal, loneliness, hurt, and longing for attachment wait in the wings while the therapist works to help them receive their just due. As a safe space is made for both partners, the therapist becomes a detective of sorts who explores the affective terrain of each marital argument. As the process identifies interpersonal patterns full of disappointment and sadness, the therapist experiments with various words that name primary emotions. As clients are invited to partake of this affective smorgasbord, they find words and phrases that fit the complexity of their experience. Similar to White's (1986) narrative family therapy, they are introduced to new and liberating narratives that provide a new dimension to the old story. This helps spouses find their emotional voice.

There are powerful transformations that occur in relationships when couples enter a safe space and find enough calm to hear each other's pain, without defense. The therapist models systemic empathy. The couple feels this empathy and begins to *soften* in response to the narratives of longing and desired attachment. Lieberman et al. conducted a series of fMRIs while people engaged in *affect labeling*, the process of putting feeling into words during a negative stimulus exercise (Lieberman et al., 2007; Kircanski et al., 2012). They found the process calmed the amygdala-PFC circuits in a number of brain regions. Over the course of therapy, the decrease in reactivity that occurs as affect labeling behavior increases is a hallmark of EFT and restoration therapy. As Johnson (1996) intuitively knew many years ago, communication about emotion becomes the change agent, not merely part of the marital conflict (Gross & Levenson, 1997; Tabibnia et al., 2008).

The nine steps of EFT include:

1. Identify the relational conflict issues between the partners.
2. Identify the negative interaction cycle where these issues are expressed.
3. Access the unacknowledged emotions underlying the interactional position each partner takes in this cycle.
4. Reframe the problem in terms of the cycle, accompanying underlying emotions, and attachment needs.
5. Promote identification with disowned attachment emotions, needs, and aspects of self.
6. Promote acceptance by each partner of the other partner's experience.
7. Facilitate the expression of needs and wants to restructure the interaction based on the new understandings and create bonding events.
8. Facilitate the emergence of new solutions to old problems.
9. Consolidate new positions and cycles of attachment behaviors (Johnson et al., 2005, pp. 103–104).

This work focuses primarily on the here and now of marital strife. A critical part of the process involves detailed discovery of interaction cycles. These are the drama that contain an incomplete script. As the drama comes to the fore, reflections about the pattern provide therapeutic empathy. Going slowly over the story, minute by minute, includes unspoken attachment emotions that operate within the story. In EFT, *heightening* is a skill that helps the therapist achieve systemic empathy by weaving complex parts of the person's experience together with attachment emotion. The following dialogue illustrates this intervention during Step 6, Heightening Emotion (Johnson et al., 2005, pp. 155–156).

Ingrid: ... I gave a lot! I gave time and I have always been there. I don't see what she's giving—I can't give anymore.

Therapist: You gave a lot to help Frances. I would expect that you, like all of us when we join our lives with someone, had a lot of hopes of sharing your life with her and all kinds of dreams about building a future together with her, like working as a team.

Ingrid: (voice starts to calm) That's it. I don't feel like we are sharing. I am doing everything and she just goes along for the ride.

Therapist: That is so hard because this is where the cycle takes over. You see yourself alone doing all the work and Frances is not there. The resentment starts to build and suddenly you are caught in your anger. You want to share with Frances but you really don't expect she'll be there, so you up the ante so that she will respond—to which Frances withdraws, shuts down, and she is even more unavailable. Is that how it is?

Ingrid: (starting to tear) Yes, she is nowhere, I never know what is going on with her. . . . I can't do everything. Frances just expects me to swallow it up and not say anything and just carry on like I always do.

Therapist: Hmm . . . so on one hand you need to be with Frances and share with her. But on the other, it's like you are not supposed to speak or be able to say what you need and actually the cycle gets in the way of that

Ingrid:
really happening, getting your needs met. Once it takes hold you are off and running and you end up nowhere but frustrated, distant and alone.

Ingrid: (crying, nodding).

In this interaction, the therapist gives voice to aspects of the pattern, implicit thoughts, and emotions that lead to systemic empathy, in which Ingrid feels felt. This minute-by-minute analysis is a basic skill that leads to partners being able to label affect and express this to the other. The therapist identifies the unspoken dilemma, having wants and needs for the other person, and feeling restrained from speaking these. In family psychopolitics, all children need love, thus, they express their individuality at the risk of rejection. For the interaction to be complete, the same dialogue continues with Frances and her frustration with the criticism she perceives from Ingrid.

As the therapist models *empathic conjecture*, the process moves from anger and hopelessness to needs and intentions. Softening occurs as each begins to see the real intent and the primary emotion that is underneath the conflict. In the language of attachment, the process begins with a sound behavioral exploration of attachment attempts. Then, therapeutic attunement identifies underlying attachment emotions. Safety provided by the therapist invites vulnerability and connection, which ultimately lead to mutual attunement and a secure bond.

The Psychobiological Approach (PBA)

Solomon & Tatkin (2011) approach couple therapy with an explicit attention to the physiology that exists in each session. They integrate attachment theory with mindfulness and movement as they address the conflicts of intimate partners. *Core dynamics* are the dreams, longings, disappointments, and coping strategies that emerge from childhood attachment, separation, and loss. These become the plot in each marital drama. Many times it may be abandonment or lack of attunement. Assessment questions come from the Adult Attachment Interview (AAI) and assess family of origin experiences related to attachment processes. After identifying these dynamics, the therapist might say,

> You both have the capacity to encourage the strengths of each other. To make your relationship deeper, Richard, you need to allow Christine's learning, growing, and becoming autonomous. Christine, you need to know Richard beyond his outward self of strength, to know that inside there is an abandoned little boy who is as vulnerable as your abandoned little girl. If you attune to each other and encourage each other's dreams, you will grow together in a partnership of trust and security.
>
> (Solomon & Tatkin, 2011, p. 96)

A central belief of this approach is that intimate partners have a powerful influence on each other and this resource can help people heal attachment wounds. Thus, the couple is the primary focus. *Home* is partners becoming "two best friends celebrating profound companionship while maturing and growing together" (Solomon & Tatkin, 2011, p. 166). They work with early attachment histories, helping the couple to work together in the session to resolve historical wounds and bring about a safe haven. The relationship becomes a catalyst for growth and change. As core elements become linked to here and now conflicts, there is a focus on developing reciprocity to meet each person's core needs (Solomon, 1994).

Initially, the therapist develops safety and security to regulate the arousal of both parties. Then, as conflicts emerge in session, the therapist watches for sympathetic (fight–flight–freeze) or parasympathetic (lower) arousal. In this approach, clinicians want to intervene with high arousal states immediately as they occur. Physiologically, each partner learns to stay with a state of arousal long enough to develop new options for old triggers. Affectively, each learns to identify and discuss the core issues that prevent secure attachment. The therapist becomes a narrator of process, explaining and reflecting on internal and interpersonal processes during the session. Then the goal is to recognize and repair the unmet needs so that secure attachment can occur. Failure to do this results in ongoing battles that become dead ends. Old triggers reenact old wounds. As with restoration therapy and EFT, great care is taken to avoid blame and shame.

The therapist educates the couple on how to tune in to their bodies during conflict. Like personal trainers at the local gym, therapists provide coaching in the moment to tolerate emotional arousal in a nonjudgmental way. The therapist also prompts couple dialogue during these times of arousal that lead to corrective emotional experiences. In this model, individual therapy may interfere with the primary processes that emerge in couple sessions. Therapists learn to work with moments of high arousal that are often the basis for traditional symptoms that bring people into therapy. Instead of addressing these symptoms in isolation, the attachment relationship becomes the main source of healing. Attachment and arousal become main themes.

The therapist might ask partners to face each other to discuss areas of importance or conflict. When the nervous system reacts to this type of intensity, a psychobiological therapist will work with these dynamics to shift body and mind in the moment. This type of highly experiential intervention addresses fast-acting, survival-oriented, nonverbal biology. Interventions include conflict enactments, nonverbal communications, movement exercises, and psychodrama. Then, there is attention to breathing, with exercises similar to the felt sense activities in other chapters of this book. Reflecting on the Gottman discoveries with violent men, this attention to whole body within a safe therapeutic structure could become ground-breaking treatment for problems that currently challenge domestic violence services. Chapter 8 discusses brain-informed recommendations for program developers.

Solomon & Tatkin (2011) suggest that teaching clients to be aware of shifts in their arousal is the "royal road" to connecting the affective processes that interfere with love (p. 179). Thus, early stages of the work include attention to breathing and mindfulness. This links the PFC with other regions of the body. Integrating these parts by a focus on the present settles arousal and prepares couples for emotional balance and empathy. Self-observation in a safe environment expands the capacity to tolerate a new range of emotions without too much reactivity. This is important for the healing process.

A unique feature of the process involves longer initial sessions to allow primary emotion to surface. Interventions for cycles of arousal do not fit neatly into 50-minute hours. Accordingly, sessions may be 2–4 hours to provide a safe space for a complete cycle and to process it in a transformative way. In describing the rationale for this experiential structure, the authors note that eye-to-eye contact and skin contact are basic forms of human connection. Body and mind need them. Bowlby (1969) documented that children separated from parents would go through protest, withdrawal, and detachment over time. The same was true for those who were not held by parents or loved ones. Thus, this approach allows time for therapists to explore deep affective experiences during conflicts with questions like, "As you look at him, what's coming up for you right now?" In an environment of reflection, answers about core issues surface such as "Will he be there when I need him? Can my true self be loved?" The following dialogue from Solomon & Tatkin (2011, pp. 151–157) illustrates the process.

Are there any images or memories, any emotions or thoughts? . . . stay with the emotion in your bodies . . .

"Finally Richard began to weep, with deep gasping noises. He was having trouble crying and breathing at the same time.

"My father died all alone . . . My mother got a call from his girlfriend that she had taken him to the hospital . . . I went over as soon as I got the message, but he had died before I got there. His girlfriend had left him there, I didn't make it on time. He was only 45 years old, and he died alone. I think of what that must have felt like for him. What it must be like to be dying and all alone. I don't want that to happen to me. But I'm afraid it will." Christine, now crying with him, says over and over again, "How awful," and "I didn't understand." Through a series of understanding reparative responses, the brain's plasticity can result in changes in early imprints. They are each experiencing something different, the beginning of a reorganization.

"Do you see Christine's response to what you are feeling?" I ask him, wanting to make this reorganization conscious. Toward the end of this session, I ask them to look at each other again and alternate starting some sentences with the words, I want. "See what comes up."

CHRISTINE: I want to see more of the you that has needs and feelings, not just anger.

RICHARD: I want you to promise to be with me, and not disconnect from me, when I get upset.

CHRISTINE: I want to be able to make my own decisions.

RICHARD: I want you to know how much I love and respect you.

CHRISTINE: I want to be there for you.

RICHARD: I want your help to talk to my mom. She listens to you.

CHRISTINE: I want us to have another child.

RICHARD: I want us to have a happy family.

The conversation then becomes playful, and sexual, their body language much more open to each other. For the time being, the war is over. Their brains, bodies, and minds are not repeating the wounds.

GUIDELINES FOR COUPLE THERAPY

Brain-motivated couples therapists can learn from the similarities and differences of these cutting-edge models. RT takes a developmental approach to helping adults identify issues of love and trustworthiness. There are many narratives that identify childhood losses and begin healing the limbic system. EFT focuses on the here and now, taking minute pieces of current interactions and linking them to attachment conflicts. PBA strikes a balance between the two with attention to emotions in cycles that relate to developmental experiences. PBA therapists are more experientially oriented. RT attends to physiology through self-affirmations and assignments. EFT narratives attend indirectly to physiology through the slow-paced explorations of relationship cycles. The following guidelines encourage practitioners to consider the developmental readiness of each couple, then explore with them what might fit best.

1. Screen for trauma. When trauma is a factor, RT is good preparation for more intensive work and can be integrated with felt sense exercises. It can be easily used in individual sessions as preparation for conjoint sessions. RT models calm, centered interaction. This is important for trauma survivors.

2. Be active in modeling trustworthiness and reframing stressed behaviors. All three models do this well. Practice the language of attachment theory. Belonging, identity, safety, and love resonate with both genders and provide nonjudgemental interpretations of the most challenging behaviors.

3. Allow space in therapeutic conversations for silent reflection and attunement to primary emotions. RT and PBA do this well. Writing with the nondominant hand can also introduce space for reflection.

4. Appeal to the highest aspirations that humans have. Each couple is a miracle of human achievement, deserving of the best that life can offer. RT and EFT emphasize this. This can calm an anxious amygdala and invoke the expectation of dopamine.

5. Center the self of the therapist and work on your own core issues. Sincere, calm, acceptance of others' behavior during their turmoil can engage mirror neurons. It is most effective when we live what we desire for others (Grepmair et al., 2007).

6. Use metaphors of cavemen and women, babies, and animals. In general, metaphor engages the right brain.

7. Experiment with movement and action in sessions. Activate the PLAY system for each couple.

7

Family Therapy as Transformation of the Tribe

The present day hero searches for the self by reliving experience in a contractual relationship which is, by definition, removed from "real life" and artificial in the sense that the feelings and emotions it contains are not indigenous to it but belong to other primary relationships in the real world . . . Psychoanalysis (and psychiatry) is the only form of psychic healing that attempts to cure people by detaching them from society and relationships. All other forms—shamanism, faith healing, prayer—bring the community into the healing process, indeed use the interdependence of patient and others as the central mechanism in the healing process. Modern psychiatry isolates the troubled individual from the currents of emotional interdependence and deals with the trouble by distancing from it and manipulating it through intellectual/verbal discussion, interpretation, and analysis.

Veroff et al. (1981, pp. 6–7)

During the decade of the brain, a majority of voices that spoke from a mental health perspective were psychiatrists and psychologists who conceived of treatment as individuals seeking psychotherapy (Siegel, 2012; Schore, 2012). As the social brain came to the fore, the importance of family relationships became obvious, but there has been little mention of family intervention, whether the problem was trauma or child symptoms. In the family therapy community, there have been few family therapists who speak the language of neuroscience. In 1999, the International Family Therapy Association had informal discussions about why family therapists should care about brain research. This was a novel and early attempt to engage family therapists in discussions about neuroscience. With Siegel's (1999) work about to come forth, family therapists were soon to become brain-informed.

Perhaps the subtitle of this chapter should be, "Why Neuroscientists Should Care About Family Therapy." However, in the tradition of family therapists, we prefer dialogue rather than education in isolation. The variety of approaches to family therapy fall into a number of categories. Hanna (2007) provides a summary of traditional and contemporary models, advocating for the integration of common themes and interventions. This chapter provides a review of brain-friendly family therapy approaches that deserve more attention from the neuroscience community. Ecologically, inclusion of the natural support network is a powerful resource for long-term transformation. Those approaches that specifically target attachment processes are excellent resources for child and adolescent problems. In addition, there are neuro-enhancements that can make these interventions more effective for family therapists. For example, attention to brain differences between women and men can increase father involvement. Consider the following example:

> Betty's plastic surgeon referred her to a family therapist when she came seeking her sixth elective surgery at age 27. The therapist learned over the phone that she had two older, married siblings and parents living in the area. He requested that they attend with her. Upon greeting the therapist in the waiting room, Betty's father asked, "How do you feel about Archie Bunker?" The thera-pist replied by describing his favorite episode of the T.V. series. Archie and his son-in-law, Meathead, were accidently locked in a refrigerated room together. As the time wore on, Archie's desper-ation led to the bearing of his soul about his tough childhood and punitive father. Touched by this glimpse of humanity, Meathead hugged Archie at the end of the ordeal, exclaiming, "Archie, you're finally human. I love you."

Upon hearing this story, Betty's father turned to his family and said, "Gang, this guy is O.K. Let's get in." What ensued were several sessions in which Betty was able to express hurt and anger at her father in an environment that was safe for both. His past alcohol use and verbal abuse left deep wounds. He was now in a place where he could apologize. Empowered by the process and support from her family, Betty extended to her father a number of requests. Over the next few weeks, they went to playgrounds, movies, and other venues that she had longed to visit with him when she was young. She felt as though she finally had the father she had always wanted. This attachment injury was on the way to healing.

(Rueveni, 1992)

Part of this story is about Betty's healing. The other part is about what it takes to engage men in therapy. While there was a certain amount of serendipity to the therapist's creativity, it's entirely possible for a young, female, beginning family therapist to facilitate similar results by resonating with male energy and meeting men on their own emotional terms. As this case illustrates, stories and narratives can touch people in deep ways. The average psychotherapist today might not be comfortable with the thought of family therapy. As we saw with models of couple therapy, brain-informed approaches usually have elements of experiential, affective intensity. The more common clinical scenario would be for Betty to attend individual sessions without ever involving her father. Very likely, she knew about the individual approach. In hindsight, which one do you think she would prefer? Sadly, most clients never know there is an option of family growth and healing—one that will not scare away the men in their lives, but will provide safety and attunement for them.

Trauma screening for parents and children can alert practitioners to the potential of arousal states that may interfere with problem-solving. Whole body interventions can remove a number of affective obstacles. When parents are already victims of trauma and are re-traumatized by child behavior problems, there are brain-friendly guidelines as to how multigenerational pain can become an arena for transformation in families with symptomatic children. In

Chapter 6, RT gave us a glimpse of how specific self-healing strategies for parents can have a positive impact on their children.

Often, parent burnout behaviors elicit criticism from child advocates who are unaware that a family healing process can conjointly address parent and child well-being. Cutting edge family therapy approaches transform the future of many troubled youth (Hanna, 2009). Engagement of parents and parent figures is an important skill that is central to these approaches and has lasting effects on developing children (Henggeler et al., 1998; Dakof et al, 2001; Liddle, 2000; Landau-Stanton et al., 2000; Smith & Meyers, 2004; Stanton & Todd, 1982).

With the hope of stimulating dialogue between the communities of neuroscience and family therapy, this chapter highlights a few family therapy approaches through the eye of neuroscience and describes how integration of whole body interventions can strengthen their effect. Affect, meaning, memory frame the content of attachment in every family session. Their substance fuels the process. Affect is the biological state that prompts the body to SEEK attachment. Meaning and memory provide predictability. All work together for survival.

AFFECT

What does family therapy have to say about affect, as neuroscientists understand it? In addition to the couples' therapists in Chapter 6, two approaches conceptualize attachment processes at the center of the process. One addresses the affect of parent-adolescent attachments when substance abuse becomes a symptom. The other addresses ruptured attachments outside the family to reduce violence. Both are examples of gut-level approaches that attune to the deepest wounds that adolescents may sustain.

Multidimensional Family Therapy (MDFT)

This approach works with substance abusing teens and their families (Liddle & Schwartz, 2002). During the joining phase, the therapist works with parents and youth separately in addition to conjoint sessions. One of the goals of these sessions is to access primary emotions on each side. In the safety of separation, each subsystem is free to disclose potentially risky emotions. Burned out parents may have anger and even contempt for the teen. Before they are able to develop empathy for their child, they need empathy and support for their own stress and trauma. Their PFCs cannot come back online without the safety of the therapeutic relationship.

Parent engagement. For some, parenting has become a battleground of failure and discouragement, with parents just bracing for blame to come from outside parties. Their behavior is easily understood through the lens of attachment theory and RT. What happened to love and safety in their lives? Without attention to their affect, progress will be slow. MDFT therapists attend to parental affect and to the burdens of physical survival. Case management services provide help to navigate school, social, and economic systems. Some family therapists are unaware of how important these outside systems become to a family's survival. As one client put it, "I don't need this therapy stuff, Doc. Money and power is all I need. That's the best medicine."

If clinicians only define themselves by their own preferences in practice, we fail to serve the whole body. The threat-survival system traverses the realm of economic survival, as the most basic need. Waldegrave (1990) notes that traditional therapists often treat someone's depression and then expect them to go home and be happy in poverty. Even when a therapist might be powerless to provide tangible

Discrepancy
Distress
Discouragement
Despair

relief, clients still welcome empathy for their heroic survival under adverse circumstances. Clinicians can attune to this affect and encourage survivor's pride.

This attunement says, "I get it." Those acknowledgments help parents feel felt so they can trust the therapist with additional affective experiences. The ensuing down regulation enables the PFC to bring some perspective to the situation. Then, in cases where parents have extreme pain and hurt, it is helpful to conduct a *parental reconnection intervention* (Liddle, 2000; Diamond et al., 2000). The exercise invites parents to retrieve memory of an earlier time when they felt closer to their child and didn't have such hostility. The therapist guides a meditation through parents' affective experiences during those times. In neuroscience terms, the parent reaches deep into the compost pile of their memory and grabs a handful of mulch, shakes off the most recent debris and finds moist and fertile ground, still full of potential. The guided imagery is not a fantasy. It accesses real experiences that can soothe a wounded parent's heart. With the addition of the felt sense, this becomes the perfect blend of neuroscience and family intervention. Therapists can heighten these memories by asking parents to feel these memories in their bodies. How do they feel and where in their body do they feel it? Can they take a few minutes and a few breaths to just feel these memories?

Preparing for enactments. During individual sessions with the adolescent, the therapist joins, creates a safe place, and explores strengths and vulnerabilities in the teen's life. The goal is to discover and give voice to the *4Ds: discrepancy, distress, discouragement, despair* (Liddle, 2000, pp. 63–69). As the therapist looks for these, a sense of entitlement becomes leverage for how it could benefit the youth to share these experiences with his or her parents. Meanwhile, as parents become soothed and supported in their sessions, they learn empathy skills and strategies for how to listen to their child before launching into problem-solving or debate. Launching is a sign of emotional reactivity. The therapist helps them redirect their affect toward attachment first, problem-solving second. When the time is right, the therapist convenes family sessions in which *enactments* lead to *attachment repairs*. Allen-Eckert, Fong, Nichols, Watson and Liddle (2001) developed an enactment rating scale through which therapists receive a map for conducting successful enactments. MDFT practitioners consider parent-adolescent attachment during enactments to be a central element in successful substance abuse treatment (Diamond & Liddle, 1999). A productive enactment is when

> (a) the conversation was two-sided, meaning that both partici-pants expressed their points of view; (b) clients agreed to work together to resolve the problem under discussion, or at least one of them acknowledged his or her role in the problem under discussion; or a meaningful breakthrough in either content or process occurred.
>
> (Allen-Eckert et al., 2001, p. 471)

The intervention also specifies four phases, pre-enactment phase, initiation phase, facilitation stage and summary statement. These have specific guidelines as to how the therapist can maximize impact of the enactment (see Box 7.1). The researchers note that an enactment is not just a directive for family members to talk to each other. Rather, it is a carefully monitored process that addresses affect and communication to increase attunement.

Box 7.1 MDFT enactments

Pre-enactment phase:	Two minutes preceding initiation. Prepare family members to talk. Inquire about concerns. Explore the extent to which issues have been discussed previously. Emphasize the need for communication and understanding.
Initiation phase:	Direct clients by word or gesture to being talking. Specify which family members are to participate. Clarify the topic for discussion. Request that clients change seats or turn their chairs to face each other. Pull back or look away to discourage family members from talking to the therapist instead of to each other.
Facilitation stage:	The period between initiation and closing of an enactment.

	Avoid interrupting until clients change the subject, stop talking, appear not to listen, or start to attack one another.
	Urge clients not to change the subject, to keep talking even though they feel like giving up.
	Prompt to say more about their feelings, to listen to each other.
	Encourage continued focus on each other rather than the therapist.
Conclusion:	Make a summary comment.
	Praise clients for making an effort to communicate.
	Note impediments to communication.
	Make suggestions for further progress.
	(Allen-Eckert et al., 2001)

Traditional models of family therapy such as Minuchin's (1974) and Satir's (1972) often addressed attachment issues and created in-session changes through enactments. However, pioneering family therapists kept a distance from the language of attachment. As social constructionists developed more reflective styles during sessions, the directive approaches from structural and experiential models seemed to fade from view in published work. Now, MDFT provides the content and process to have an effect on the substance, those affect states of PANIC/GRIEF and FEAR that limit the body's supply of serotonin. The focus stays on affect, communication, and fostering systemic empathy within the relationship (CARE). This process also occurs in the work of Hardy and Laszloffy (2005) who describe their work with violent teens. They bring these issues to bear as they analyze social factors that lead to attachment ruptures, PANIC/GRIEF and RAGE.

Four Factor Model of Violence (FFM)

In response to the increase in violence among adolescents, from the formation of gangs in neighborhoods to the lone-wolf gunmen of schools, Hardy & Laszloffy (2005) outline their violence reduction model for youths who cycle through as victims and perpetrators. In the FFM, RAGE results from the *three Ds, devaluation, disruption of community,* and *dehumanization of loss.* These practitioners outline the formation of these factors as the foundation for empathy and attunement. Then, they describe their three-step process of working with youth, the Validation, Challenge, Request (VCR) Model for parents and therapists.

Devaluation Disruption of community Dehumanization of loss

Devaluation. This is an assault to one's dignity and worth. It may include racism, sexism, homophobia, poverty, and other forms of marginalization. However, it also goes beyond these group dynamics to more personal transactions that lead to shame, fear, grief and pain, the precursors of rage. *Situational devaluation* includes abandonment, abuse, and social ostracism.

Societal devaluation occurs because of racial or ethnic identity with a disadvantaged group. Classism occurs when a community "confuses class with character" (Hardy & Laszloffy, 2005, p. 55). A great deal of societal devaluation results in school violence and peer rejection. Adolescent brains are primed to connect outside the family. With underdeveloped PFCs, rejection and bullying can lead a person to be obsessed with gaining respect. This can become destructive entitlement in the form of violence to self or others.

Disruption of community. This arises from abuse, divorce, separation, abandonment, illnesses, and drug addiction at home. Abuse and neglect may lead to foster placements. Broader social behaviors include racial, gender, and economic oppression. These lead to neighborhood and community neglect in which communities feel devalued and forgotten. Disruption at multiple levels becomes a significant risk factor for many different adjustments. As Chapter 5 discussed, multiple factors can reach a level of trauma (overwhelm) in the body. Without screening for trauma, these complex layers of activation lead to a revolving door of social services or criminal justice actions. Our prisons have become modern-day insane asylums and the number of African American men who become imprisoned represent a mental health catastrophe that begins with the lack of brain-informed, culturally attuned services for families with African American boys (Woods et al., 2012).

Dehumanization of loss. This is lack of awareness that an experience involves loss or lack of empathic response to a known loss. *Intangible loss* is emotional and psychological. It relates to loss of respect, dignity, hope, and voice. *Tangible loss* may be physical and emotional, related to divorce, significant others, relocations, and deaths.

> Loss of any kind is painful, but even more painful than loss itself is when it remains unacknowledged, un-mourned, and therefore unhealed ... repeated experience with unacknowledged, unmourned, and unhealed losses contribute to the dehumanization of loss, which is a precursor to violence.
>
> (Hardy & Laszloffy, 2005, p. 91)

Bowser, Word, Stanton & Coleman (2003) studied HIV risk behaviors (IV drug use and unsafe sex). Among 3,000 drug users, they found two strong predictors of HIV risk behaviors, 1) death of a significant other prior to age 15 and 2) whether the person attended the funeral. Funeral attendance was an indicator of healthy grieving. These data illustrate the profound effects of losses in the lives of children. They also underscore the need for family therapists to assess losses and their impact. Neuroscience shifts our thinking from disease to injury. Trauma-informed work shifts our thinking from "What is wrong?" to "What happened?"

Vulnerable emotions and rage. These emerge when individuals experience devaluation, disruption of community, and dehumanization of loss. Shame, fear, grief, and pain are some of the most vulnerable of all emotions which many hide with secondary emotions of anger and rage (Hardy & Laszloffy, 2005; Johnson,

1998; Hargrave & Pfitzer, 2011; Panksepp, 2011). The FFM suggests that RAGE is the product that emerges from the confluence of the 3Ds. RAGE is a natural and inevitable response to experiences of pain and injustice. When it is suppressed, the risk of violence is greater because the underlying emotions of shame, fear, grief, and pain are also suppressed. When it is recognized and validated, it can be channeled into constructive transformations (Panksepp, 2009; Hardy & Laszloffy, 2005).

Panksepp (2009) reports that RAGE and FEAR are closely associated in brain regions. Although amygdala activity is high with both states, the activity of each occurs in different regions of the amygdala and descend to different circuits. He notes that when RAGE is inhibited, internalized hatred and resentments occur. This suggests the importance of therapeutic interventions that validate RAGE and foster the energy into a sense of empowerment.

Validation, Challenge, and Request (VCR)

Hardy & Laszloffy (2005) use the three-step VCR process. As a way to address the 3Ds and diffuse the affective energy from them, they begin with VCR in response to an adolescent's problem behavior. Because the 3Ds have a domino effect, it is crucial for therapists to bring a sense of valuing, systemic empathy, and attunement into the room. Once devaluation is counteracted, the problem is addressed from a strength perspective and requests become a face-saving way to correct the behavior. The down regulation that can occur from VCR lays a foundation for other interventions that address disrupted relationships and traumatic losses. Therapists, parents, and teachers can make a significant contribution to a transformative process when they are willing to learn VCR. All three components should focus on the same issue or behavior. On a scale of severity, these may range from irritating or inappropriate behavior, to the healing of deep wounds.

Validation. This step involves attunement and acknowledging strengths that are woven into the complicated behaviors of violent youth. Often, love, loyalty, leadership, creativity, and innovation are easy to recognize. Conversations that hold these up as important contributions are the first step toward earning trust. Trust is not an event. It is earned. The authors emphasize that it may take weeks just to earn the trust of a troubled youth. This step must proceed with patience and goodwill while the youth determines whether the clinician is "for real." As an intervention for attachment difficulties, validation addresses the "adolescence of attachment." At each developmental stage of growth, humans need safe havens that attune to the needs of infancy, childhood, adolescence, and adulthood. The key to validation as part of correction is to always see the glass as half full. For example, if the topic or behavior involves an aggressive act, validation can be about the person's good intentions.

Validation strikes a delicate balance between a need for empowerment and for safety. First, recognizing strengths develop narratives of his or her abilities. Second, acknowledging rage can lead to explorations of vulnerable emotions. Similar to Hargrave and Pfitzer (2011), therapists can emphasize the entitlement to have these emotions and provide a narrative of respect and reverence for youths' ordeals. Acknowledging that they are worthy of love and safety can be reassuring. Far from melodrama for its effect, therapists can serve as witnesses to the horrible atrocities that many of our youth have survived. Later in this chapter, a discussion of celebrations for brain health illustrates how these validate and help to heal the wounds of developmental trauma.

Challenge. This step requires a balanced and paced introduction. After youthful aggressions have challenged family, school, and neighborhood, the idea of challenging a youth may be all too welcome for a wounded warrior, be they parent, teacher, or therapist. However, Hardy and Laszloffy's version of

> . . . challenge assumes a careful position that is entirely dependent upon the success of the validation step.

challenge assumes a careful position that is entirely dependent upon the success of the validation step. Without this, challenge may risk becoming counter-aggression, when adult caregivers have been taxed to their limit. For this step to be effective, it is wise for the professional or parent to . . . close your eyes, take a deep breath, feel your feet on the floor, etc.

Once validation brings nonverbal messages that the youth feels appreciated, challenges describe the issue in question. Statements such as "I think there is a better way to get what you want." "You have a lot of good intentions and I'm concerned about how you keep hurting yourself." "Even though you have a right to feel angry, it's not appropriate to return violence with violence." "I think you can use your talents to solve this problem in a different way." This type of communication avoids use of the word, "but." "But" can negate all that went before it. Linguistically, the authors stress the importance of using "and" whenever possible and incorporate the youth's strengths into the challenge and request.

Request. This is a problem-solving skill. Given whatever the issue might be, the question now is how the adult can request a solution that validates the worth of the person and provides some direction for change. Examples of these are requests 1) to sit and brainstorm other ways of handling the incident, or 2) to follow some specified guidelines, or 3) to use their talents and strengths in a relevant task. These acknowledge the value of what the person wanted. They also value the character of the youth. Finally, they take a stand that the youth is capable of appropriate behavior. The following example illustrates how VCR fit together with a youth who wants revenge for the murder of his friend:

> Validation: I can really see how much you loved Hank and how close the two of you were. We can't even begin to imagine how intense your loss and pain must be. I know you probably feel like you have to hold it all together now and be strong . . . you must really be hurting inside . . . we really admire your devotion to your friend . . . It makes sense that you would want to strike back against the person who hurt him and hurt you . . .

Challenge: I know how important loyalty is to you, and how devoted you were and still are to Hank . . . I know your commitment to Hank is so strong you would sacrifice yourself. I do not doubt your willingness to die for him—I just doubt whether it's the best way to honor him. After all, if you die, Hank will die with you. No one knew him like you did, and no one understood his dreams like you did. If you die there will be no one to carry on for him . . .

Request: I know the most important thing to you is being loyal to Hank, and we know you have the courage to die for him. I hope that you have enough courage to live for him . . . Could you carry on in his honor, in his footsteps, so his life won't be truly lost forever? I know it's a harder path because it doesn't have a quick 'payoff' . . . but could you love Hank enough to hang in there and deal with the tougher path for his sake?

(Hardy & Laszloffy, 2005, pp. 164–166)

The order of VCR follows the order of trauma in the brain. First, validation immediately speaks to the amygdala by acknowledging pain and rage. There is no attempt to "reason" with a person or to "cheer up." The therapist describes the state of activation in the amygdala. Second, challenge attunes to attachment and loss issues by acknowledging them and then extending them into the future. This tests the water to engage the PFC. The affirming language of the therapist leaves nothing to debate. The narration continues to attune to the affective state in this young man's trauma. It will take every ounce of energy in the PFC to deactivate the PANIC/GRIEF-RAGE circuit. Third, request appeals to his character. He is already courageous. Can that courage be tested further? Can the love for Hank be stretched? The PFC sends electrochemical surges of reason and judgment informed by memory. Request reaches into the compost heap and shovels as much memory (love of Hank), reason (becoming Hank's surrogate), and motivation (honoring Hank) as the amygdala will accept. There is no suppression of the rage. Instead, therapists are witnesses to the rage, legitimize it, and foster its transformation into constructive action. These steps are necessary to address devaluation, and as rage enters the drama, specific measures allow its expression and channel its energy into transformative healing.

Rechanneling Rage

Rechanneling relies heavily on a knowledge of the youth's interests, talents, and specific history of injustices. The <u>content</u> comes from injustices as themes for new directions. The <u>process</u> involves recruiting the talents and interests of the adolescent in creative, expressive, social activities. Community activism, athletics, and artistic expressions provide nonviolent ways to externalize rage. The <u>substance</u> comes from the mindful focus on the connection between loss, rage, and action. As a literal neuroaffective circuit, the five senses, limbic system and motor neurons encode possible responses to vulnerable affective states. Shaping the safe expression of rage comes about through helping the youth to

1. Verbalize the connections between inner experience and behavior.
2. Think about possible positive activities for the rage.
3. Physically connect rage to positive action.

This blend of mindfulness about rage and conscious association with constructive activities develops circuits that loop through Panksepp's (2009) biological systems of RAGE, CARE, and PLAY. While PLAY is not explicitly addressed in the FFM, it would be an easy integration to include what he describes as PLAY in a final step toward the healing of rage. All mammals engage in PLAY behaviors. When rage is connected physically to action that includes PLAY circuits as part of the total treatment plan, Panksepp suggests this circuit is rich in opioids and activates the dopamine system that provides sensations needed for the "joy of laughter" (p. 16). In addition, this circuit does not use the neocortex, thus, the body can be freed momentarily from the work required by the PFC.

In reviewing the 7Ds from both models, there is a cascading effect that should make reasonable people shutter at the thought that some adolescents are burdened with enormous losses at multiple levels. When our youth endure the tragic domino effect of these misfortunes, their personal disasters become society's loss. There is a critical need for a "disaster relief program" that acknowledges and attends to the affective dimensions of their lives. Specifically, the interpersonal ruptures that warrant repair.

A number of neuroscientists emphasize the fact that these and other indicators of affective dysregulation and attachment injuries receive no attention in the DSM-V (Panksepp, 2009; van der Kolk, 2009; Beauchaine, 2001). Nevertheless, these models demonstrate how attachment theory and social justice theory can lead to important outcomes for youths at risk. These approaches address the deep issues of identity and belonging that bring children secure attachments. They also illustrate an oft forgotten fact: Despite their developmental needs for autonomy and risk-taking, adolescents still need parents, family, and a nurturing community. Interventions that heal attachment and cultural wounds at this formative stage can create new brain circuitry that is balanced and resilient for future life stages.

> Interventions that heal attachment and cultural wounds at this formative stage can create new brain circuitry that is balanced and resilient for future life stages.

Between them, MDFT and FFM contribute important interventions that focus on affect. The steps toward addressing these Ds follow the processes of developing secure attachment, which in turn, calms the nervous system and injects positive affect into the equation. Both models are quick to seek out and name the Ds. Helping young people develop their voices around the 7Ds is an important part of affective regulation. Affect is the state of the body that first signals a survival need. Efforts toward meeting the need lead to a "thumbs up or thumbs down" response. Either way, the mind tallies these votes and meaning emerges from these evaluations. As the votes collect, they are stored as patterns of memory that become learning. Just as in any compost pile, there is fertile ground containing the seeds of endless possibilities. These seeds are part of brain plasticity and await the gardener's hand to foster germination. Transformations within the field of family therapy have occurred in much the same way as those in the human brain. Over many decades, from a fertile mix of germinating ideas, developmental stages, and real-world experience, the field has been on a trajectory to bring meanings and memories into the body.

MEANING AND MEMORY

Pioneering approaches to family therapy brought the excitement of communication and relationship analysis to the worlds of mental health, child behavior problems, and marital distress (Hanna, 2007). At the time, the need for professional differentiation and identity overshadowed developments in family treatment occurring globally. "Insight" was thought by some to be the realm of psychoanalysis, the very movement against which early family therapists rebelled. "History" was also suspect for the same reason. For a large segment of the profession, the primary focus was on innovative strategies for behavior change. Even the term *reframing* only hinted at the cognitive elements of meaning and experience that were central to its success (Watzlawick, 1967).

However, the imbalances of these creative mavericks eventually came into view as the international community cross-fertilized with family therapists in the U.S. First, the Milan Team in Italy began to explore the interplay of meaning, interaction, and presenting problems (Selvini Palazzoli et al., 1980). Social constructions came to the fore:

Who first noticed the problem?
Who agrees and disagrees that this is a problem?
What would happen if . . .?

They developed interview tools called *circular questions* that enabled therapists to deconstruct the finer points of meaning and memory within the collective experience of the family (Fleuridas et al., 1986).

Michael White and Narrative Family Therapy (NFT)

Then, the late Michael White in Australia sought to lower defenses of his clients by helping them *restory* their lived experience. His approach came in the form of questions. As I sat in the audience of a presentation, I watched White present a video session with a family in the U.K. who was despondent and in a state of despair. As I recall, their six-year-old son stabbed a classmate with a pencil. The pattern and intensity of his escalating aggression unnerved school personnel and family, becoming a straw that was about to break the back of their hope. It was just a nondescript, black and white film of an interview. People were talking. White was listening. Close ups showed a tearful mother, a fearful father, a silent child. Then, White began to work his magic. It happened through the use of questions that framed and reframed their story. I don't remember his exact line of questioning, but an example of his social constructions would be something like this:

> Which of these pictures do you prefer for your son? The one as a pencil fighter or the one as a pencil writer?
>
> If you prefer the pencil writer, what difference would this make in how he thinks of himself? If we were to keep this picture of the pencil writer in front of us, how might this picture frame his future?
>
> How would this picture affect your relationship with him?
>
> What times have you seen when he was more the pencil writer?
>
> Who is most likely to notice when he is writing rather than fighting.
>
> If he were writing his story, what would he say about how he put the pencil fighter down?

White's questions set a trend in what came to be known as *relative influence questioning*. While the decade of the brain was capturing the attention of larger health arenas, social constructionist approaches like NFT captured the attention of many family therapists who were ready for greater attention to the meaning, lived experience, and narratives of their clients. From dark despair, we watched the U.K. family come back from the dead right before our very eyes. There was relief and hope. They saw a new way out besides placing their son outside the home. Not only could we see it in their faces and hear it in their voices, we could feel it in our bodies. Would this have been mirror neurons? Back then, we had no language for our own somatic experience. From the lens of attachment, there was resonance. It vibrated between White and the family. Then, between the audience and White. When there is resonance, the whole body lights up (Siegel, 2012). We had witnessed transformation.

What made Michael White's work so powerful? He created new meanings from existing narratives and intuitively understood that consciousness was, indeed, a compost heap waiting to produce additional meaning—empowering meaning. Developmentally, he was informed by Bateson (1972) and first-generation family therapists, but went on to integrate ideas from additional anthropologists, philosophers, and phenomonological psychologists (Bruner, 1986; Foucault, 1973). In retrospect, he may have been the equivalent in the family therapy movement of Daniel Siegel in the neuroscience movement. Specifically, he brought numerous disciplines together under the tent of family therapy, and later, psychotherapy in general. His integration of language from various knowledge bases kept family therapists connected to a larger picture of hope, resilience, and healing.

He often wrote about those "absent, but implicit" aspects of narratives that he invited into a therapy session (White, 1995). In addition, his personal presence with clients has always been notable. A commitment to social justice led him to consider each therapy session as a political event. Consequently, he had a knack for leveling the playing field between himself and clients. This was a personal style, consistent with his belief that new stories, co-constructed by clients and therapists, belonged to the people, not the experts.

Understandably, one can argue that he didn't need brain science to be successful. His work, by all accounts, changed the language and narratives of family therapy forever. As a clinician, he brought a sense of humanity to a session that made NFT empowering for the underdog in all of us. Looking ahead now, a desire for cross-fertilization prompts these questions: Does NFT affect brain functioning? Is there room in this approach for the substance of family therapy? Is there room in neuroscience for the nuanced artistry in NFT? Can a whole body narrative be liberating for those who are oppressed by dominant discourses that fragment the body? Yes. Yes. Yes. Yes. Through the lens of neuroscience, it is possible to examine the characteristics of NFT alongside our cast of characters in the brain. In particular, neuroscientists are very interested in the role of meaning, memory, and coherent narratives in healthy development. I would hope that nothing could honor the memory of Michael White more than the adventure of linking these two worlds together.

NFT and the Amygdala

As a watchdog of the whole body, the amygdala is a central player in the formation of implicit memory, the unconscious performance of procedures and emotions that become systematized under a variety of conditions. For example, once a person learns to ride a bicycle, the ability and memory never leave. However, performance becomes unconscious. There is a sense of balance and coordination that enables the person to pedal, even between long intervals of use. The amygdala works with the PFC to assign meaning to various stimuli. Siegel (2012) suggests that after any experience of pain, the amygdala automatically signals fight/flight circuits to prevent future occurrences. With respect to conscious, verbal, contextual, explicit memory, the amygdala sorts and encodes experiences of high arousal. Many significant experiences are held in both levels of memory. It is at the intersection of these two modes that NFT has relevance.

White emphasizes the importance of identity emerging from narratives (White & Epston, 1991). The questions for the pencil writer are examples of identity emerging from narratives. Transformational narratives emerge from a process that begins with *dominant* or *problem-saturated stories.* These would be amygdala-activated narratives. The language of these problem stories are part of explicit memory. The emotional activation in the body that biases the selective recall of details is part of implicit memory. White had an interesting habit of writing down the exact words used by clients in these initial narratives. He used their phrases as he began to expand the story. His questions brought forth information about the situation that was not as spontaneously retrieved by stressed family members. This would become the *alternate,* or *subjugated story*, one that provided a different identity for each person involved in the pattern. Using client language, these new stories tapped into overlooked details of the original story. These details transformed the story into a few standard plots.

A common theme in NFT is that a condition or circumstance has overpowered the family and they need help to fight it off. Sounds like the HPA axis! The condition receives a name, such as bickering, Sneaky Poo, etc. Weaving these elements into the plot is termed *externalization.* This parallels the threat-survival function of the amygdala. The suggestion that family members can unite to throw off the shackles of the enemy contains attachment themes and survival themes that access conscious and unconscious meaning. This matches the processes already happening in the limbic system, since these are not under conscious control. The enhanced story recruits all the PFCs in the room to fight the battle. Language with clients is literary and story-telling. There is scant mention of standard mental health terms or jargon unless it comes from family. In devising a plan of action, the condition or situation might become a mythic or metaphoric character. The victory in battle, nothing less than numinosum.

During times of stress, CORT may slow explicit memory and the amygdala may secrete noradrenaline that speeds up implicit memory (Siegel, 2012). This juxtapositioning can lead to gaps in the detail of collective experience, leading to fragmented narratives, lacking coherence. Attachment theorists note the importance of coherent narratives as a sign of healthy identity development. Theoretically, these narratives pull together episodes of experience in explicit memory. Then, the hippocampus and PFC assign meaning and put them in perspective (e.g., I had a good day today. My teacher likes me. Our marriage is secure.). Narratives become fragmented when episodes of experience fail to produce a pattern of belonging, identity, love, or safety. A state of threat or anxiety ensues and the amygdala overtakes the PFC.

As a family seeks therapy under duress, NFT practices may soothe the amygdala through the humility of the practitioner who begins to frame the effects of the problem situation as one of oppression. No one is to blame. The meaning attached to this expanded story gives the PFC a coherent narrative. In NFT, a narrative is incomplete if it lacks detail about family attempts to overcome the condition. Narratives must include episodes of competence and strength. The therapist draws out these details and invites parents to expand their view of possibilities. These *unique outcomes* lead to a thickening of the plot in which new scripts amplify abilities that may have been ignored by gyrations of the amygdala. This amplification of overlooked abilities has been a hallmark of strength-based work (de Shazer & Berg, 1992; White & Epston, 1991). However, in this approach, it is important to maintain a sincere sense of drama and wonder because it attunes to the distress of parents while constructing a way out. It is the combination of novelty, repetition, and affective intensity (focus) that maximizes neuroplasticity (Rossi, 2002).

White (1995) was known for his narratives of oppression. Sometimes the oppression is from larger politicized societal systems and always, there is the oppression of the problem that has taken on a life of its own. Repeating the family's words is attunement to the PFC by staying with client explicit memory. Then, sympathizing with the oppression that has overtaken the family speaks to the implicit, affective state that triggers threat-response associated with the problem. In fact, behaviors that are tied to implicit, emotional memory do have a biological life of their own. The invoking of oppression attunes to implicit memory, regardless of the stimulus. Feeling "one-down" has a universal resonance to those who seek therapy services. NFT practices have a knack for highly individualized conversations anchored in clients' narratives. Simultaneously, these also tap into the generalized sense of "every man." In one fell swoop, the amygdala rests!

Next, as families settle in for the middle stage of NFT, questions add distinctions to the story. A catalogue of questions draws out detail of interactions. From this information, a plan of attack comes into view. Since there is strength in numbers, each family member pitches in to help as their contribution to the team. The therapist invites each team member to commit to the plan. At this point, the reader can invoke a favorite action story in which one side prepares for battle. Picture the legions lined up on their horses or behind their cannons ... CHARGE! Biologically, Panksepp's (2011) index of basic mammalian functions might view RAGE and PLAY systems connected to this activity. Similar to Hardy & Laszloffy's (2005) focus on rage, these activities in NFT can acknowledge primary emotion and connect the energy to positive activity.

Among family therapists, White received national attention for his work with children when he demonstrated a number of case examples that took the form of a game or an epic journey for the youth. Parents and others are recruited to assume roles in the game or story. These PLAY experiences help parents share the alternate reality and allow everyone to bypass blame, shame, and fear (White, 1986). A famous case worked to outsmart Sneaky Poo (for encopresis). For his starring role, the child received an award. Sharing the joy of laughter and victory as a family is good medicine for the soul.

The Dopamine Fix and Transformation

Now that we know something about dopamine and expectancy, it is easy to see how NFT, with attention and hope toward the future victory, transformed the despairing family with the pencil fighter. The audience could see the physical transformation that came from acknowledging oppression and expanding the narratives to include tangible elements of hope. This, in turn, gave the audience a new hope, possibly from mirror neurons. Their drama had a new chapter in which allies came to share their battle and defeat the enemy. Evolutionary biologists and anthropologists can resonate to these narratives!

The therapist becomes a troubleshooter to help families with the plan from week to week. Girls provide their own metaphors and stories. There are enough female heroines with magical powers from which to choose. Given the developmental risk factors for boys that Chapter 6 outlined, there is a distinct need for therapists to respond to the content, process, and substance that leave boys at greater risk. Then, during adolescence, the risks for girls increase and the need to engage families around the oppression of girls becomes important.

Victory over the presenting problem is not the end of the story. NFT contributed a generation of therapists who learned to celebrate successes in concrete, socially supported ways. Award ceremonies, rites of passage, and rituals of healing anchor success in the body and in the tribe as a prelude for the journey ahead (Imber-Black et al., 1988). Maintaining the flow of dopamine connected with new behaviors is an important part of the work. Certificates of achievement, special tokens, and the applause of a small audience can help the state of pride in the body to linger and later, to trigger that same feeling of achievement all over again.

The protagonist may be a conquering hero who receives a medal. For children with enuresis or encopresis, they may conquer Sneaky Wee or Sneaky Poo. They may also become an expert at monster taming and receive an award or certificate (White & Epston, 1991). He purposely avoided traditional terms like "termination" and stayed with the universal themes of the tribe, such as rites of passage, graduation, etc. Thus, the content of NFT is about universal themes such as oppression and heroism. The process is one of creating expanded narratives with new scripts anchored in the language and experience of the family. The substance is the transfer of energy from threat-survival circuits to the feeling of safety in the body, and finally, the pure joy of transformation.

Reflecting on these narrative practices and neuroplasticity, Sluzki (1992) suggests that transformation comes from taking enough elements of the old story so that it remains familiar and adding new elements that are hidden between the lines. These hidden elements can come from almost any approach to family therapy, as long as they resonate with family experience. As an example, RT might take the old story and add narratives about love, safety, and entitlement. When these enriched stories resonate with the attachment needs and identity issues of families, they plant the seeds of transformation.

With this process in mind, it makes sense that brain-informed practices can simply add a narrative about emotion and physiology that our clients already feel, but have no words to describe. Felt sense exercises can be as simple as just savoring sensations in the body that come from accepting the award or the applause. Mindfulness can be a quick footnote that simply gives the body its just due. When these are facilitated as part of an attachment experience, interpersonal physiology strengthens the circuits. Then, affect, meaning, and memory form circuits of secure attachment through belonging and identity. This is when our ancient ancestors would use the primacy of the tribe. Social networks have a potent potential for healing.

TRANSFORMATION AND THE TRIBE

Around the world, there are numerous family configurations, but it is safe to say that most provide necessary interpersonal attachments that are necessary for survival. In industrialized societies, these necessities become obscure with consumerism that invites people to value their own dwellings, separate from the group, and many times, separate from the village. In addition, other threats to survival, such as scarcity of food, have been replaced by refrigeration and fast food. In the face of this progress, an unintended consequence has been the way in which these basics have migrated from our explicit memory to our implicit memory. Most food and shelter seeking happens unconsciously, without much strategy or problem-solving from the PFC. Even if we want to remember the location of a favorite restaurant, this hardly reaches the level of threat-survival in our bodies. More likely, it would activate the dopamine circuits of expectation for gratification.

American society has promoted the value of autonomy and independence for centuries (Bellah et al., 1985). As threats from revolution and civil war receded, Americans sought greater independence and privacy from each other. European visitors noted the contrasts in culture and speculated as to whether this independence-seeking was behind the general malaise they found in various parts of the country. Compared to their homelands, they found less community (Bellah et al., 1985). Somehow, amid all the progress America had to offer, some felt isolated. With that isolation comes depression.

Perhaps this is why anthropologists note that the need for social connection has survived throughout every major transition that the world has experienced (Fisher, 2004b; Small, 2011). Humans feel the danger of isolation and instinctively want to bond. Eventually, something shifts to bring about homeostasis. In psychotherapy, the isolation of psychoanalysis begs for more inclusion of the tribe. This is not far from the minds of researchers who see the importance of social activity for brain health in older adults. James, Boyle, Buchman & Bennett (2011) found that seniors reduced their risk of disability with increased social activity. As Chapter 2 notes, relationships are complicated and stimulating. This is good for the brain.

Many believe that our larger brain size is needed for increased social capacity. The electrochemical energy that fires off between two, three, and four minds can be just like a modern-day dam. When coordinated, they can be a reservoir for life-giving water. When fragmented, the reservoir may burst under a flood of life-threatening weight. Thus, societal changes can threaten our capacity for survival if relationships become sparse. Recall the research in Chapter 3 on social support. The density of our support, just like the density of our brain circuits, fortifies us against a flood of stress. As the quote at the beginning of this chapter suggests, traditional psychotherapy may contribute to sparse social networks by ignoring the power of the tribe. Boyd-Franklin and Bry (2000) note the importance of including the network for treatment with Black families. Sometimes clinicians go into the waiting room to get a child for therapy and walk past aunts, uncles, and cousins to get her. It is clear that there is a role for family therapists to play by validating and using what already exists—extended families, kinship circles, and social networks.

We have modern day tribes that are as resilient as the human race. In the absence of an agrarian society when everyone knew where everyone was, we now have cell phones and the internet. Is it possible that these technologies have not replaced anything? Instead, they may be compensating for thin social networks that have been evolving over time. Is it possible that the latchkey kids of this generation are more connected than before? Do we have a virtual village because social transitions leave gaps in the density of our networks? Before these social connectors, the babysitter was our television with little opportunity for social interaction. Despite troubling excesses and predatory practices on the internet, the rising generation continues to demonstrate the power of connection.

However, there is still something missing. Random connection is not necessarily the power of the tribe. Tribes have history, tradition, and shared genes (and maybe jeans!). Tribes have the wisdom of the elders. They provide ritual. They care for each other. They adapt to changing circumstances without losing connection. In 1978, journalist Jane Howard traveled across America interviewing modern day tribes. Some of them were extended family, others were families of choice. She found they all had these characteristics. Our brains need them. These are social connections that bring belonging and identity. This final review of selected family therapy approaches illustrates how tribes help us thrive and why family therapists should help their clients strengthen them.

Who is the Tribe?

It is surprising how often we overlook some of the most important people in our clients' lives. After years of hearing the treatment community stereotype drug addicts as those without family, Stanton & Todd (1982) reported on a number of surveys that found 80–60 percent of drug users averaged weekly contacts with one or more family members. Not only do substance users have families, but many have ongoing contact with them. In these cases, the tribe is the family and extended family. All tribes have saints and sinners. Some are banished from the community, others choose to leave. However, in most cases, tribes are diverse enough so that everyone has somebody. As Hardy & Laszloffy (2005) contend, when the tribe breaks down, rage may not be far behind. However, some of their work helps people to find new tribes. In the case of a gay adolescent who was ostracized at home, he found a gay community that provided belonging and identity for him.

In families of choice, friends, neighbors, and non-blood kin are the tribe. Reeb et al. (1986) studied primary care patients and asked who is <u>like</u> family? They found that health outcomes related more to quality of that group, rather than to household composition or blood kin. Therapists using transitional family therapy (TFT) ask women with HIV "Who cares about you?" These are the people they engage (Landau-Stanton et al., 1993).

A final characteristic of the tribe is those who have influence. They may not be blood kin, but they may have more identity power than traditional family. The case of Kevin, 38, is an example of those with influence. Kevin's wife, Ellen, was ready for divorce. She had reached her limit with his broken promises over late night bar escapades. He would get drunk after his softball games. His team members knew about his one-night stands and just looked the other way. A close examination of Kevin's tribe found the following features. He was an only child. Father and grandfather were both widowed at an early age. He was raised motherless, in a three generational male household. He had been on the same softball team since the ninth grade. These were his brothers, his identity, his roots. The idea that he would have to quit the team for his marriage was an unspeakable dilemma. Having lost his mother and grandmother, his teammates and their families were the only family he knew.

With this background, it was possible to see the team as taking the place of in-laws. Despite having looked the other way at the bar, they had the potential to be resources because they were a diverse group, yet most were married, and Kevin had his strongest ties to a select few. Ellen liked a couple of his closest married friends and knew that they had tried to stop his drinking in the past. A two-step plan involved having the couple reach out to the supportive couples and socialize with them in between games, so that his only avenue for connection was not the games. Then, he experimented with coming home right after the games. Experimentation is a way for the PFC to deactivate the amygdala when new behavior brings some unknowns. It didn't have to be permanent, he still had options. After a month, his wife was more integrated into the friendship circle and the importance of the team began to dwindle as he strengthened the brotherly bonds with his closest friends.

Marital sessions explored major transitions in his life, including the death of his grandfather and the impending care that his father would need as he aged. These explorations drew upon explicit memory. Within them, it was possible to find the absent, but implicit aspects of his story. When his grandfather aged, his father was in the house to care for him. As his father aged, Kevin and his wife were there for him. With the threat of divorce hanging over his head, I asked, "So, who is going to take care of you, when you're old? Have you thought about the future and whether your teammates might be there for you under those circumstances?" He feared abandonment by his brothers because of his losses in the past, but had never thought about the loss of his marriage.

His irrationality is perfectly understood in light of what the amygdala does to prevent past pain. From the ninth grade on, his circuits of belonging and identity were anchored in the team. However, this had blocked his view of the future, a function of the PFC. As I questioned him about this, he began to hyperventilate. Now, the PFC had a visual genogram that plotted implications of the future that lay before him. Since men process visual stimuli more intensely, the power of the tribe began to dwindle in light of his genogram and the reality that he could lose his wife and two daughters. The role of the tribe became more balanced. This often happens with in-laws who need to renegotiate boundaries after marriage. Just like family of origin, there was no need for cut off, once it was clear how Kevin had become so attached. His transformation involved proper identification of his tribe, using the resources within it, and structuring sessions around visual stimuli that enabled his explicit memory of intergenerational transitions to inform his assessment of the future.

Discovering the influence of the tribe can have an important effect on violent men as well. In one domestic violence case, White (1990) explores a man's attitudes toward women and the traditions that prevent him from a more respectful relationship with women. His peer group is a significant influence in his life. The defining questions are these:

1. Are there certain people in your life that have invited you to adopt that way of thinking? Who are they and what is your relationship to them now?

2. Are there experiences you've had that have led to this way of thinking? What were they and how did they affect you?

3. If you were to adopt a different way of thinking now, would it cause problems within your group? Would you be facing some flak if they thought you were drifting in your views?

4. How would you cope with such flak, if it came your way? Would it be too costly to risk a challenge to this group? What would you need to help you cope if you did decide to break away from the group?

The first two questions evoke stories that provide the context for a certain mindset. There is no direct challenge to his views. Instead, listening to his stories of influence and attachment to the tribe provides a map of his mental process that is tied to his identity. Question 3 assesses the flexibility of the tribe and the degree of his attachment. This signals potential amygdala interference. Question 4 explores the possibility of an amygdala anecdote. Instead of challenging his views directly, the therapist can work with the restraints that keep him from new ways of thinking.

Often, those who are labeled as "resistant" or "in denial" are really just the tip of the iceberg. Their tribe is the rest of the iceberg and the therapist may not realize who is the tribe and what is the person's position in it. A case study in Chapter 8 illustrates how important this can be. By deconstructing experiences and relationships that influence current thinking, the therapist can explore the disadvantages to change and how one might cope with the social consequences (threat) of change. Especially for boys and men, peer groups can be brutal and bullying. There can be implicit memory (autonomic knee jerk reactions) from past peer encounters that leave a male in a hypervigilant state regarding his place in the group. The process of therapy must respect this possibility and avoid judgment of overt behavior (Jenkins, 1991). Then, as the context becomes clear, it is possible to sympathize with the unspoken dilemma and comment on how much courage it might take to strike out on his own and risk isolation or worse from the group. Thus, the restraint becomes the first problem to tackle. Thereafter, the "problem" becomes the second problem. In addition, a safe therapeutic relationship (see Chapter 4) may allow for some mindfulness and felt sense exercises to ground a person and allow them to feel their somatic resources. An initial trauma assessment may also alert the practitioner as to the best order of interventions when a person becomes more aware of gender-based traumas and their impact on current behavior.

Tribal Rituals for Healing

There are two approaches from the family therapy community that provide excellent guidelines for extended family, group, and network interventions. During these, the therapist offers to help families organize important ceremonies. One of the most overlooked mental health needs in America relates to proper grieving for traumatic deaths in a way that will lead to healing and peace. American society has evolved a set of values that leads to many counterproductive practices regarding death and dying. The medicalization of dying makes it difficult to have personal moments of connection, with the living or the dead. When there are suicides, untimely, or violent deaths, there may be so much shame, guilt, or rage to process that social and religious circles may be unprepared as to how to comfort those that mourn. As mentioned above, the dehumanization of loss is a precursor to rage. Children are at particular risk when they lose an important family member early in their lives. It is crucial for therapists to assess these influences and provide education and guidance.

Transitional family therapy (TFT). This approach developed as an intervention for substance abusers, based on the premise that substance abuse is a symptom of unresolved losses in the intergenerational family. Research documents that substance abusers have high rates of premature deaths at early ages (Bowser et al., 2003). TFT is an integration of structural/strategic family therapy with intergenerational interventions that address grief and loss issues. The former addresses current relationship conflicts, especially at the parent-adolescent level, when the substance user is a minor. This approach uses enactments, similar to MDFT, but families are kept together in conjoint sessions. The reason for this is because one goal is to identify losses and transitions in a family's history that have led to unresolved grief. The process enables an adolescent to become a witness to parents' losses in childhood and the focus shifts to a family's history of coping with losses or transitions (Horwitz, 1997; Seaburn et al., 1995).

Frequently, families have circumstances that prevent memorial services from becoming a healing ritual. As family members discuss these experiences, they are invited to describe what they wish could have happened to properly honor their loved one. Sometimes, they were so young that there was no way to benefit or grieve. Thus, the current experience provides an opportunity to honor and reflect on the person. Extended family figure prominently in this process, especially when older relatives are still alive who can share new stories and add new dimensions to what parents knew about the lost loved one. The therapist takes responsibility for educating families about the benefits of the process and stimulating motivation to organize an event. Sometimes the event may be as simple as inviting extended family to a few sessions to reminisce and answer questions from clients and therapist. At other times, there may be a service with clergy or other leaders that provide the support of the family's social network. In cases of suicide, it is important to find those people who can reflect on aspects of the person apart from the suicide, since shame often overshadows any honor that should be given.

Regardless of the form it takes, the process of planning, convening, and participating in the event is therapeutic and invokes the presence and support from the tribe. This is a time for the wisdom of the elders to come forth and provide an intergenerational perspective on the person's life. As a witness to parents reconnecting with aspects of their past, the adolescent shifts from their focus on present conflicts to a broader identity within the tribe. Parents think through the effects of the loss, how they coped, and how it affects their current relationships. Each generation has an opportunity to reflect on the larger context of their family heritage, not just day-to-day conflicts.

In one case, an aunt had been brutally murdered. Jerry, 16, developed his substance abuse problem in the wake of this family trauma. He was trying to protect his single-parent mom from having to address his grief issues while she was still mourning her sister's death. There had been such a focus on the trial and conviction of the murderer that her sister's personhood had gotten lost. They found tremendous energy and joy from bringing her "back to life" in a way that allowed them to reconnect with her presence and energy (White, 1988). They celebrated favorite foods, jokes, memories, and personality traits. These became rituals for ongoing enjoyment.

White (1988) speaks of the tendency for people to promote the Freudian idea of "letting go" instead of "holding on" to the lost loved one. Many rituals can resist the former and help families develop new ways to hold on to the person. In one case, a juvenile sex offender discussed the deaths of his "daddy and granddaddy" with the therapist. They had both committed suicide at different times during his childhood. This dialogue invited the boy to hear what his daddy and granddaddy would say to him now. It gave him permission to put them back in his life and put down the shame that had come between them (Schauer, 1993).

These events become powerful times of transformation. They form a new culture for the witnessing of losses that encourages families to develop new narratives about who the person was and how their legacy can shape the future. As these events occur, there is a shifting of the adolescent's role in the family from one of burdened silence to active participation with permission to share their own grief and insights. The family of Marty, 12, provides another view of how participatory grieving can be therapeutic. His mother had lost her way with drugs when he was a baby. As an only child, he was raised by his father, a truck driver. Extended family helped with Marty's care when his father was on the road.

While on a trip, his father died suddenly from a heart attack. Because Marty had always been part of this tribe, the transition involved people that knew and loved him from birth. His new guardians, an aunt and uncle, understood how important it would be to include Marty in the funeral planning and service. Marty spoke at the funeral. The family came together to honor and remember him. The aunt and uncle helped Marty obtain his father's possessions. He kept his wallet in his pocket. He wore his watch. There were pictures in the house so he could know that his father would always be with him.

Through the lens of attachment, it makes sense to hold on, rather than let go. In a number of societies outside the U.S., lost loved ones are remembered at anniversaries and with daily incense at home-based shrines. American families would do well to break the silence of grieving in this culture and bring their lost loved ones back into their lives. A coherent narrative includes the meaning of important relationships and the ability to reflect on autobiographical memory over time. These narratives can be especially important when chronic illness threatens the identity of families during the course of conditions such as schizophrenia, PTSD, and bipolar disorder.

Multifamily psychoeducational groups (MFG) as ritual. Earlier chapters mention McFarlane's (2002) model of multi-family groups for those with schizophrenia. There is probably no other diagnostic category that challenges the mental health treatment community like schizophrenia. There are two reasons for reviewing this approach. First, family therapy's relationship with schizophrenia dates back to the beginning of the profession when federal funding initiated a number of projects to explore schizophrenia. Those early projects brought teams of researchers together. They became the founding fathers of marriage and family therapy (Bateson et al., 1956).

Thirty years later, the study of *expressed emotion (EE)*, a measure of criticism and interpersonal involvement, led to consistent findings that lower EE related to lower relapse rates (Anderson et al., 1986). Regardless of etiology, low EE appeared to foster recovery. McFarlane's (2002) approach to multifamily groups saw the need for families to receive better support for the stresses of living with a symptomatic family member. Over the past twenty years, this multifamily group format has achieved consistent positive results in numerous clinical trials (McFarlane et al., 1995). When family members receive education and support, symptoms decrease.

The second reason for including this model is because of its integrative, client-centered, brain-informed process. Many studies find an imbalance of dopamine levels in schizophrenic patients. It is too high in limbic regions (high activation) and too low in the PFC (low activation). Most anti-psychotic medications address this imbalance. Medication combined with MFG achieves better results than medication alone, or medication with assertive community treatment (McFarlane et al., 1993). Although the mechanisms of action remain speculative, as a model of clinical wisdom, MFG deserves more attention from family therapy and neuroscience communities because of its outcomes and adaptability for use with other problems (Steinglass, 1998). To date, MFG adaptations exist for bi-polar disorder, major depression, obsessive-compulsive disorder, and a range of medical problems (McFarlane, 2002). Woods et al. (2012) recommend this program as one that is relevant for adaptations in African American communities because of the emphasis on creating community, attention to outreach, and modeling calm, friendly interactions.

As a model for network therapy and convening the tribe, MFGs use carefully scripted engagement skills that are designed for people with high levels of distrust and social isolation. These skills convey understanding and sympathy for the burden of caring for a person with schizophrenia. The therapist becomes a witness to their pain. As family members agree to experiment with the program, group interactions follow a sequence that attunes to experiences of social anxiety, stress, and stigma. Schizophrenia involves a sensitivity to sensory stimulation. Thus, group processes are structured, predictable, and focused on a specific outcome. In contrast to the experiential models in this book, MFGs seek a low level of affective intensity to match a person's capacity for social stimulation. Becoming brain friendly involves an understanding of when to allow emotional expressions and when to control them. Over time, these social rituals become informal as trust increases within the group and symptoms stabilize in the family member.

Table 7.1 summarizes the main components of MFGs with their desired biosocial effects. The components resulted from years of trial and error work in reaching out to families. Hence, the goal of joining sessions is motivation and attachment. The goal of the education seminar is to provide a rationale for new problem-solving behaviors with the family (PFC). The goal of session one is to have everyone return for session two. This means it must be safe and meaningful. Everyone is invited to put their best foot forward by describing who they are and what they enjoy in life.

The goal of session one is to have everyone return for session two.

As a pragmatic response to client feedback, the program attunes to the unique sensitivities that families develop over the course of their member's condition. Low emotional risk is an important component in the early stages of group formation. The goal of session two is to develop a list of experiences that schizophrenia has stolen from their lives. This list becomes a set of goals for each group member to accomplish. For example, if schizophrenia has stolen some opportunities for travel, the goal of the group will be to help that family reclaim

Table 7.1 Desired biosocial components of multifamily groups

Stages	Tasks	Attachment Effects	Biological Effects
Single-family joining sessions	Learn the family's story; Provide sympathy, empathy; Explain purpose of the program related to family's story.	Feeling felt; Attunement.	Hope: Dopamine SEEKING state; CARE state.
One-day education seminar	Powerpoint presentation; Educational atmosphere; Low risk, friendly environment; No one is asked for personal disclosures.	Feeling safe; Protected; Attunement.	PFC engaged-novelty; Amygdala calmed.
Role of facilitators	Host and hostess; Credible facilitator; Maximize social interaction and social rewards, matchmaking; Lower stigmatization; Model low EE; Facilitate brain-storming activity; Between-session outreach and crisis intervention.	Feeling welcome; Belonging; Trustworthiness.	Serotonin; Brain plasticity; Limbic system calm; Endorphins; PLAY state; CARE state; Mirror neurons from demonstrations.
Session 1:	Introductions: Who am I?	Positive identity; Belonging.	Engage explicit memory.
Session 2:	Introductions: How has schizophrenia affected me? Plans to reclaim losses.	Attunement; Entitlements; Coherent narratives.	Engage implicit memory; CARE state.
Sessions 3+	1. Socializing; 2. Go-around; 3. Selecting problem; 4. Formal problem-solving with markers and an easel; 5. Socializing—Celebrating.	Community; Attunement; Belonging; Identity; Numinosum.	PLAY state; Serotonin; "Community PFC"—novelty, focus, planning, mental stimulation.

their right to travel. If someone is afraid to leave home to socialize with old friends, the goal will be to reclaim that part of their life. In addition to the general goal of symptom reduction, each family member receives encouragement and social support for increasing their personal rewards in life (dopamine).

Session three introduces the repetition and ritual that continues for each session thereafter. Chapter 3 referred to this as a "community frontal lobe." With these functions of the PFC in mind, witness a typical 90-minute group session:

Functions of PFC
Establishing a cognitive set
Problem-solving
Planning
Attention
Initiative
Motivation
Integration of thought and affect
Mental liveliness

---

1. Socializing
2. A go-around, in which members take turns checking in, reviewing their week.
3. Selecting one representative problem that has wide applicability to the group.
4. Formal problem-solving with markers and an easel using the following steps:
   a. problem definition
   b. listing possible solutions, each member taking a turn giving one suggestion
   c. listing pros and cons beside each suggestion
   d. reviewing the lists and allowing the person to choose what fits best for them
   e. assigning tasks and support people to help with implementation
5. Socializing

Socializing at beginning and end is intentional and facilitators are trained to use this time productively. Families have had their lives stolen away. This time is to reintroduce PLAY as part of the healing process. The problem-solving section, while some might think overly structured, provides just what the frontal lobe is supposed to do. Repetition encourages brain plasticity. Social support tags new memories.

Here, I suggest that these groups have many characteristics of a tribe. While not blood kin, families share the same stresses, shame, and stigma. These are powerful isolators and hence, they become powerful unifiers. They do not have a shared history, but they have shared experiences that have been life-changing. In many ways, these groups help families to externalize the problem and create new identities for themselves and their family member.

The unique role of facilitators in *matchmaking* helps families to connect between sessions in personal, day-to-day ways over hobbies, interests, and shared needs. Perhaps a few people begin golfing together. Families may provide respite for each other to allow more freedom. Facilitators encourage this environment and explore opportunities for friendships to develop. At the end of 12–18 months of twice-monthly sessions, various families may maintain the group as a social outlet away from the treatment facility (McFarlane, 2002). By now, they have shared birthdays, anniversaries, weddings—all the rituals that are important to a tribe.

Tribes prize their rituals. There is extensive attention to these in anthropological literature. Social support research reveals how basic and simple support relates to illness and death rates. As an alternative to traditional forms of group therapy, and as a model of limbic system deactivation, MFGs contain many important features. At the affective level, there is support for the PFC and a cooling of the amygdala. At levels of meaning and memory, the collective becomes an audience to healing, making a big deal out of small, but important steps. As time goes on, cultural wisdom develops from narratives of healing. When progress is punctuated with ceremony, memories are more vivid. Finally, helping members reclaim lost aspects of their lives addresses the PLAY system noted by Panksepp (2007) as the most therapeutic and healing of all brain systems. In his opinion, the notion of restoring PLAY does not get enough "play" in mental health treatment systems today.

PRINCIPLES OF TRANSFORMATION

1. From the beginning, identifying all members of the tribe will help clinicians develop strategies for involvement.
2. Initially, every client question is a potential message from the amygdala.
3. Attuning to women's focus on relationship detail and men's focus on visual-spacial detail can enhance the engagement of parents.
4. Attunement to the 3Ds and autobiographical histories of oppression calm the amygdala and improve coherent narratives.
5. As preparation for enactments, individual sessions that focus attunement on the 4Ds can deescalate negative affect in parents and adolescents.
6. During times of emotional activation, grounding and resourcing can synchronize the body into balanced flows of energy.
7. Validation is the first step toward a successful request for change.
8. Successful enactments involve intentional preparation and lead to the healing of attachment injuries.
9. During times of high burden, integration with case management is a vital part of transformation.
10. PLAY circuits begin deep in the limbic and primitive regions of the brain. Activity in these regions sends energy to the cortex for better problem-solving.
11. Holding on to lost loved ones accesses implicit memory tied to the limbic region. This, in turn, energizes explicit

memory to include belonging and identity attached to lost loved ones, ancestors and legacies.

12. Creating community and convening audiences of healing thicken neural net profiles that broaden options and mindsets.

13. When therapeutic process mimics functions of a targeted brain region, the region grows new circuits from repetition, novelty, and creativity.

8

Neurobiology and Community
From Family Therapy to Program Development

> The brain did not evolve to see the world the way it really is—we can't. We . . . see things according to history—our own history and that of our ancestors—because we are defined by ecology. Not by our biology, not by our DNA, but by our history of interactions.
>
> (Lotto, 2012, p. 1)

This chapter steps back and reviews body, survival, attachment, circuits, and transformation. As concepts that shape the content, process, and substance of family therapy work, these become a framework to understand the lives of our clients (what is happening) and the possibilities for transformation (what can happen). Without them, therapy can be a nonverbal obstacle course for clients who are already struggling to make sense of their experience. One way to integrate these ideas is to think:

Content = Body, Survival
Process = Attachment, Belonging, Identity
Substance = Circuits, Transformation

First, these describe the stories our clients bring to us. Second, these become a template for family therapy that follows the lived experience of therapist and client. A case example from start to finish will illustrate this integration. Toward the end of this chapter, Table 8.1 integrates these interventions and concepts into the main tasks of family therapy process. Then, using the neurobiology of substance abuse, a proposal outlines how program developers can include brain-friendly components in a cost-effective manner.

For a program to be brain-friendly, it must

1. deactivate threat-survival circuits in the body,
2. address attachment issues in clients' stories and in the therapeutic process, and
3. activate new circuits that involve physical, affective, and interpersonal transformation.

Chapters 6 and 7 illustrate several interventions that achieve these results. They serve as illustrations for practitioners as they integrate program components that fit with their style and the client's neurobiological needs.

CASE STUDY: ELSIE

This story includes Elsie's story and my story, two minds that traveled together, looking for places of healing and growth. On the way, there were systemic dilemmas, high drama, noble intentions, and heroic acts. It was my privilege and honor to walk with Elsie and her tribe as they made a perilous transition after coming to America.

The Plot

Elsie, 30, came to a facility for homeless women after she had been on the street for two years. We began work as a requirement of the homeless facility and continued sessions after she left the facility and lived with friends. Pregnant at the time, she delivered a baby girl about four months into treatment. The father of her unborn child threatened to kill her when he learned she would not have an abortion. With nowhere else to turn, she came to our facility (survival). My work with her continued intermittently for

18 months, until she reunited with her mother, who had custody of her oldest daughter (transformation). Despite all she endured, she was charming, respectful, and had a sense of humor (resilience). During our many home visits, she liked to mention neighbors' curiosities about this "white lady" that was coming to see her (PLAY). She was motivated to receive "help for her emotions" and wanted to regain her independence and custody of her daughter.

> As I reviewed the self of the therapist, my affective activation, and survival history, these affirmations came to mind: This home-based case will be an adventure, just like when I once helped my mom rescue a battered woman. With my teenage sense of wonder, I look forward to what I will learn. Just as I bring my mother's voice with me, I ask, "What inspiration will I take from this person?

Upon meeting Elsie, I described my services as case management, counseling, and family therapy. People with high levels of burden need integrated services because of whole body survival needs (Brown et al., 2000; Hennkeler et al, 1998; Liddle, 2000). Waldegrave (1990) notes that, too often, psychotherapists expect depressed people to feel better from treatment and then go home and be happy in poverty. I knew she needed help to find housing. Elsie shared her sense of betrayal and rage about the circumstances that led to her mother gaining custody of her daughter. She wanted to have a healthy baby, regain custody of her daughter, and move on with her life, independent of her mother (resilience). Thinking about the amygdala and how it processes data from the five senses, I thought about how her safety and attachment needs could filter her perceptions of me (circuits, triggers):

> You've really been through a lot (3Ds). If you want to talk about your feelings here, you're welcome to do that (belonging). In our work together, I'm here for you and you call the shots (amygdala, safety, identity-autonomy). There are a couple of things I have to do to maintain my legal responsibilities as a licensed practitioner,

such as ... but, other than those things, I want to know what's important to you right now (desire to attune; I'm a guest in her "house").

The Cast

Elsie was born in the U.S. after her parents came from South Africa during the apartheid oppression. Her older siblings were born there and were school age when they moved. All three were 9–11 years older than Elsie. Her father studied at a university and returned to his homeland as the couple divorced after years of domestic violence. Elsie was born just before the height of that violence after her mother was pushed down a flight of stairs, breaking her leg. Her mother went on to obtain graduate degrees in political science and became an advocate for her country from her new-found status in America.

Many of her mother's seven siblings had come to America. Elsie described interactions that highlighted fear that her mother had turned them against her (dominant story, influence of the tribe). They were close knit and had regular communication. She heard her mother vent to aunts and uncles about her "disrespect." She commented regularly on how her family would never approve of her seeing a counselor. This was highly shameful. A child out of wedlock was also shameful. This tribe had a responsibility to their homeland and ancestors, in view of their suffering under apartheid. In this world, age takes precedence over any other priority. Honoring those who are older, whether parents or siblings, is paramount. Her honest appraisals of a situation were one of the seven resiliencies. However, this brought condemnation from the elders.

> As a rationale for my assessment process, I made this request: Your life has a lot of twists and turns. You've really been through a lot! I want to help you get your daughter back and get on with your life. It would be helpful to me if I could hear the rest of your story so that I'll know exactly where you're coming from when we talk about your emotions and how to calm yourself down

(attunement, triggers, snapshot of the body). May I draw out your family tree and fill in the details on this chart (explicit memory, snapshot of the environment)? I also have some surveys that would save some talking, if you don't mind answering those questions. These are completely confidential. You deserve the best service I can give you and this just helps to make sure I'm covering all the bases and not missing anything (worthiness, entitlement).

She was pleased that I wanted to hear her life story (Over the first 3 sessions, I charted her story on a timeline and drew a genogram as she talked (Hanna, 2007)). She scored moderately high on the PCL, had elevated depression scores, and RES items suggested family of origin pain.

From the genogram, Elsie introduced me to each member of the family. I was looking for someone who might be able to step outside the tribe and enter Elsie's world. A few female cousins were possibilities because they had come to visit a few years before and Elsie thought they had empathy, but didn't want to rock the intergenerational boat. Later, I would learn that I overlooked a cousin because my questions relied on Elsie's preferences and experience without also looking for new possibilities within the tribe (creating new circuits). As she described people and experiences, the conversations with her mother were clearly dialogues about old world/new world values (dilemmas).

The Story

Elsie was robbed of her status in the tribe due to circumstances beyond her control. I could see this tribe had cultural wounds. The violence in her immediate family affected everyone's affective regulation. Father against mother; brother bullying Elsie, and Elsie reacting to boyfriends (intergenerational trauma). The tribe was so preoccupied with protecting and defending their own that the battlefront left them no opportunity to reflect on Elsie's challenges, from her brain surgery (age 11), to the losses, lack of belonging and attunement (age 12 on). Elsie began to relax as I presented these narratives and pointed to various aspects of her genogram and timeline (3Ds). I introduced her explicit memory to her implicit memory. A coherent narrative was forming that would connect the dots for her (heightening, externalization, restorying).

> Have you ever thought of yourself as a trauma survivor? These are some really heavy things that happened to you (validation). Did you know that trauma can actually affect your emotions so much that it makes it hard to think (psychoeducation)?

Elsie liked the idea that she had been through trauma. This was a new concept for her (novelty). The first event she considered traumatic was when her mother graduated and got a job. They were uprooted to a far-away city. Her brothers, now in college, had always been her caregivers and she had never been alone with her mother, who was strict and traditional. They would argue, sometimes to the point of physical aggression on both sides.

> She said, "My mother couldn't understand that I was from the hood. I'm not African! I never lived there! I was born here! This is all I know (family psychopolitics)!

Within months after moving to the family's new home, Elsie, now 11, developed symptoms from a tumor and underwent brain surgery. She appeared to make a nearly complete recovery, other than some mild tremors on one side of her body that remained after the surgery. Within a year, she was suicidal. She was also entering puberty. I did an internet search of her diagnosis and found some pioneers working with the rare condition. They warned of mental health risks and recommended follow-up and assessment for mood disorders. I noticed her tremors were more pronounced when she spoke of painful experiences (whole body). She lived through some very dark times with courage and resilience. I complimented her on her heroic efforts in the face of great odds (validation).

The relationship with her mother continued to deteriorate beyond middle school. Elsie took refuge with friends and developed close confidants in high school and college. She kept in touch with her high school friends and was good at making friends and attracting boyfriends. It was at this point she had her first baby. She and the father hoped to marry, but both had emotional outbursts that became so extreme neighbors would call the police (trauma triggers). Elsie spoke with great pain about the fact that one of these encounters led to the arrest of her boyfriend, and ultimately, some jail time. She felt responsible. She grieved that relationship as the only one in which she ever really felt understood (loss of attunement).

I reflected on her genogram and reminded her that her second brother had been violent and abusive to her during the long hours of babysitting. I explained the effects of such violence, even though he was just an adolescent. In her childhood mind (explicit memory) he was just a mean brother looking for trouble after school. However, as we filled in trauma-related details, she began to see the connections between her current affective states and the experiences she had with her brother (triggers, attachment). The role of adrenaline was especially relevant to explain (psychoeducation). When the body goes into high gear from an unexpected assault, there is a drug reaction that goes unnoticed in a child's awareness, but becomes a triggered pattern after repeated episodes. With her brother, she fought back in futility. Once she encountered conflict with boyfriends, it was easy to have the "fight trigger" go off.

About this time, her mother got a new job in a bigger city and encouraged Elsie to move with her. She was hesitant to go, given their strained relationship. Her mother was persuasive. For the second time, she was all alone with only her mother for support. She enrolled in the community college and found a part-time job. However, an auto accident led to lack of transportation, which led to job loss. It was at this point she lost custody of her daughter.

Her mother told her to leave her house because she was taking her daughter to friends' houses after school and staying out late

(SEEKING, attachment). After leaving the house, she stayed with friends and visited her daughter every day when her college classes were over (resilience, heroism). She was devastated when she received a summons to attend a hearing. Her mother was seeking legal guardianship of her daughter. She was shocked, intimidated, depressed, and couldn't bring herself to attend (attachment injury, 3Ds; HPA axis, PANIC/GRIEF). I continued to insert trauma and attachment narratives to the story.

> I'm sorry things went so badly with your mother. It must have been hard to need her support, but at the same time, be at an age where you needed your independence, too (dilemma, systemic empathy). Don't be too hard on yourself for not going to the court hearing. From the things you've already told me, it sounds like you had a series of traumas that were weighing you down. It's understandable that you were alone, with no family support, depressed because you didn't have any friends you could count on, and exploited by the people on the street who did show up (systemic empathy, heightening, restorying).

She described a dark time. In addition to the shock of the court summons, she remembered a deeply painful event, in which she was homeless and penniless. Her mother agreed to meet and talk. At the restaurant, she watched while her mother ordered food for herself, never offering anything to Elsie (attachment injury, RAGE, PANIC/GRIEF). This led to the cut off, in which Elsie stopped communicating with her mother and visiting her daughter. She fought back tears as she told the story.

This story was particularly poignant. After learning about implicit memory as a "compost heap," I didn't need to worry about the actual facts or another's perceptions. What activates in the body is purely phenomenological. Elsie was caught between longing for inclusion and understanding, but feeling deep pain from these betrayals. In trauma work, developing experiences of protection and safety is the first step toward recovery (survival). I asked if she would like to be able to protect herself from her mother's betrayals so that she couldn't get to her. "Yes!"

The Plot Thickens

We began a review of her family information, looking for ways that Elsie could develop protective strategies. It seemed like it was time to meet the tribe and enhance the story with information she missed because of the large age difference between siblings. Elsie was deeply depressed at not having access to the rest of her family. It was clear that her rage at her mother was a combination of the 3Ds. She assured me that contact with her mother was not an option. I agreed. There were too many possibilities for retraumatizing Elsie. The cultural shame over counseling was also too much for her to bear. She knew her mother couldn't save face in a counseling environment and she was a proud woman.

However, her nonviolent brother, Samuel, and his wife lived in a large, modern city. He had a government job. Regardless of his cultural script, he was assimilated enough that he married an African American woman. Family psychopolitics placed him in a position of trust and credibility, since he was the oldest male child. I could speak indirectly to her mother through this favored son. Elsie still hoped that he could learn to understand her. "What about a Skype session with Samuel over the internet?" She agreed to ask and he agreed to meet. I was worried about Elsie's vulnerability with an older sibling, so I emailed an agenda and ground rules for the meeting. The purpose of the meeting was to get Samuel's help in completing Elsie's life story. There were insights he had about her mother and about life when she was a child. After all, he was the father figure. The only ground rule was that we were there to get information about the family and reflect on her history, not to discuss her current difficulties. Samuel agreed and we met three times.

Elsie learned a lot about her family that she didn't know. From listening to Samuel's telling of the family's violent history, it was clear that her mother had moderate to severe trauma symptoms from apartheid and the domestic violence. At times, her strong emotions were unpredictable and puzzling to those around her.

By this time, I hoped that Samuel would be describing the process to his mother, but it was best not to openly acknowledge this, given the stigma that existed about counseling. During the meetings in which we reviewed Elsie's history, there were many opportunities to illustrate some of her dilemmas for Samuel.

> Were you aware of how much she missed you? I imagine it was difficult for your mother to be far away from you, too. Have you heard much recently about how those brain surgeries affect a child's emotions? I understand Elsie had some hard times afterward. I imagine that was really tough for your mother, too.

I also emailed him a PowerPoint presentation on trauma, and a list of nodal events in Elsie's life, taking care to avoid criticizing anyone, but stating the facts, including her suicidality after surgery. With no comment, criticism, or interpretation, the facts spoke for themselves.

Suspense

Samuel shared his perceptions of how traditional his mother was and how he had to draw some boundaries with her. It was helpful for Elsie to hear this, even though he enjoyed more status as a male and she never expected to have the same respect.

> During the third session with Samuel, I made a process error. By this time, information was flowing freely between Elsie and Samuel. I thought of this as progress and began to relax. Then, Samuel began to lecture Elsie about something and she abruptly got up and left the room. She was having an acute trauma reaction and I had not safeguarded her from it. By the time I concluded the meeting with Samuel and found her outside, she was smoking, holding back tears, and pacing.

That day, intergenerational trauma produced very extreme symptoms in the current generation. Careful timing and pacing of emotional content is very important. Some might say this is a reason to avoid family therapy. However, the eventual turning point for Elsie's mental health came in a later family therapy session.

> In the meantime, I took <u>full responsibility</u> for allowing a conversation that triggered her pain and explained how her trauma symptoms were not a weakness. In fact, they were a red flag signaling how much she had endured and how complicated her pain was (affirmation; van der Kolk, 2009). It was extremely important to have a narrative for her symptoms that would not shame her. I apologized for not anticipating the risks with Samuel (validation of her pain; attachment repair). Elsie was generous in forgiving me.

In this experience I saw sudden flashes of emotion as symptoms, not "temper." Since then, I have opted for a longer go-between process in cases of intergenerational trauma when there have been cut-offs. Had I met with Samuel individually, I could have monitored his affective state and assessed his potential for empathy and learning new skills. Subsequent to this session, I obtained Elsie's permission to meet with Samuel without her and report back. After two more meetings, he confided his own sense of burden in the family. As the oldest son, he had the weight of the world on his shoulders. In addition to his mother calling and needing support regarding Elsie, a younger brother was in some trouble. His wife and son needed time with him. He was stretched thin and exhausted. His lecture to Elsie was about more than just her. I could see he was too distraught to learn empathy or problem-solving under so much stress (HPA axis). I thanked him for his time and sympathized with his dilemmas. Little did I know that some other help was just around the corner . . .

Shortly before she delivered her baby, an aunt telephoned, urging her to change the chosen name for the baby. It was not from their tribe and she was concerned it might originate with an enemy tribe. Elsie took this as an all out assault on her autonomy. She was enraged. She was certain her mother had prompted the aunt to call. She expressed anger, outrage, and betrayal to her aunt. I could see empowerment in her anger and validated her right to be upset. Repeated validations without problem-solving was important as this point. Without supporting her sense of entitlement, I would run the risk of being too much like family, in which she felt her anger was never understood. Also, there was a physiological component to her anger. Validating her feelings increased her sense of entitlement. In her case, where silence was expected as a sign of respect, I wanted her to have the <u>release of entitlement</u> for her body, something she could savor and relish (see RT, Chapter 7).

Transformation

Elsie gave birth to her baby and proudly gave her the name she had researched months earlier. While she was still in the hospital, her mother came to visit. She brought gifts and money. She brought good wishes from other family members. This was a grandmother who was terrified that she would be cut off from her granddaughter (the tribe, transformation). She sprang into action and began visiting each week so Elsie's oldest daughter could see the new baby. Elsie gained new power as she lived with friends and allowed her mother to visit. She realized she had leverage in the relationship through this baby and planned how to protect herself from any further betrayal from her mother (survival).

Her childhood powerlessness was giving way to a new awareness of her options (transformation). She submitted a request to the court for expanded visitation with her older daughter and she began to explore the possibility of a new start with a friend in another state who had a job for her. Her sense of betrayal and distrust of her mother's overtures continued to motivate her toward independence, but she was tolerating conversations with her mother for the first time in over a year. At the same time, she could tell her mother was being very careful. She was changing. During a holiday visit at her mother's house, her cousin, Albert, visited. She described Albert as removed from the family, involved in entrepreneurial activities, and "cool."

I'm ashamed to admit, as a "die-hard" family therapist, during our discussions of her genogram, I failed to notice that the oldest cousin in her mother's clan was only 50 miles away. This is the type of tribe member that deserves exploration. Often, those who are removed from the day-to-day dramas of the nuclear family have a helpful outsider's view. This person's perspective, coupled with their history inside the family, can often provide important insight to someone who feels disenfranchised. In this case, he was oldest of the cousins and Elsie was youngest. The wisdom of the elders was about to come forth.

I didn't want to repeat a painful experience, like that with Samuel, so I took some time to explore exactly who Albert was and what Elsie thought about him. Four conversations planted seeds, explored, and suggested that a meeting with Albert might be helpful. After the trauma with Samuel, it was important for me to walk through an agenda that would guarantee her safety. She was comfortable with Albert and didn't have the same triggers as she did with Samuel. During the fourth conversation, she felt strong enough to explore this suggestion.

Albert was very reluctant to meet with us. According to Elsie, he gruffly asked, "What are you doin' hanging around this white lady? Is she some kind of phony crusader?" Elsie reassured him that I was different than that. She mentioned the family's history and her life story. Family is family. If it meant that much to her, he would do it for her. In a 90-minute session, Albert provided more therapy for Elsie than ten individual sessions, combined. The most dramatic moments came as he gave her his take on his mother, her mother, and the uncles in the clan. Shaking his head, "didn't you know that we gave up listening to these drama queens years ago! We know we can't get the straight story from them. They exaggerate everything! If I want to know something, I go to my dad or Uncle Henry. I can't trust a thing they say."

Elsie was stunned. Her mother didn't have as much power as she thought. Albert's candor took the lid off her mother's traditional world and the isolation Elsie felt as a "prisoner of war." She was free! She had no idea how much empathy this far-away family member could have. The next moment of drama came as he gave his impressions of Samuel. "Samuel is so tied up in knots. He had a childhood of living through the trauma of your parents' violence. He hasn't even begun to deal with his shit." Elsie giggled. Was this her brother, her former protector? Mother's senior advisor? Her childhood mind would have never thought of him in this way. As the oldest cousin, Albert had a perspective more powerful than any therapist. Indeed, his perspective led to some of his alienation in the family. But for Elsie, it was a breath of fresh air. Literally. Her body relaxed and she couldn't stop giggling.

Her system was discharging the energy she stored from being frozen in the war zone with her mother's traumas. As a child, she was unable to escape the lack of attunement. The only ways she knew how to signal distress were with unacceptable behavior. This new perspective took away her shame. I couldn't have scripted a better dialogue. I was prepared to intervene if Albert became critical. Instead, he was fatherly, gave her advice, and laughed about memories of her as a little girl. He said she was never as happy as when she had the whole extended family around her. She hated to be alone. He helped me understand how profound the losses were for Elsie when she first moved away from her tribe.

From this point on, Elsie's perceptions of her mother continued to change. Over the next six months, while she continued to live with friends, she became assertive and defended her decision to seek counseling. She guarded her baby closely and watched for any sign that her mother might betray her again or allege any parenting weaknesses. I affirmed these as healthy defensive and protective measures that kept her calm in the face of danger. She declared her interest in moving out of state to find new opportunities. As this became a serious reality, she received a letter from her mother.

Written in beautiful prose were the reflections of a remorseful mother. There were tender memories from Elsie's childhood, the angst of wondering how things got off track after her brain surgery, declarations of love, and a commitment to work on the barriers, "piece by piece, and however long it takes . . . I believe it's never too late," she wrote. After 12 heart-wrenching years, a mother extends the olive branch.

Elsie had mixed feelings, but she felt ready to return to her mother's home "temporarily," with the understanding she would still see her counselor and she would still explore new places to live. Her coherent narrative now included the effect of her traumas, her mother's traumas, what works as a recovery process for her (protection and defense), and Albert's insights about her immediate family. By this time, her oldest daughter was 11, her baby, 15 months. The family moved a third time for another job opportunity. Elsie wrote to say she was back in school taking computer classes and liked the big city environment.

CONTENT, PROCESS AND SUBSTANCE

Elsie's experience of pain was clearly focused on family relationships. The content of this case includes the experiences that Elsie shared as she constructed her autobiography and themes from Elsie's attachment history entwined with the sequence of traumas that peppered her growth into adulthood. These themes were provided by the therapist. In the past five years, when I have identified trauma symptoms and experiences, I have never had a client who rejected the possibility that trauma was part of their problem, even when it was not their description of the presenting problem. When the information is there, it's an easy "sell" and I have never had a client who didn't find relief in naming this reality.

Therapeutic process began as an intermittent blend of case management and restorying with the elements of Elsie's heroism, determination, and commitment to children and family. It evolved into sessions of psychoeducation about trauma symptoms in the moment. Given the tremendous cultural stigma for stereotypic counseling, it was very important to mix activities that matched Elsie's affect on a given day. There were weeks, even a few months when we did not meet. Without closing the case, contact balanced her initiation and my outreach. This is when case management activities are a critical component for facilitating a long enough process for deeper parts of the healing to take place. As time went on, it was comfortable to attend to the substance of Elsie's traumas, bringing in attention to the felt sense during times of joy, insight, and achievement. At the time, I was not certified to provide more indepth SE, so I encouraged protection and defense as a way of respecting the attachment vulnerabilities that need physical protection.

The influence of the tribe is a confluence of content, process, and substance. History deserves new recognition in clinical process (Hanna, 1997). So-called "psychosocials" are forms that bureaucracies advance as their best effort at capturing context. Brain-informed intake processes are merely a form away! As mesmerizing as these become for entry-level and experienced clinicians alike, they do not capture the cultural histories, traditions, or family resources that are likely to exist. In their absence, families of choice and networks of belonging may be as close as the waiting room! As a way of accessing implicit and explicit memory, the exploration of social networks is a critical part of the process. Those who receive help from attending Alcoholics Anonymous (AA) groups are recipients of these benefits. However, when they do not lead to interpersonal healing, participants may remain fragmented, neurologically.

As a revision of current agency documents, client background data can focus on survival histories and those who have provided secure attachment. "Who cares about you?" "With whom do you feel safe?" If there is no one, "With whom do you feel most safe?" The survival questions at the beginning of Chapter 4 provide a menu of interpersonal information that has somatic implications. Also, circular questions can quickly pinpoint nodal points of history.

Has it always been this way?

When did things change?

What was happening around that time?

These lead to treatment plans that honor the importance of explicit memory on the way to accessing important parts of implicit memory. These revisions don't require practitioners or administrative staff to have a complicated understanding of neuroscience. Instead, they provide a different emphasis that allows an understanding of symptoms in the context of survival, attachment, and affective circuits. As these elements become part of the client's dominant story, it expands into a coherent narrative that includes all levels of functioning. Table 8.1 is a cumulative outline of whole body principles and approaches integrated with the tasks of therapy sessions. Now, as we turn our attention to the challenges of substance abuse treatment in America, these paradigm shifts stretch the outer reaches of our conscious imagination, and institutional histories that rest on the same universal survival needs as individuals.

SUBSTANCE ABUSE TREATMENT: A PROPOSAL FOR PROGRAM DEVELOPMENT

The community of substance abuse treatment services is a tribe. There is a distinct culture that has evolved, just like our prehistoric ancestors who roamed the earth looking for safety, protection, and food. In 1935, explorers wandered out of a jungle, weakened by existing strategies of survival that were leading them toward the edge of extinction. Through faith in God, themselves, and ingenuity, Bill W. led them into a tribal adaptation that came to be known as Alcoholics Anonymous (AA). First, AA was an encampment on the edge of American civilization. Some heard about it and passed through out of curiosity. Others came, stayed, and put down roots in this place that seemed like an oasis in their personal deserts. The movement

Table 8.1 Integration of principles and processes

Process	Primary Focus	Relevant Instruments/ Techniques
Therapist preparation	Self of the therapist, affective activation, survival history.	Felt sense exercises, grounding, resourcing.
Initial contact	Speak to the amygdala; Attune to attachment needs; Tranquility and hope; Negotiate a tangible plan.	Host and Hostess; Credible facilitator.
Engagement	Continued attunement to attachment; Gendered engagement; Parent engagement; Attune to trauma, affect & trust; Acknowledge unspeakable dilemmas.	Easel—diagrams, lists; Parental reconnection; Motivational interviewing; Empathic conjecture; Mindfulness.
Assessment	Social support—Who is the tribe? Trauma occurrence and symptoms; Affective tolerance; Love and trustworthiness; Core dynamics; 7Ds; Intergenerational losses; Major transitions.	Berkman & Syme Scale; PCL-Civilian; RES; Table 5.2 Survey Stories; Clean questions; SE basics; Pendulation; Genograms; Timelines.
Mapping interpersonal terrain	Pain and peace cycles; Mapping interactional cycles (the dance); Pursuit-distance; Deconstructing influence of the tribe.	Genograms; Sequence questions; Influence questions.
Accessing memory and triggers	Survival narratives; Exploring the dominant story.	Survival questions; Timelines; Drawing with non-dominant hand; SE basics, pendulation.

Accessing primary emotion	RT; Heightening; Tolerating cycles of arousals; Exploring 7Ds.	Checklist of 7Ds; SE basics, pendulation; Empathic conjecture.
Creating new circuits	Realign messages and needs with generations; Access resilience; Highlight safety, defense, protection; Facilitate self-healing; Integrate trauma.	Entitlement narratives; Enactments; VCR; Rechannel rage; Restorying; MFG; Metaphors of ancestors, babies & animals; Matchmaking; Drawing with non-dominant hand; Nostril breathing; Mindfulness; SE basics; Grief and loss rituals.
Enhancing transformation	Assemble the tribe; Facilitate compensation and entitlements; Facilitate celebrations of transformation; Grief and loss rituals.	"I want" exercise; Celebrate survivor's pride; SE basics; Invoke spirit of adventure; Invoke spirit of ancestors.

grew exponentially, remaining a peer-led, mutual help, world-wide "fellowship" of men and women. There was no money exchanged. "Recovery, unity, and service" was their creed. Although the primary influence was a religious group, it claims no denomination and mentions God as an individual's personal concept of a higher power.

In the early years, the AA *disease model* of alcoholism met with resistance from other tribes, such as the mental health establishment of the day. Ironically, neuroscientists now consider substance impact on the brain as just that, a disease. Who knew? Back then, a number of psychotherapists like myself considered

AA nothing more than the trading of one addiction for another. Neurobiologically, Panksepp (2011) suggests that attachment is the ultimate addiction. Who knew? One of the ironies regarding disease model debates is that trauma specialists think of trauma as "physiology, not pathology" (Levine, 1997). For those who are not comfortable with the disease model, a focus on physiology may provide a middle ground. No one can argue with the physiology of addiction.

Thus, the grassroots movement that has created communities all over the world continues to flourish in its own right. However, the success of AA led to other tribes of the day becoming jealous of that success. These tribes have other creeds. As dominant professional tribes intermarried with the original model, they hijacked the original creed and developed variant strains of the fellowship. Now, substance abuse treatment services employ countless professionals who are tied to monetary systems, from tax dollars to upscale private fees. Recovery has turned into a mandate. Unity has turned into institutionalized forms of confrontation. Service has turned into professional education and salaries. Where have all the flowers gone? Thus is the story of civilization.

However, all is not lost. As Chapter 1 described, principles of neuroscience hold the potential to unify disparate approaches and to help us benefit from the best of both worlds. AA is not effective with everyone and neither are the evidence-based models that exist in a few centers of excellence. Both camps developed without any brain science behind them. Thus, the following is a flight of fancy as to how the transparent brain can guide the development of more effective substance abuse programs. From current literature, the following is a brief proposal.

Think Whole Body

The physiology of addiction is described in detail by Maté (2010) and Panksepp (2011) from the perspective of affective neuroscience. Briefly, there are differences between the effects of stimulants (cocaine, amphetamines) and opiates (heroin, morphine, pain-killers). Somatic interventions should consider the fact that opiates lead to pleasure, relaxation, and bonding with the substance itself (CARE). Stimulants lead to the expectation of additional social, sexual, or other environmental rewards (SEEKING). Many who are addicted to stimulants report a dislike for the actual effect. The differences between these mechanisms can lead to program enhancements, based on drug of choice.

The binding process of both types of drugs is also important to know. Prior to addiction, research shows lower numbers of dopamine receptors in the body. This suggests an inability of the body to benefit from natural endorphin (CARE) and dopamine (SEEKING) surges during normal activity. Then, as addiction sets in, receptors actually decrease further, leaving a greater need for the substance as a substitute. Thus, depending on the drug of choice, the body's need for relaxation or social reward could be the first element in treatment. As a moment of temporary insanity, consider the following questions: Based on the physiology of reward centers, what would happen if treatment involved spas with holistic approaches to healing? What if addicts had whirlpool baths, massage, or even small steps like pedicures and manicures for those with primary trauma symptoms? What other substances might a recovering person bond with? There may be foods, incense, oils, lotions, etc. What resiliencies can be celebrated immediately to enhance social rewards and status? The repetition of praise is equal to money and can compensate for a lack of naturally occurring dopamine.

Think Survival

Maté (2010) cites research about how opioid and dopamine receptors decrease prior to addictions. Bottom line: the 7Ds. Thus, what addicts really want is attachment, a tribe, and the joy of numinosum (SEEKING, CARE, & PLAY). These are pre-requisites for survival. Some of this explains AA's success with so many people. However, with the growing numbers of those with co-morbidity, trauma-informed thinking leads us to consider low-key practices such as MFGs integrated with holistic and somantic approaches. Since cocaine can impair frontal lobe functioning from one year to permanently, it would seem useful to provide a community frontal lobe along with somatic sources of soothing and pleasure that can rebuild SEEKING, CARE, and PLAY circuits.

If treatment was reframed as "protection," how would this look? Perhaps each addict would receive a welcome from the host or hostess who runs a "safe house" where they can rest from the battle. If they landed in the Land of Oz, perhaps there would be people to shine their shoes and give them respite from the storms. After all, these are heros coming in from the battles of losses, traumas, and triggers. However, our war heros from recent military assignments find that a hero's welcome is not enough. Even the celebrity addictions centers lack a full, cutting-edge interdisciplinary approach. The social environment must attune to deeper needs. Perhaps a little soul food is in order.

Think Attachment

The case examples throughout this book provide the range of healing possibilities that await drug abusers, if only their treatment facilities could provide them. From rituals that help to heal tragic losses, to conversations that claim or reclaim love, belonging and identity, these would not cost a single penny more to implement. After initial training, they may actually reduce costs. The tribe of origin can have powerful healers. These are overlooked in traditional treatment. A large part of the brain stays attached to its roots. When family of origin is not an option, extended family often contains viable resources that go unnoticed. These relationships already exist as circuits in the brain. The longing for attachment repairs and making things right can provide all family members with more of what they each deserve, not the addict alone.

Think Circuits

The associations that formed during a person's life story include moments of triumph and tragedy. These may be triggers of relapse or hidden clues to a better recovery. Addressing addictions in the context of a complete life story provides opportunities to discover naturally existing resources for recovery and relapse prevention. When substance abuse is secondary to trauma, it is insanity not to address the trauma in concrete, coordinated ways.

Think Transformation

The concept of numinosum can lead us into a sense of wonder about the inconquerable human spirit. Do those in recovery see themselves as creative artists? As important contributors in the drama of life? Can we provide them with a safe place to explore the ultimate? To allow their fondest hopes to be spoken like an exciting adventure? What myths and metaphors move them? What inspires them? What avenues for self-expression help to define and redefine their identities?

WHEN SPA MEETS TRIBE

In all organizational transitions, there are steps that increase the likelihood that changes will achieve desired results and become sustainable. All change must promise some improvement in the workplace (dopamine). Focus groups and needs assessments often provide the content (rationale) needed to explain new initiatives. Without the expectancy that a change will make someone's life better (survival, dopamine), there is little chance of support. However, once these assessments provide the language and context for change, everyone can become interested (SEEKING).

The fellowship model of AA promotes peer support. Thus, many former addicts become drug counselors. The new tribe that formed when AA met up with institutions consisted of a culture of drug counselors who promoted the importance of staff being former addicts. Conceptually, they learned from an experiential model of practice. Participants are led through a certain experience with modeling and demonstration. Then, they move on to apply this experiential learning to their trade. However, this mixed the fellowship model with economics, something that Bill W. deliberately avoided.

Learning opportunities emerge when the current generation of staff become stressed from the new generation of meth addicts and those with co-morbid trauma symptoms. The physiology of these conditions is foreign to the experience of some. However, since this experiential model has promoted the importance of individual experience as a vehicle to learn new skills, why not provide whole body staff education and free whole body services in the work-place? One only need to go to the nearest shopping mall to find massage therapists providing massage chairs and 15-minute sessions. The cost of employing professionals who are certified in the healing arts would be minimal, compared to the collection of licensed staff required for the certification of many facilities.

As a first step, providing these minimal services to staff would begin the whole body campaign in a revolutionary, but noncon-troversial way. Given caseload stresses for most staff, holistic staff development could provide encouragement for stress manage-ment that would be beneficial at home and work. This would begin the education process in a low demand way. As responses to these human resource initiatives became part of a dialogue toward change, additional steps and formal training could occur. From this, program components could evolve.

As the workplace in America continues to diversify, it should also be noted that many cultures who immigrate to America value and embrace a number of holistic practices and already embrace the collective intelligence of the body. They just have never had their native beliefs affirmed in the workplace! As workplaces look for loyalty, commitment, and productivity, perhaps these ideas can foster tribes at work, in addition to those at home.

ONE FINAL PAUSE

It is intentional that a book like this would end with ideas that some will think outlandish. However, they are part of novelty and numinosum during the journey. Just food for thought and a moment of pause to think outside the box. Perhaps some will consider them on a rainy day, and still others might sit back and take a few deep breaths. Please join me for a final moment to let our bodies speak. Close your eyes, take a few deep breaths, and see how these ideas feel in your body. What comes up? Is there a particular area of distress or comfort? Choose one spot and focus on it. Keep your mind focused on that spot and just see what happens. As you focus on it, whether you chose a place of distress or a place of comfort, note your breathing. Let your focus stay long enough so that you really give it a place. There may be sensations, colors, textures, thoughts, or stories that come up. These are worth noting. If you chose a place of distress and your body says, "enough," then move your focus to a comfortable place or look around the room and find something pleasant to watch. Regardless of your response at this moment—if you took a moment to let your body speak, you're on your way! Best wishes as the whole body guides you toward your place in history, your place in the tribe.

Appendix A
Berkman-Syme Social Network Index (SNI)

PhenX Toolkit Supplemental Information
Domain: Social Environments
Release Date: October 8, 2010
Social Support

	About the Measure
Domain	Social Environments
Measure	Social Support
Definition	This measure is a questionnaire to assess the type, size, closeness, and frequency of contacts in a respondent's current social network. In contrast to the Social Networks measure which captures each network member, this measure allows researchers to categorize individuals based on social connectedness and can highlight those at risk for social isolation.

About the Protocol

Description of Protocol

The Berkman-Syme Social Network Index (SNI) is a self-reported questionnaire for use in adults aged 18–64 years old that is a composite measure of four types of social connections: marital status (married vs. not); sociability (number and frequency of contacts with children, close relatives, and close friends); church group membership (yes vs. no); and membership in other community organizations (yes vs. no). SNI allows researchers to categorize individuals into four levels of social connection: socially isolated (individuals with low intimate contacts—not married, fewer than six friends or relatives, and no membership in either church or community groups), moderately isolated, moderately integrated, and socially integrated.

Protocol text

The following two-page questionnaire asks about your social support. Please read the following questions and circle the response that most closely describes your <u>current</u> situation.

1. How many *close friends* do you have, people that you feel at ease with, can talk to about private matters?
[ ] 0 None
[ ] 1 1 or 2
[ ] 2 3 to 5
[ ] 3 6 to 9
[ ] 4 10 or more
[ ] 9 Unknown

2. How many of these *close friends* do you see at least once a month?
[ ] 0 None
[ ] 1 1 or 2
[ ] 2 3 to 5
[ ] 3 6 to 9
[ ] 4 10 or more
[ ] 9 Unknown

3. How many *relatives* do you have, people that you feel at ease with, can talk to about private matters?
[ ] 0 None
[ ] 1 1 or 2
[ ] 2 3 to 5
[ ] 3 6 to 9
[ ] 4 10 or more
[ ] 9 Unknown

4. How many of these *relatives* do you see at least once a month?

[ ] 0 None

[ ] 1 1 or 2

[ ] 2 3 to 5

[ ] 3 6 to 9

[ ] 4 10 or more

[ ] 9 Unknown

5. Do you participate in any groups, such as a senior center, social or work group, religious-connected group, self-help group, or charity, public service, or community group?

[ ] 0 No

[ ] 1 Yes

[ ] 9 Unknown

6. About how often do you go to religious meetings or services?

[ ] 0 Never or almost never

[ ] 1 Once or twice a year

[ ] 2 Every few months

[ ] 3 Once or twice a month

[ ] 4 Once a week

[ ] 5 More than once a week

[ ] 9 Unknown

7. Is there someone available to you whom you can count on to listen to you when you need to talk?

[ ] 0 None

[ ] 1 1 or 2

[ ] 2 3 to 5

[ ] 3 6 to 9

[ ] 4 10 or more

[ ] 9 Unknown

8. Is there someone available to give you good advice about a problem?

[ ] 0 None

[ ] 1 1 or 2

[ ] 2 3 to 5

[ ] 3 6 to 9

[ ] 4 10 or more

[ ] 9 Unknown

9. Is there someone available to you who shows you love and affection?

[ ] 0 None

[ ] 1 1 or 2

[ ] 2 3 to 5

[ ] 3 6 to 9

[ ] 4 10 or more

[ ] 9 Unknown

10. Can you count on anyone to provide you with emotional support (talking over problems or helping you make a difficult decision)?

[ ] 0 None

[ ] 1 1 or 2

[ ] 2 3 to 5

[ ] 3 6 to 9

[ ] 4 10 or more

[ ] 9 Unknown

11. Do you have as much contact as you would like with someone you feel close to, someone in whom you can trust and confide?

[ ] 0 None

[ ] 1 1 or 2

[ ] 2 3 to 5

[ ] 3 6 to 9

[ ] 4 10 or more

[ ] 9 Unknown

Scoring Instructions:

Loucks et al. (2006) scored as follows: Married (no = 0; yes = 1); close friends and relatives (0–2 friends and 0–2 relatives = 0; all other scores = 1); group participation (no = 0; yes = 1); participation in religious meetings or services (less than or equal to every few months = 0; greater than or equal to once or twice a month = 1). The latter two categories were mutually exclusive from each other. Scores were summed: 0 or 1 being the most isolated category; and 2, 3, or 4 formed the other three categories of increasing social connectedness.

Psychometrics on the Berkman-Syme Social Network Index (SNI) and additional evidence for the scale's predictive validity are available in Berkman & Breslow (1983).

Participant	Adults, aged 20–65 years old
Source	U.S. Department of Health and Human Services; National Institutes of Health; National Heart, Lung and Blood Institute; and Boston University. (YYYY). Framingham Heart Study (FHS), Exam 27. Berkman-Syme Social Network Questionnaire, Part I and Part II, questions 1–6, 9–13 (questions 7–11).
Language of Source	English
Personnel and Training Required	None
Equipment Needs	The respondent will need a copy of the questionnaire.
Protocol Type	Self-administered questionnaire
General References	Berkman, L. F., Blumenthal, J., Burg, M., Carney, R. M., Catellier, D., Cowan, M. J., Czajkowski, S. M., DeBusk, R., Hosking, J., Jaffe, A., Kaufmann, P. G., Mitchell, P., Norman, J., Powell, L. H., Raczynski, J. M., & Schneiderman, N.; Enhancing Recovery in Coronary Heart Disease Patients Investigators (ENRICHD) (2003). Effects of treating depression and low-perceived social support on clinical events after myocardial infarction: The enhancing recovery in coronary heart disease patients (ENRICHD) randomized trial. *Journal of the American Medical Association, 289*(23), 2106–3116.
	Berkman, L. F. & L. Breslow (1983) *Health and ways of living.* New York, NY: Oxford University Press.
	Berkman, L. F. & Syme, S. L. (1979). Social networks, host resistance, and mortality: A nine-year follow-up of Alameda county residents. *American Journal of Epidemiology, 109,* 186–204.
	Biordi, D. L. & Nicholson, N. R. (2008). Social isolation. In P. D. Larsen & I. M. Lubkin (Eds.), *Chronic illness: impact and intervention* (7th ed.; pp. 85–117). Boston: Jones and Bartlett.
	Brissette, I., Cohen, S., & Seeman, T. (2000). Measuring social integration and social network. In S. Cohen, L. Underwood, & B. Gottlieb (Eds.), *Social support measurement and interventions: A handbook for health and social scientists* (pp. 53–85). New York: Oxford University Press.

Kawachi, I., Colditz, G. A., Ascherio, A., Rimm, E. B., Giovannucci, E., Stampfer, M. J., & Willett, W. C. (1996). A prospective study of social networks in relation to total mortality and cardiovascular disease in men in the USA. *Journal of Epidemiology and Community Health, 50,* 245–251.

Loucks, E., Sullivan, L., D'Agostino, R., Larson, M., Berkman, L., & Benjamin, E. (2006). Social networks and inflammatory markers in the Framingham Heart Study. *Journal of Biosocial Science, 38*(6), 835–842.

Lubben, J. & Gironda, M. (2004). Measuring social networks and assessing their benefits. In C. Phillipson, G. Allan, & D. H. J. Morgan (Eds.), *Social networks and social exclusion: sociological and policy perspectives* (pp. 20–35). Hampshire, United Kingdom: Ashgate.

Michael, Y., Colditz, G., Coakley, E., & Kawachi, I. (1999). Health behaviors, social networks, and healthy aging: Cross-sectional evidence from the Nurses' Health Study. *Quality of Life Research, 8,* 711–722.

Appendix B
Checklist of
Experiences (CE)

☐ war
☐ racism
☐ cultural wounding
☐ persecution
☐ gender discrimination
☐ class discrimination
☐ sexual orientation discrimination
☐ natural disasters
☐ incarceration
☐ homicides
☐ assaults
☐ immigration
☐ auto accidents
☐ falls
☐ medical procedures

☐ life-threatening illnesses
☐ chronic pain
☐ losses
☐ drowning

☐ suffocation
☐ childhood abuse & neglect
☐ foster placements
☐ sexual abuse
☐ domestic violence
☐ rape
☐ bullying
☐ being lost
☐ animal attacks
☐ failure to meet others' expectations
☐ death of important family member
☐ teacher/school relationships
☐ peer or romantic rejection
☐ internet violence & exploitation
Type of Shock (can be part of any experience)
☐ high impact
☐ inescapable attack
☐ physical injury

Appendix C
Post-traumatic Stress Checklist (PCL)

Weathers, F.W., Huska, J.A., Keane, T.M. *PCL-C for DSM-IV*. Boston: National Center for PTSD—Behavioral Science Division, 1991.
This is a government document in the public domain.

INSTRUCTIONS: Below is a list of problems and complaints that people sometimes have in response to stressful experiences. Please read each one carefully, circle the number to indicate how much you have been bothered by that problem in the past month.

1. Repeated, disturbing *memories, thoughts,* or *images* of a stressful experience?
   1. Not at all   2. A little bit   3. Moderately   4. Quite a bit   5. Extremely
2. Repeated, disturbing *dreams* of a stressful experience?
   1. Not at all   2. A little bit   3. Moderately   4. Quite a bit   5. Extremely
3. Suddenly *acting* or *feeling* as if a stressful experience *were happening again* (as if you were reliving it)?
   1. Not at all   2. A little bit   3. Moderately   4. Quite a bit   5. Extremely
4. Feeling *very upset* when *something reminded you* of a stressful experience?
   1. Not at all   2. A little bit   3. Moderately   4. Quite a bit   5. Extremely
5. Having *psychical reactions* (e.g. heart pounding, trouble breathing, sweating) when *something reminded you* of a stressful experience?
   1. Not at all   2. A little bit   3. Moderately   4. Quite a bit   5. Extremely
6. Avoiding *thinking about* or *talking about* a stressful experience or avoiding *having feelings* related to it?
   1. Not at all   2. A little bit   3. Moderately   4. Quite a bit   5. Extremely
7. Avoiding *activities* or *situations* because *they reminded you* of a stressful experience?
   1. Not at all   2. A little bit   3. Moderately   4. Quite a bit   5. Extremely
8. Trouble *remembering important parts* of a stressful experience?
   1. Not at all   2. A little bit   3. Moderately   4. Quite a bit   5. Extremely
9. *Loss of interest* in activities that you used to enjoy?
   1. Not at all   2. A little bit   3. Moderately   4. Quite a bit   5. Extremely
10. Feeling *distant* or *cut off* from other people?
    1. Not at all   2. A little bit   3. Moderately   4. Quite a bit   5. Extremely
11. Feeling *emotionally numb* or being unable to have loving feelings for those close to you?
    1. Not at all   2. A little bit   3. Moderately   4. Quite a bit   5. Extremely
12. Feeling as if your *future* will somehow be *cut short*?
    1. Not at all   2. A little bit   3. Moderately   4. Quite a bit   5. Extremely
13. Trouble *falling* or *staying* asleep?
    1. Not at all   2. A little bit   3. Moderately   4. Quite a bit   5. Extremely
14. Feeling *irritable* or having *angry outbursts*?
    1. Not at all   2. A little bit   3. Moderately   4. Quite a bit   5. Extremely
15. Having *difficulty concentrating*?
    1. Not at all   2. A little bit   3. Moderately   4. Quite a bit   5. Extremely
16. Being *"super-alert"* or watchful or on guard?
    1. Not at all   2. A little bit   3. Moderately   4. Quite a bit   5. Extremely
17. Feeling *jumpy* or easily startled?
    1. Not at all   2. A little bit   3. Moderately   4. Quite a bit   5. Extremely

Appendix D
Relational Ethics Scale (RES)

Name_____ID#_____   **Relational Ethics Scale**

These questions are about some of the emotions in your childhood family and in other current relationships. Since each family is unique, there are no right or wrong answers. Just try to answer as honestly as you can. Please answer as many questions as you can. In reading the following statements, apply them to yourself and your family and then circle the rating that best fits.

5 = STRONGLY AGREE	4 = AGREE	3 = NEITHER AGREE NOR DISAGREE	2 = DISAGREE	1 = STRONGLY DISAGREE

Rate the following statements as they apply to the _family and parent(s) with whom you spent most of your childhood._

						TJ	L	E
1. I could trust my family to seek my best interests.	5	4	3	2	1			
2. Individuals in my family were blamed for problems that were not their fault.	5	4	3	2	1			
3. Pleasing one of my parents often meant displeasing the other.	5	4	3	2	1			
4. I received the love and affection from my family I deserved.	5	4	3	2	1			
5. No matter what happened, I always stood by my family.	5	4	3	2	1			
6. At times, it seemed one or both of my parents disliked me.	5	4	3	2	1			
7. Love and warmth were given equally to all family members.	5	4	3	2	1			
8. At times, I was used by my family unfairly.	5	4	3	2	1			
9. I felt my life was dominated by my parents' desires.	5	4	3	2	1			
10. Individuals in my family were willing to give of themselves to benefit the family.	5	4	3	2	1			
11. I continue to seek closer relationships with my family.	5	4	3	2	1			
12. I often felt deserted by my family.	5	4	3	2	1			

Rate statements 13–24 as they apply to _one important relationship in your life now._ If you are _DIVORCED, SINGLE OR UNMARRIED,_ apply them to your closest relationship, except parents and children.

Circle one: friend, family member, sponsor, work associate, other (list: _____). If you are *MARRIED or have a PARTNER of more than 2 YEARS,* apply them to this relationship. If you are *WIDOWED,* apply them as you can recall to your spouse. In reading the following statements, apply them to yourself and the appropriate relationship and then circle the rating that best fits.

						TJ	L	E
13. I try to meet the emotional needs of this person.	5	4	3	2	1			
14. I do not trust this individual to look out for my best interests.	5	4	3	2	1	☐		
15. When I feel hurt, I say or do hurtful things to this person.	5	4	3	2	1			☐
16. This person stands beside me in times of trouble or joy.	5	4	3	2	1			
17. Before I make important decisions, I ask for the opinions of this person.	5	4	3	2	1			
18. There is unequal contribution to the relationship between me and this individual.	5	4	3	2	1	☐		
19. When I feel angry, I tend to take it out on this person.	5	4	3	2	1			☐
20. We are equal partners in this relationship.	5	4	3	2	1			
21. We give of ourselves to benefit one another.	5	4	3	2	1			
22. I take advantage of this individual.	5	4	3	2	1			☐
23. I am taken for granted or used unfairly in this relationship.	5	4	3	2	1	☐		
24. This person listens to me and values my thoughts.	5	4	3	2	1			

Relational Ethics Scale (RES) Scoring

There are 8 subscales:

1. Vertical total, add items 1-12.
2. Horizontal total, add items 13-24.
3. Vertical Trust/Justice, add the TJ column for items 1-12.
4. Vertical Loyalty, add the L column for items 1-12.
5. Vertical Entitlement, add the E column for items 1-12.
6. Horizontal Trust/Justice, add the TJ column for items 13-24.
7. Horizontal Loyalty, add the L column for items 13-24.
8. Horizontal Entitlement, add the E column for items 13-24.

Begin subscale scoring by transposing REVERSED ITEMS.
REVERSE SCORING is indicated for the DOUBLE BOXES in columns labeled TJ, L, and E.
This can be done by

Using these new numbers: **1 2 3 4 5**
Instead of original numbers: 5 4 3 2 1

Approximate General Population Percentile Norms for Raw Scores

%ile	Vert	Hor	Vert TJ	Vert L	Vert E	Hor TJ	Hor L	Hor E
100	60	60	30	15	15	30	15	15
75	52	53	27	13	12	27	13	12
50	45	47	23	11	10	25	11	10
25	33	36	16	8	7	17	9	8

References

Acevedo, B.P., Aron, A., Fisher, H.E., & Brown, L.L. (2012a). Neural correlates of long-term intense romantic love. *Social Cognition of Affective Neuroscience, 7*(2), 145–59.

Acevedo, B.P., Aron, A., Fisher, H.E., & Brown, L.L. (2012a). Neural correlates of marital satisfaction and well-being: Reward, empathy, and affect. *Clinical Neuropsychiatry: Journal of Treatment Evaluation, 9*, 20–31.

Ader, R. (2007). *Psychoneuroimmunology*. San Diego, CA: Elsevier Academic Press.

Ainsworth, M.S. (1989). Attachments beyond infancy. *American Psychologist, 9*, 709–16.

Ainsworth, M.D.S., Blehar, M.C., Walters, E., & Wall, S. (1978). *Patterns of attachment: A psychological study of the Strange Situation*. In Anonymous, Hillsdale, NJ: Erlbaum.

Alim, T., Charney, D. S., & Mellman, T. (2006). An overview of post traumatic stress disorder in African Americans. *Journal of Clinical Psychology, 9*, 801–13.

Allen-Eckert, H., Fong, E., Nichols, M.P., Watson, N., & Liddle, H.A. (2001). Development of the family therapy enactment rating scale. *FamilyProcess, 40*(4), 469–78.

Amedi, A., Merabet, L.B., Bermpohl, F., & Pascual-Leone, A. (2005). The occipital cortex in the blind: Lessons about plasticity and vision. *Current Directions in Psychological Science, 14*(6), 306–11.

Amen, D.G. (1998). *Change your brain change your life: The break-through program for conquering anxiety, depression, obsessiveness, anger and impulsiveness.* New York: Three Rivers Press.

Amen, D.G. (2002). *Healing the hardware of the soul.* New York: Free Press.

Anderson, C.M. (2000). *The ones we left behind: Family therapy and the treatment of mental illness.* Paper presented at the annual meeting of the American Association for Marriage and Family Therapy. Denver, CO.

Anderson, C., Reiss, D., & Hogarty, G. (1986). *Schizophrenia and the family: A practitioner's guide to psycho-education and management.* New York: Guilford Press.

Andreano, J.M., & Cahill, L. (2009). Sex influences on the neurobiology of learning and memory. *Learning and Memory, 16*(4), 248–66.

Andreano, J.M., & Cahill, L. (2010). Menstrual cycle modulation of medial temporal activity evoked by negative emotion. *Neuroimage, 53*(4), 1286–93.

Arnsten, A.F. (2009). Stress signalling pathways that impair prefrontal cortex structure and function. *Nature Reviews Neuroscience, 10*(6), 410–22.

Atkinson, B. (2005). *Emotional intelligence in couples therapy: Advances from neurobiology and the science of intimate relationships.* New York: W.W. Norton.

Baron-Cohen, S. (2002). The extreme male brain theory of autism. *Trends in Cognitive Sciences, 9* (6), 248–54.

Barraza, J.A., & Zak, P.J. (2009). Empathy toward strangers triggers oxytocin release and subsequent generosity. *Annals of the New York Academy of Science, 9,* 182–9.

Bateson, G. (1972). *Steps to an ecology of mind.* New York: Dutton.

Bateson, G. (1979). *Mind in nature: A necessary unity.* New York: Dutton.

Bateson, G., Jackson, D., Haley J., & Weakland, J. (1956). Toward a theory of schizophrenia. *Behavioral Science, 1*(4), 251–64.

Beauchaine, T. (2001). Vagal tone, development, and Gray's motivational theory: Toward an integrated model of autonomic nervous system functioning in psychopathology. *Development and Psychopathology, 9,* 183–214.

Bechara, A., Damasio, H., & Damasio, A.R. (2000). Emotion, decision making and the orbitofrontal cortex. *Cerebral Cortex, 10*(3), 295–307.

Bechara, A., Damasio, H., & Damasio, A.R. (2003). Role of the amygdala in decision-making. *Annals of the New York Academy of Science, 9,* 356–69.

Bellah, R., Madsen, R., Sullivan, O., Swidler, A., & Tipton, S. (1985). Reaching out. In R. Bellah, R. Madsen, O. Sullivan, A. Swidler, & S. Tipton (Eds.), *Habits of the heart: Individualism and commitment in American life.* New York: Harper & Row.

Berg, I.K., & Dolan, Y.M. (2001). *Tales of solutions: A collection of hope-inspiring stories.* New York: W.W. Norton.

Berkman, L., & Glass, T. (2000). From social integration to health: Durkheim in the new millennium. *Social Science and Medicine, 15*(6), 843–58.

Berkman, L., & Syme, S. (1979). Social networks, host resistance, and mortality: A nine-year followup of alameda county residents. *American Journal of Epidemiology, 9,* 186–204.

Bickart, K.C., Wright, C.I., Dautoff, R.J., Dickerson, B.C., & Barrett, L.F. (2011). Amygdala volume and social network size in humans. *Nature Neuroscience, 9,* 163–4.

Block, R.A., Arnott, D.P., Quigley, B., & Lynch, W.C. (1989). Unilateral nostril breathing influences lateralized cognitive performance. *Brain Cognition, 9,* 181–90.

Blond, B.N., Fredericks, C.A., & Blumberg, H.P. (2012). Functional neuroanatomy of bipolar disorder: Structure, function, and connectivity in an amygdala-anterior paralimbic neural system. *Bipolar Disorders, 9,* 340–55.

Bos, P.A., Terburg, D., & van Honk, J. (2010). Testosterone decreases trust in socially naive humans. *Proceedings of the National Academy of Sciences of the United States of America, 107*(22), 9991–5.

Boszormenyi-Nagy, I., & Krasner, B. (1986). *Between give and take: A clinical guide to contextual therapy.* New York: Brunner/Mazel.

Bowen, M. (1978). *Family therapy in clinical practice.* New York: Aronson.

Bowlby, J. (1944). Forty-four juvenile thieves: Their characters and home lives. *International Journal of Psychoanalysis, 9,* 19–52.

Bowlby, J. (1949). The study and reduction of group tensions in the family. *Human Relations, 9,* 123–8.

Bowlby, J. (1969). *Attachment and loss: Vol. 1. Attachment.* New York: Basic Books.

Bowser, B.P., Word, C.O., Stanton, M.D., & Coleman, S.B. (2003). Death in the family and HIV risk-taking among intravenous drug users. *Family Process, 42*(2), 291–304.

Boyd-Franklin, N., & Bry, B.H. (2000). *Reaching out in family therapy: Home-based, school, and community interventions.* New York: Guilford Press.

Brehm, S. (1985). *Intimate relationships.* New York: Random House.

Bretherton, I. (1992). The origins of attachment theory: John Bowlby and Mary Ainsworth. *Developmental Psychology, 9,* 759–75.

Brody, S. (2007). Vaginal orgasm is associated with better psychological function. *Sexual and Relationship Therapy, 22*(2), 173–91.

Brooks, G.R. (1998). Why traditional men hate psychotherapy. *Psychotherapy Bulletin, 33*(3), 45–9.

Brooks, G.R. (2012). Male-sensitive therapy for the returning veteran and his partner. In D.S. Shepard & M. L. Harway (Eds.), *Engaging men in couples therapy* (pp. 279–99). New York, NY US: Routledge/ Taylor & Francis Group.

Brown, V.B., Melchior, L.A., Panter, A.T., Slaughter, R., & Huba, G.J. (2000). Women's steps of change and entry into drug abuse treatment. A multidimensional stages of change model. *Journal of Subst Abuse Treat, 18*(3), 231–40.

Bruner, J. (1986). *Actual minds, possible worlds.* Cambridge, MA: Harvard University Press.

Bryant-Davis, T. (2007). Healing requires recognition: The case for race-based traumatic stress. *Counseling Psychologist, 9,* 135–43.

Buck, C. (2003). Smallpox inoculation—should we credit Chinese medicine? *Complementary Therapeutic Medicine, 9,* 201–2.

Buehlman, K.T., Gottman, J.M., & Katz, L.F. (1992). How a couple views their past predicts their future: Predicting divorce from an oral history interview. *Journal of Family Psychology, 9*(3–4), 295–318.

Bulhan, H.A. (1985). *Franz Fanon and the psychology of oppression.* New York: Springer.

Butts, H.F. (2002). The black mask of humanity: Racial/ethnic discrimination and post-traumatic stress disorder. *Journal of the American Academy of Psychiatry and the Law, 9,* 336–9.

Cahill, L. (2003). Sex- and hemisphere-related influences on the neurobiology of emotionally influenced memory. *Progress in Neuro-Psychopharmacology & Biological Psychiatry, 9,* 1235–41.

Cahill, L. (2006). Why sex matters for neuroscience. *Nature Review of Neuroscience, 7*(6), 477–84.

Cahill, L., Gorski, L., Belcher, A., & Huynh, Q. (2004a). The influence of sex versus sex-related traits on long-term memory for gist and detail from an emotional story. *Consciousness and Cognition, 13*(2), 391–400.

Cahill, L., Haier, R.J., White, N.S., Fallon, J., Kilpatrick, L., Lawrence, C., Potkin, S.G., & Alkire, M.T. (2001). Sex-related difference in amygdala activity during emotionally influenced memory storage. *Neurobiology of Learning and Memory, 75*(1), 1–9.

Cahill, L., Uncapher, M., Kilpatrick, L., Alkire, M.T., & Turner, J. (2004b). Sex-related hemispheric lateralization of amygdala function in emotionally influenced memory: an FMRI investigation. *Learning and Memory, 11*(3), 261–6.

Carlson, E.B. (1997). *Trauma assessments: A clinician's guide.* New York: Guilford.

Capacchione, L. (2001). *The power of your other hand.* Revised edition. Franklin Lakes, NJ: The Career Press, Inc.

Carre, J.M., & Mehta, P.H. (2011). Importance of considering testosterone-cortisol interactions in predicting human aggression and dominance. *Aggressive Behavior, 37*(6), 489–91.

Cassidy, J., & Shaver, P.R. (1999). *Handbook of attachment: Theory, research, and clinical applications.* New York: Guilford Press.

Chapman, L. (2012). *Strengthening sensory-motor systems, part I.* Redwood Valley, CA, Art Therapy Institute of the Redwoods.

Chapman, L. (2013) *Neurobiologically informed trauma treatment with children and adolescents: Understanding mechanisms of change.* New York: W.W. Norton.

Chein, J., Albert, D., O'Brien, L., Uckert, K., & Steinberg, L. (2011). Peers increase adolescent risk taking by enhancing activity in the brain's reward circuitry. *Developmental Science, 9*, F1–F10.

Chopra, D. (1997). Forward. In C.B. Pert (Ed.), *Molecules of emotion: Why you feel the way you feel.* New York: Scribner.

Clark, C.F. (2000). *What men hate about psychotherapy.* Tucson, AZ: Psychotherapy and Organizational Development (www.psychod. com).

Cohen, J.D., McClure, S.M., & Yu, A.J. (2007). Should I stay or should I go? How the human brain manages the trade-off between exploitation and exploration. *Philosophical Transactions of the Royal Society B Biological Sciences, 9*, 933–42.

Cooley, C.H. (1902). *Human nature and the social order.* New York: Scribner.

Cozalino, L.J. (2006). *The neuroscience of human relationships: Attachment and the developing social brain.* (1st edn) New York: W.W. Norton.

Cross, T.L. (1995). Understanding family resiliency from a relational world view. In H.I. McCubbin, E.A. Thompson, A.I. Thompson, &

J.E. Fromer (Eds.), *Resiliency in ethnic minority families: Native and immigrant American families* (pp. 143–57). Madison, WI: University of Wisconsin-Madison Center for Family Studies.

Cunningham, P.B., & Henggeler, S. (1999). Engaging multiproblem families in treatment: Lessons learned throughout the development of multisystemic therapy. *Family Process, 38*(3), 265–81.

Dakof, G.A., Tejeda, M., & Liddle, H.A. (2001). Predictors of engagement in adolescent drug abuse treatment. *Journal of the American Academy of Child and Adolescent Psychiatry, 40*(3), 274–81.

Damasio, A.R. (1994). *Descartes' error: Emotion, reason, and the human brain.* New York: G.P. Putnam.

Damasio, A.R. (2003). *Looking for Spinoza: Joy, sorrow, and the feeling brain.* Orlando, FL: Harcourt.

Damasio, A. (2010). *The self comes to mind.* New York: Pantheon.

Darwin, C. (1859). *The origin of species.* London: John Murray.

Davis, K.L., & Panksepp, J. (2011). The brain's emotional foundations of human personality and the Affective Neuroscience Personality Scales. *Neuroscience and Biobehavioral Review, 35*(9), 1946–58.

de Quervain D.J., Roozendaal B., Nitsch R.M., McGaugh J.L., & Hock C. (2000). Acute cortisone administration impairs retrieval of long-term declarative memory in humans. *Nature Neuroscience, 3*(4), 313–14.

deShazer, S., & Berg, I.K. (1992). Doing therapy: A post-structuralist re-vision. *Journal of Marital and Family Therapy, 18*(1), 71–81.

Diamond, G., & Liddle, H.A. (1996). Resolving a therapeutic impasse between parents and adolescents in multidimensional family therapy. *Journal of Consulting and Clinical Psychology, 64*(3), 481–88.

Diamond, G.M., Diamond, G.S., & Liddle, H.A. (2000). The therapist-parent alliance in family-based therapy for adolescents. *Journal of Clinical Psychology, 56*(8), 1037–50.

Diamond, G.S., & Liddle, H.A. (1999). Transforming negative parent-adolescent interactions: from impasse to dialogue. *Family Process, 38*(1), 5–26.

Diamond, L.M. (2004). Emerging perspectives on distinctions between romantic love and sexual desire. *Current Directions in Psychological Science, 9*, 116–19.

Doidge, N. (2007). *The brain that changes itself: Stories of personal triumph from the frontiers of brain science.* New York: Penguin Books.

Ekman, P. (2007). *Emotions revealed: Recognizing faces and feelings to improve communication and emotional life.* (2nd edn) New York: Henry Holt and Company.

Engel, G.I. (1977). The need for a new medical model: A challenge to biomedicine. *Science, 9,* 129–36.

Epston, D., & White, M. (1992). *Experience, contradiction, narrative and imagination.* Adelaide, Australia: Dulwich Centre Publications.

Erickson, C.K. (2007). *The science of addiction: From neurobiology to treatment.* New York: W.W. Norton.

Erickson, M., & Rossi, E. (1979). *Hypnotherapy: An exploratory casework.* New York: Irvington.

Evans, D. (2002). The search hypothesis of emotion. *British Journal for the Philosophy of Science, 9,* 497–510.

Ferree, N.K., & Cahill, L. (2009). Post-event spontaneous intrusive recollections and strength of memory for emotional events in men and women. *Consciousness & Cognition, 9,* 126–34.

Fincher, J. (1981). *The brain: Mystery of matter and mind.* Washington, D.C.: U.S. News Books.

Fishbane, M.D. (2008). News from neuroscience: Applications to couple therapy. *American Family Therapy Academy Monograph Series,* (Winter), 20–8.

Fishbane, M.D. (2007). Wired to connect: Neuroscience, relationships and therapy. *Family Process, 9,* 395–412.

Fisher, H. (2004a). Dumped! *New Scientist, 181*(2434), 40–3.

Fisher, H.E. (2004b). *Why we love: The nature and chemistry of romantic love.* New York: Holt.

Fisher, H.E. (2004c). Your brain in love. *Time, 163*(3), 80–3.

Fisher, H.E. (2009). Why him? Why her? *Psychotherapy Networker, 33*(3), 28–59.

Fisher, H., Aron, A., & Brown, L.L. (2005). Romantic love: An fMRI study of a neural mechanism for mate choice. *Journal of Comparative Neurology, 493*(1), 58–62.

Fisher, H.E., Aron, A., & Brown, L.L. (2006). Romantic love: a mammalian brain system for mate choice. *Philosophical Transactions of the Royal Society of London B: Biological Science, 361*(1476), 2173–86.

Fisher, H.E., Aron, A., Mashek, D., Li, H., & Brown, L.L. (2002). Defining the brain systems of lust, romantic attraction, and attachment. *Archives of Sexual Behavior, 31*(5), 413–19.

Fisher, H.E., Brown, L.L., Aron, A., Strong, G., & Mashek, D. (2010). Reward, addiction, and emotion regulation systems associated with rejection in love. *Journal of Neurophysiology, 104*(1), 51–60.

Fivush, R. (2011). The development of autobiographical memory. *Annual Review of Psychology, 9*, 559–82.

Fleuridas, C., Nelson, T., & Rosenthal, D.M. (1986). The evolution of circular questions: Training family therapists. *Journal of Marital and Family Therapy, 12*(27), 113–28.

Foerschner, A.M. (2010). The history of mental illness: From 'skull drills' to 'happy pills'. *Student Pulse, 9*, 1–4.

Ford, J.D. (2008). Trauma, Posttraumatic stress disorder and ethnoracial minorities: Toward diversity and cultural competence in principles and practices. *Clinical Psychology: Science and Practice, 9*, 62–67.

Forgeard, M.J., Haigh, E.A., Beck, A.T., Davidson, R.J., Henn, F.A., Maier, S.F. et al. (2011). Beyond depression: Towards a process-based approach to research, diagnosis, and treatment. *Clinical Psychology, 9*, 275–99.

Foucault, M. (1973). *The birth of the clinic: An archaeology of medical perception.* London: Tavistock.

Frank, C. (2001). Why do we fall in—and out of—love? Dr. Helen Fisher unravels the mystery. *Biography Magazine, 9*, 86–7.

Franklin, A.J., Boyd-Franklin, N., & Kelly, S. (2006). Racism and invisibility: Race-related stress, emotional abuse and psychological trauma for people of color. In L.V. Blitz & M.P. Greene (Eds.), *Racism and racial identity: Reflections on urban practice in mental health and social services* (pp. 9–30). Binghamton, NY US: Haworth Maltreatment and Trauma Press/The Haworth Press.

Friel, J.C. & Friel, L.D.O. (2012). *The power and grace between nasty or nice.* Deerfield Beach, FL: Health Communications, Inc.

Gendlin, E.T. (1996). *Focusing-oriented psychotherapy.* New York: Guilford.

Gecas, V. & Schwalbe, M.L. (1983). Beyond the looking-glass self: Social structure and efficacy-based self-esteem. *Social Psychology Quarterly, 9*, 77–88.

Gershon, M. (1998). *The second brain.* New York: HarperCollins.

Goldstein, J.M., Jerram, M., Abbs, B., Whitfield-Gabrieli, S., & Makris, N. (2010). Sex differences in stress response circuitry activation dependent on female hormonal cycle. *The Journal of Neuroscience, 30*(2), 431–8.

Gong, G.H., & Yong Evans, A.C. (2011). Brain connectivity: Gender makes a difference. *The Neuroscientist, 17*(5), 575–91.

Gottman, J.M. (1993). The roles of conflict engagement, escalation, and avoidance in marital interaction: a longitudinal view of five types of couples. *Journal of Consult Clin Psychol, 61*(1), 6–15.

Gottman, J.M., & Levenson, R.W. (1985). A valid procedure for obtaining self-report of affect in marital interaction. *Journal of Consult Clin Psychol*, *53*(2), 151–60.

Gottman, J.M., Jacobson, N.S., Rushe, R.H., Shortt, J.W., Babcock, J., La Taillade, J.J., & Waltz, J. (1995). The relationship between heart rate reactivity, emotionally aggressive behavior, and general violence in batterers. *Journal of Family Psychology*, *9*(3), 227–48.

Gottman, J.M., Katz, L.F., & Hooven, C. (1997). *Meta-Emotion: How families communicate emotionally*. Mahwah, New Jersey: Lawrence Erlbaum Associates.

Grepmair, L., Mitterlehner, F., Loew, T., Bachler, E., Rother, W., & Nickel, M. (2007). Promoting mindfulness in psychotherapists in training influences the treatment results of their patients: A randomized, double-blind, controlled study. *Psychotherapy Psychosomatics*, *76*(6), 332–8.

Griffith, J.L., & Griffith, M.E. (1994). *The body speaks*. New York: Basic Books.

Gross, J.J. (1998). Sharpening the focus: Emotion regulation, arousal, and social competence. *Psychological Inquiry*, *9*(4), 289–90.

Gross, J.J., & Levenson, R.W. (1997). Hiding feelings: The acute effects of inhibiting negative and positive emotion. *Journal of Abnormal Psychology*, *106*(1), 95–103.

Gross, J.J., & Munoz, R.F. (1995). Emotion regulation and mental health. *Clinical Psychology: Science & Practice*, *2*(2), 151–64.

Grove, D. (1988). *Healing the wounded child within*. Edwardsville, IL: David Grove Seminars.

Hamlin, J.K., Wynn, K., & Bloom, P. (2007). Social evaluation by preverbal infants. *Nature*, *450*(7169), 557–9.

Hamlin, J.K., Wynn, K., & Bloom, P. (2010). Three-month-olds show a negativity bias in their social evaluations. *Developmental Science*, *13*(6), 923–9.

Hanna, S.M. (1995). On paradox: Empathy before strategy. *Journal of Family Psychotherapy*, *6*(1), 85–8.

Hanna, S.M. (1997). A *developmental-interactional model*. In T.D. Hargrave & S.M. Hanna (Eds.), *The aging family: New visions in theory, practice and reality*. (pp. 101–30). New York: Brunner/Mazel.

Hanna, S.M. (2007). *The practice of family therapy: Key elements across models*. (4th edn). Pacific Grove, CA: Thomson/Brooks Cole.

Hanna, S.M. (2009). *Why evidence-based family therapies work: Simple truths*. Presented at the American Association of Marriage and Family Therapy Annual Conference, Sacramento, CA.

Hanna, S.M. (2010). *Implications of neuroscience for couples therapy.* Alexandria, VA: American Association for Marriage and Family Therapy.

Hanna, S.M., Harper, J.M., & Nelson, N.J. (2011). *Neurocybernetics and siblings: New maps for family therapy.* Presented at the American Association for Marriage and Family Therapy Annual Conference. Fort Worth, TX.

Hardy, K.V., & Laszloffy, T.A. (2005). *Teens who hurt: Clinical interventions to break the cycle of adolescent violence.* New York: Guilford.

Hargrave T.D. (1994). *Families and forgiveness: Healing wounds in the intergenerational family.* New York: Brunner/Mazel.

Hargrave, T.D., & Pfitzer, F. (2003). *The new contextual therapy: Guiding the power of give and take.* New York: Routledge.

Hargrave, T.D., & Pfitzer, F. (2011). *Restoration therapy: Understanding and guiding healing in marriage and family therapy.* New York: Routledge.

Hargrave, T.D., Jennings, G., & Anderson, W.A. (1991). The development of a relational ethics scale. *Journal of Marital and Family Therapy, 7*(2), 145–58.

Hebb, D.O. (1949). *The organization of behavior: A neuropsychological theory.* New York: John Wiley and Sons.

Heinrichs, M., & Domes, G. (2008). Neuropeptides and social behaviour: Effects of oxytocin and vasopressin in humans. *Progress in Brain Research, 9,* 337–50.

Heller, L., & LaPierre, A. (2012). *Healing developmental trauma: How early trauma affects self-regulation, self-image, and the capacity for relationship.* Berkeley, CA: North Atlantic Books.

Henggeler, S.W., Pickrel, S.G., & Brondino, M.J. (1999). Multisystemic treatment of substance-abusing and dependent delinquents: outcomes, treatment fidelity, and transportability. *Mental Health Services Research, 9,* 171–84.

Henggeler, S.W., Schoenwald, S.K., Borduin, C.M., Rowland, M.D., & Cunningham, P.B. (1998). *Multisystemic treatment of antisocial behavior in children and adolescents.* New York: Guilford Press.

Hiller, J. (2004). Speculations on the links between feelings, emotions and sexual behaviour: Are vasopressin and oxytocin involved? *Sexual and Relationship Therapy, 19*(4), 393–429.

Hoizey, D., & Hoizey, M.-J. (1993). *A history of Chinese medicine.* Vancouver, Canada: UBC Press.

Hong, F.F. (2004). History of medicine in China: When medicine took an alternative path. *McGill Journal of Medicine, 9,* 79–84.

Hood, B. (2012). *The self illusion: How the social brain creates identity.* New York: Oxford University Press.

Horwitz, S.H. (1997). Treating families with traumatic loss: Transitional family therapy. In C.R. Figley, *Death and trauma: The traumatology of grieving.* New York: Routledge, 211–30.

Howard, J. (1978). *Families.* New York: Simon & Schuster.

Hubbard, I.J., Harris, D., Kilkenny, M.F., Faux, S.G., Pollack, M.R., & Cadilhac, D.A. (2012). Adherence to clinical guidelines improves patient outcomes in Australian audit of stroke rehabilitation practice. *Archives of Physical Medical Rehabilitation, 93*(6), 965–71.

Imber-Black, E., Roberts, J., & Whiting, R. (1988). *Rituals in families and family therapy.* New York: W.W. Norton.

Ishak, W.W., Berman, D.S., & Peters, A. (2008). Male anorgasmia treated with oxytocin. *Journal of Sexual Medicine, 5*(4), 1022–4.

Ishii, H., Nagashima, M., Tanno, M., Nakajima, A., & Yoshino, S. (2003). Does being easily moved to tears as a response to psychological stress reflect response to treatment and the general prognosis in patients with rheumatoid arthritis? *Clinical and Experimental Rheumatology, 9,* 611–16.

Izuma, K., Saito, D.N., & Sadato, N. (2008). Processing of social and monetary rewards in the human striatum. *Neuron, 9,* 284–94.

Jack. F., MacDonald, S., Reese, E., & Hayne, H. (2009). Maternal reminiscing style during early childhood predicts the age of adolescents' earliest memories. *Child Development, 80*(2), 496–505.

Jackson, J.S., Knight, K.M., & Rafferty, J.A. (2010). Race and unhealthy behaviors: chronic stress, the HPA axis, and physical and mental health disparities over the life course. *American Journal of Public Health, 100*(5), 933–9.

James, B.D., Boyle, P.A., Buchman, A.S., & Bennett, D.A. (2011). Relation of late-life social activity with incident disability among community-dwelling older adults. *The Journals of Gerontology Series A: Biological Sciences and Medical Sciences, 66A* (4), 467–73.

Jäncke, L. (2009). The plastic human brain. *Restorative Neurology and Neuroscience, 9,* 521–38.

Jella, S.A. & Shannahoff-Khalsa, D.S. (1993). The effects of unilateral forced nostril breathing on cognitive performance. *International Journal of Neuroscience, 9,* 61–8.

Jenkins, A. (1991). *Invitations to responsibility: The therapeutic engagement of men who are violent and abusive.* Adelaide, Australia: Dulwich Centre Publications.

Johnson, S.M. (ed.). (1996). *The practice of emotionally focused marital therapy: Creating connection*. New York: Bruner/Mazel.

Johnson, S.M. (1998). Listening to the music: Emotion as a natural part of systems theory. *Journal of Systemic Therapies, 9*, 1–18.

Johnson, S.M. (2002). *Emotionally focused couple therapy with trauma survivors: Strengthening attachment bonds*. New York: Guilford Press.

Johnson, S.M., Bradley, B., Furrow, J., Lee, A., Palmer, G., Tilley, D., & Woolley, S. (2005). *Becoming an emotionally focused couple therapist: The workbook*. New York: Routledge.

Johnson, S.M., Makinen, J.A., & Millikan, J.W. (2001). Attachment injuries in couple relationships: A new perspective on impasses in couples therapy. *Journal of Marital and Family Therapy, 27*(2), 145–56.

Kabat-Zinn, J. (2006). *Coming to our senses: Healing ourselves and the world through mindfulness*. New York: Hyperion.

Kantor, D., & Lehr, W. (1975). *Inside the family: Toward a theory of family process*. New York: Harper and Row.

Kiecolt-Glaser, J.K. (2009). Psychoneuroimmunology psychology's gateway to the biomedical future. *Perspectives in Psychological Science, 4*(4), 367–9.

Kiecolt-Glaser, J.K. & Newton, T.L. (2001). Marriage and health: his and hers. *Psychological Bulletin, 9*, 472–503.

Kiecolt-Glaser, J.K., Bane, C., Glaser, R., & Malarkey, W.B. (2003). Love, marriage, and divorce: newlyweds' stress hormones foreshadow relationship changes. *Journal of Consulting Clinical Psychology, 9*, 176–88.

Kiecolt-Glaser, J.K., Glaser, R., Cacioppo, J.T., & Malarkey, W.B. (1998). Marital stress: immunologic, neuroendocrine, and autonomic correlates. *Annals of the New York Academy of Science, 9*, 656–63.

Kiecolt-Glaser, J.K., Loving, T.L., Stowell, J.R., Malarkey, W.B., Lemeshow, S., Dickinson, S.L., & Glaser, R. (2005). Hostile marital interactions, proinflammatory cytokine production, and wound healing. *Archives of General Psychiatry, 62*(12), 1377–84.

Kircanski, K., Lieberman, M.D., & Craske, M.G. (2012). Feelings into words: Contributions of language to exposure therapy. *Psychological Science, 23*(10), 1086–91.

Konorski, J. (1948). *Conditioned reflexes and neuron organization*. Cambridge: University of Cambridge Press.

Kropotkin, P. (1902). *Mutual aid: A factor of evolution*. London: Heinemann.

Laird, R.D. (2011). Teenage driving offers challenges and potential rewards for developmentalists. *Child Development Perspectives, 9,* 311–16.

Landau, J., Garrett, J., Shea, R.R., Stanton, M.D., Brinkman-Sull, D., & Baciewicz, G. (2000). Strength in numbers: the ARISE method for mobilizing family and network to engage substance abusers in treatment. A relational intervention sequence for engagement. *American Journal of Drug Alcohol Abuse, 26*(3), 379–98.

Landau-Stanton, J., Clements, C.D., & Stanton, M.D. (1993). Psychotherapeutic intervention: From individual through group to extended network. In J. Landau-Stanton & C.D. Clements (Eds.), *AIDS, health and mental health: A primary source book.* (pp. 214–65). New York: Brunner/Mazel.

Laws, E., Ezzat, S., Asa, S., & Rio, L. (2013). Pituitary disorders: Diagnosis and management. New York: John Wiley & Sons.

LeDoux, J. (2003). The emotional brain, fear and the amygdala. *Cellular and Molecular Neurobiology, 9,* 727–38.

Levine, P.A. (1997). *Waking the tiger: Healing trauma.* Berkeley, CA: North Atlantic Books.

Levine, P.A. (2010). *In an unspoken voice: How the body releases trauma and restores goodness.* Berkeley, CA: North Atlantic Books.

Levine, P.A., & Kline, M. (2008). *Trauma-proofing your kids: A parents' guide for instilling confidence, joy and resilience.* Berkeley, CA: North Atlantic Books.

Lieberman, M.D., Eisenberger, N.I., Crockett, M.J., Tom, S.M., Pfeifer, J.H., & Way, B.M. (2007). Putting feelings into words. *Psychological Science, 9,* 421–8.

Liddle, H.A. (2000). *Multidimensional family therapy treatment manual.* Rockville. MD: Center for Substance Abuse Treatment.

Liddle, H.A., & Schwartz, S.J. (2002). Attachment and family therapy: clinical utility of adolescent-family attachment research. *Family Process, 41*(3), 455–76.

Lincoln, K.D., Taylor, R.J., Bullard, K.M., Chatters, L.M., Woodward, A.T., Himle, J.A., & Jackson, J.S. (2010). Emotional support, negative interaction and DSM IV lifetime disorders among older African Americans: findings from the National Survey of American Life (NSAL). *International Journal of Geriatric Psychiatry, 25*(6), 612–21.

Lloyd-Fox, S., Blasi, A., Mercure, E., Elwell, C. E., & Johnson, M.H. (2012). The emergence of cerebral specialization for the human voice over the first months of life. *Social Neuroscience, 9,* 317–30.

Lotto, R.B. (2012). Everything begins with perception. In P. Baumann (Ed.), *Being Human 2012: Science, Philosophy and Your Life* San Francisco, CA: The Baumann Foundation.

Loucks, E.B., Sullivan, L.M., D'Agostino, R.B., Sr., Larson, M.G., Berkman, L.F., & Benjamin, E.J. (2006). Social networks and inflammatory markers in the Framingham Heart Study. *Journal of Biosocial Science, 9,* 835–42.

Luders, E., Gaser, C., Narr, K.L., & Toga, A.W. (2009). Why sex matters: Brain size independent differences in gray matter distributions between men and women. *Journal of Neuroscience, 29*(45), 14265–70.

Maté, G. (2010). *In the realm of hungry ghosts.* Berkley, CA: North Atlantic Books.

Mays, V.M., Coleman, L.M., & Jackson, J.S. (1996). Perceived race-based discrimination, employment status, and job stress in a national sample of black women: Implications for health outcomes. *Journal of Occupational Health Psychology, 1*(3), 319–29.

McCarthy, M.M., Arnold, A.P., Ball, G.F., Blaustein, J.D., & De Vries, G.J. (2012). Sex differences in the brain: The not so inconvenient truth. *Journal of Neuroscience, 32*(7), 2241–7.

McDaniel, S.H., Hepworth, J., & Doherty, W. (1992). *Medical family therapy: A biopsychosocial approach to families with health problems.* New York: Basic Books.

McDaniel, S., Hepworth, J., & Doherty, W. (1997). *The shared experience of illness: Stories of patients, families and their therapists.* New York: Basic Books.

McElroy, A. & Townsend, P.K. (1989). Medical anthropology in ecological perspective. Ann McElroy and Patricia K. Townsend. *Medical Anthropology Quarterly, 9,* 405–7.

McFarlane, W. (2002). *Multifamily groups in the treatment of severe psychiatric disorders.* New York: Guilford Press.

McFarlane, W.R., Dunne, E., Lukens, E., Newmark, M., McLaughlin-Toran, J., Deakins, S., & Horen, B. (1993). From research to clinical practice: Dissemination of New York State's family psychoeducation project. *Hospital Community Psychiatry, 44*(3), 265–70.

McFarlane, W.R., Link, B., Dushay, R., Marchal, J., & Crilly, J. (1995). Psychoeducational multiple family groups: four-year relapse outcome in schizophrenia. *Family Process, 34*(2), 127–44.

MacNeilage, P.F., Rogers, L.J., & Vallortigara, G. (2009). Origins of the left & right brain. *Scientific American, 9,* 60–7.

Main, M. (1995). Attachment: Overview, with implications for clinical work. In S. Goldberg, R. Muir, & J. Kerr (Eds.), *Attachment theory: Social, developmental, and clinical perspectives* (pp. 407–74). Hillsdale, NJ: Analytic Press.

Mead, M. (1934). *Kinship in the Admiralty Islands*. New York: American Museum of Natural History.

Mehta, P.H., Jones, A.C., & Josephs, R.A. (2008). The social endocrinology of dominance: Basal testosterone predicts cortisol changes and behavior following victory and defeat. *Journal of Personality and Social Psychology*, 94(6), 1078–93.

Mehta, P.H., & Josephs, R.A. (2010). Testosterone and cortisol jointly regulate dominance: Evidence for a dual-hormone hypothesis. *Hormones and Behavior*, 58(5), 898–906.

Miller, S.D., Duncan, B.L., & Hubble, M.A. (1997). *Escape from Babel: Toward a unifying language for psychotherapy practice*. New York: W.W. Norton.

Miller, W.R., & Rollnick, S. (2013). *Movational interviewing: Helping people change* (3rd edn). New York: Guilford.

Minuchin, S. (1974). *Families and family therapy*. Cambridge, MA: Harvard University Press.

Minuchin, S. (1987). My many voices. In J.K. Zeig (Ed.), *The evolution of psychotherapy*. (pp. 5–28). New York: Brunner/Mazel.

Minuchin, S., Rosman, B.L., & Baker, L. (1978). *Psychosomatic families: Anorexia nervosa in context*. Cambridge, MA: Harvard University Press.

Mukamel, R., Ekstrom, A.D., Kaplan, J., Iacoboni, M., & Fried, I. (2010). Single-neuron responses in humans during execution and observation of actions. *Current Biology*, 9, 750–6.

Nelson, N. (2010). Personal communication.

O'Brien, L., Albert, D., Chein, J., & Steinberg, L. (2011). Adolescents prefer more immediate rewards when in the presence of their peers. *Journal of Research on Adolescence*, 9, 747–53.

O'Hanlon, S., & O'Hanlon, W. (1999). Possibility therapy with families. In S. O'Hanlon & B. Bertolino (Eds.), *Evolving possibilities: Selected papers of Bill O'Hanlon* (pp. 185–204). New York: Brunner/Mazel.

O'Hanlon, W.H. (1987). *Taproots*. New York: W.W. Norton.

O'Hanlon, W. (1999). *Frozen in time: Possibility therapy with adults who were sexually abused as children*. In S. O'Hanlon & B. Bertolino (Eds.), *Evolving possibilities: Selected papers of Bill O'Hanlon*. New York: Brunner/Mazel.

Otto, R. (1950). *The idea of the holy*. Oxford: Oxford University Press.

Panksepp, J. (2007). Can PLAY diminish ADHD and facilitate the construction of the social brain? *Journal of the Canadian Academy of Child and Adolescent Psychiatry, 9,* 57–66.

Panksepp, J. (2009). *Brain emotional systems and qualities of mental life: From animal models of affect to implications for psychotherapeutics.* In D. Fosha, D.J. Siegel, & M.F. Solomon (Eds.), *The healing power of emotion: Affective neuroscience, development and clinical practice.* New York: W.W. Norton.

Panksepp, J. (2011). Cross-species affective neuroscience decoding of the primal affective experiences of humans and related animals. *PLoS One, 6*(9), e21236.

Panksepp, J., & Bivin, L. (2012). *The archaeology of mind: Neuroevolutionary origins of human emotions.* New York: W.W. Norton.

Panksepp, J., & Watt, D. (2011). Why does depression hurt? Ancestral primary-process separation-distress (PANIC/GRIEF) and diminished brain reward (SEEKING) processes in the genesis of depressive affect. *Psychiatry, 74*(1), 5–13.

Panksepp, J. & Zellner, M.R. (2004). Towards a neurobiologically based unified theory of aggression. *Revue Internationale de Psychologie Sociale, 9,* 37–61.

Parker-Pope, T. (2010). Is marriage good for your health? *New York Times,* April 12.

Patwardhan, K. (2008). Concepts of human physiology in Ayurveda. In P.K. Roy (Ed.), *Sowarigpa and Ayurveda* (pp. 53–73). Sarnath, Varanasi: Central Institute of Higher Tibetan Studies.

Paz, R., Gelbard-Sagiv, H., Mukamel, R., Harel, M., Malach, R., & Fried, I. (2010). A neural substrate in the human hippocampus for linking successive events. *Proceedings of the National Academy of Sciences of the United States of America, 107*(13), 6046–51.

Perel, E. (2007). *Mating in captivity: Unlocking erotic intelligence.* New York: Harper Perennial.

Perel, E. (2011). Erotic fantasy reconsidered: From tragedy to triumph. *American Family Therapy Academy Monograph, 9*(Spring), 9–15.

Pert, C.B. (1997). *Molecules of emotion: Why you feel the way you feel.* New York: Scribner.

Pieterse, A.L., Carter, R.T., Evans, S.A., & Walter, R.A. (2010). An exploratory examination of the associations among racial and ethnic discrimination, racial climate, and trauma-related symptoms in a college student population. *Journal of Counseling Psychology, 9,* 255–63.

Pinker, S. (2011). *The better angels of our nature: Why violence has declined.* New York: Viking.

Porges, S.W. (1995). Orienting in a defensive world: mammalian modifications of our evolutionary heritage. A polyvagal theory. *Psychophysiology, 32*(4), 301–18.

Porges, S.W. (1997). Emotion: an evolutionary by-product of the neural regulation of the autonomic nervous system. *Annals of New York Academy of Science, 9,* 62–77.

Porges, S.W. (1998). Love: an emergent property of the mammalian autonomic nervous system. *Psychoneuroendocrinology, 23*(8), 837–61.

Porges, S.W. (2001). The polyvagal theory: phylogenetic substrates of a social nervous system. *International Journal of Psychophysiology, 42*(2), 123–46.

Porges, S.W. (2007). The polyvagal perspective. *Biological Psychology, 74*(2), 116–43.

Porges, S.W. (in press). *Clinical insights from the polyvagal theory: The transformative power of feeling safe.* New York: W.W. Norton.

Porges, S.W. & Furman, S.A. (2011). The early development of the autonomic nervous system provides a neural platform for social behavior: A polyvagal perspective. *Infant Child Development, 9,* 106–18.

Preston, S.D., Bechara, A., Damasio, H., Grabowski, T.J., Stansfield, R.B., Mehta, S., & Damasio, A.R. (2007). The neural substrates of cognitive empathy. *Social Neuroscience, 9*(3–4), 254–75.

Reeb, K.G., Graham, A.V., Kitson, G.C., Zyzanski, S.J., Weber, M.A., & Engel, A. (1986). Defining family in family medicine: Perceived family vs. household structure in an urban black population. *The Journal of Family Practice, 23*(4), 351–5.

Rizzolatti, G., & Craighero, L. (2004). The mirror-neuron system. *Annual Review of Neuroscience, 9,* 169–92.

Robles, T.F. & Kiecolt-Glaser, J.K. (2003). The physiology of marriage: Pathways to health. *Physiology and Behavior, 9,* 409–16.

Rolland, J. (1994). *Families, illness and disability: An integrated treatment model.* New York: Basic Books.

Rose, S., Bisson, J., Churchill, R., & Wessely, S. (2002). Psychological debriefing for preventing post traumatic stress disorder (PTSD). *Cochrane Database System Review,* (2), CD000560.

Rosen, S. (1988). What makes Ericksonian therapy so effective? In J.K. Zeig & S.R. Lankton (Eds.), *Developing Ericksonian therapy.* (pp. 5–29). New York: Brunner/Mazel.

Ross, G. (2008). *Beyond the trauma vortex into the healing vortex: A guide for psychology and education.* Los Angeles, CA: International Trauma Healing Institute.

Rossi, E.L. (1983). Milton H. Erickson: A biographical sketch. In E. Rossi, M.O. Ryan, & F.A. Sharp (Eds.), *Healing in hypnosis: The seminars, workshops and lectures of Milton H. Erickson, Volume I.* New York: Irvington.

Rossi, E.L. (2002). *The psychobiology of gene expression: Neuroscience and neurogenesis in hypnosis and the healing arts.* New York: W.W. Norton.

Rothschild, B. (2010). *8 keys to safe trauma recovery: Take-charge strategies to empower your healing.* New York: W.W. Norton.

Rueveni, U. (1992). Fatherhood revisited: Intergenerational therapy in the nick of time. *GrassRoutes: Stories from Family and Systemic Therapists, 1*(1), 8.

Satir, V. (1972). *People making.* Palo Alto, CA: Science and Behavior Books.

Schauer, J. (1993). Daddy and Granddaddy. *GrassRoutes: Stories from family and systemic therapists, 2*(1), 16–20.

Schore, A.N. (2003). *Affect dysregulation and disorders of the self.* New York: Norton and Company.

Schore, A.N. (2005). Back to basics: Attachment, affect regulation, and the developing right brain: Linking developmental neuroscience to pediatrics. *Pediatrics in Review, 26*(6), 204–17.

Schore, A.N. (2012). *The science of the art of psychotherapy.* New York: W.W. Norton.

Schulte-Rüther, M., Markowitsch, H.J., Fink, G.R., & Piefke, M. (2007). Mirror neuron and theory of mind mechanisms involved in face-to-face interactions: A functional magnetic resonance imaging approach to empathy. *Journal of Cognitive Neuroscience, 19*(8), 1354–72.

Seaburn, D., Landau-Stanton, J., and Horwitz, S. (1995). Core techniques in family therapy. In Mikesell, R.H., Lustennan, D.D. and McDaniel, S.H. (Eds.) *Integrating family therapy: Handbook of family psychology and systems theory* (pp. 5–26). Washington, D.C.: American Psychological Association.

Selvini Palazzoli, M., Boscolo, L., Cecchin, G., & Prata, G. (1980). Hypothesizing, circularity, neutrality: Three guidelines for the conduct of the session. *Family Process, 19*(1), 7–19.

Siegel, D.J. (1999). *The developing mind: Toward a neurobiology of interpersonal experience.* New York: Guilford Press.

Siegel, D.J. (2010). *Mindsight: The new science of personal transformation.* New York: Bantam.

Siegel, D.J. (2012). *The developing mind: Toward a neurobiology of interpersonal experience* (4th edn). New York: Guilford.

Siegel, G.J., Agranoff, B.W., Albers, R.W., Fisher, K., & Uhler, M.D. (1999). *Basic neurochemistry: Molecular, cellular and medical aspects.* Philadelphia, PA: Lippincott-Raven.

Sluzki, C. (1992). Transformations: A blueprint for narrative changes in therapy. *Family Process, 31*(3), 217–30.

Sluzki, C.E. (2007). Interfaces: toward a new generation of systemic models in family research and practice. *FamilyProcess, 46*(2), 173–84.

Sluzki, C.E. (2008). Saudades at the edge of the self and the merits of 'portable families'. *Transcultural Psychiatry, 45*(3), 379–90.

Sluzki, C.E. (2010). Personal social networks and health: conceptual and clinical implications of their reciprocal impact. *Families, Systems, & Health, 28*(1), 1–18.

Small, M.F. (2011) The anthropology of marriage and family. In Anon., *American Association of Marriage and Family Therapy annual conference: The science of relationships.* Alexandria, VA: American Association of Marriage and Family Therapy.

Smith, J.E., & Meyers, R.J. (2004). *Motivating substance abusers to enter treatment: Working with family members.* New York: Guilford.

Solomon, M., & Tatkin, S. (2011). *Love and war in intimate relationships: Connection, disconnection, and mutual regulation in couple therapy.* New York: W.W. Norton.

Spencer, H. (1864). *Principles of Biology.* London: Williams and Norgate.

Stahmann, R.F., & Hiebert, W.J. (1998). *Premarital and remarital counseling: The professional's handbook* (3rd edn). New York: Wiley and Sons.

Stanton, M.D. (1992). The time line and the "why now?" question: A technique and rationale for therapy, training, organizational consultation and research. *Journal of Marital and Family Therapy, 18*(4), 331–44.

Stanton, M.D., & Todd, T.C. (1982). *The family therapy of drug abuse and addiction.* New York: Guilford Press.

Steinglass, P. (1998). Multiple family discussion groups for patients with chronic medical illness. *Families, Systems & Health, 9*, 55–70.

Steinglass, P., Bennett, L., Wolin, S., & Reiss, D. (1987). *The alcoholic family.* New York: Basic Books.

Suddaby, K., & Landau, J. (1998). Positive and negative timelines: A technique for restorying. *Family Process, 37*(3), 287–98.

Sweeney, M.S. (2009). *Brain: The complete mind.* Washington, D.C.: National Geographic.

Tabibnia, G., Lieberman, M.D., & Craske, M.G. (2008). The lasting effect of words on feelings: words may facilitate exposure effects to threatening images. *Emotion, 9* (3), 307–17.

Tannen, D. (1994). *Talking from 9 to 5: How women's and men's conversational styles affect who gets heard, who gets credit, and what gets done at work.* New York: Morrow.

Taylor, S.E. (2006). Tend and befriend: Biobehavioral bases of affiliation under stress. *Current Directions in Psychological Science, 9* (6), 273–7.

Taylor, S.E., Klein, L.C., Lewis, B.P., Gruenewald, T.L., Gurung, R.A.R., & Updegraff, J.A. (2000). Biobehavioral responses to stress in females: Tend-and-befriend, not fight-or-flight. *Psychological Review, 9,* 411–29.

Taylor, S.E., Lewis, B.P., Gruenewald, T.L., Gurung, R.A.R., John A. Updegraff, J.A., & Klein, L.C. (2002). Sex differences in biobehavioral responses to threat: Reply to Geary and Flinn (2002). *Psychological Review, 109*(4), 751–3.

Uckert, S., Fuhlenriede, M.H., Becker, A.J., Stief, C.G., Scheller, F., Knapp, W.H., & Jonas, U. (2003). Is there an inhibitory role of cortisol in the mechanism of male sexual arousal and penile erection? *Urology Research, 31*(6), 402–6.

van Anders, S.M., & Dunn, E.J. (2009). Are gonadal steroids linked with orgasm perceptions and sexual assertiveness in women and men? *Hormones and Behavior, 9,* 206–13.

van der Kolk, B. (2000). Posttraumatic stress disorder and the nature of trauma. *Dialogues in Clinical Neuroscience, 2*(1), 7–22.

van der Kolk, B.A. (2003). The neurobiology of childhood trauma and abuse. *Child and Adolescent Psychiatric Clinics of North America, 12*(2), 293–317, ix.

van der Kolk, B. (2005). Developmental trauma disorder: Toward a rational diagnosis for children with complex trauma histories. *Psychiatric Annals, 35*(5), 401–8.

van der Kolk, B.A. (2009). [Developmental trauma disorder: towards a rational diagnosis for chronically traumatized children]. *Prax Kinderpsychol Kinderpsychiatr, 58*(8), 572–86.

van der Kolk, B.A., Roth, S., Pelcovitz, D., Sunday, S., & Spinazzola, J. (2005). Disorders of extreme stress: The empirical foundation of a complex adaptation to trauma. *Journal Trauma Stress, 18*(5), 389–99.

van Wingen, G., Mattern, C., Verkes, R.J., Buitelaar, J., & Fernández, G. (2010). Testosterone reduces amygdala-orbitofrontal cortex coupling. *Psychoneuroendocrinology, 35*(1), 105–13.

Veroff, J., Kulka, R.A., & Douvan, E. (1981). *Mental health in America: Patterns of help-seeking from 1957–1976.* New York: Basic Books.

Waldegrave, C. (1990). Social justice and family therapy. *Dulwich Centre Newsletter, 9,* 6–45.

Wang, L.S., Hui Tang, F.Z., & Yufeng Hu, D. (2012). Combined structural and resting-state functional MRI analysis of sexual dimorphism in the young adult human brain: An MVPA approach. *NeuroImage, 61*(4), 931–40.

Watzlawick, P., Weakland, J.H., & Fisch, R. (1974). *Change: Principles of problem formation and problem resolution.* New York: W.W. Norton.

Wells, G.L., & Olson, E.A. (2003). Eyewitness testimony. *Annual Review of Psychology, 9,* 277–95.

Whipple, B., & Komisaruk. B.R. (2002). Brain (PET) responses to vaginal-cervical self-stimulation in women with complete spinal cord injury: Preliminary findings. *Journal of Sex and Marital Therapy, 9,* 79–86.

White, M. (1986). Negative explanation, restraint, and double description: A template for family therapy. *Family Process, 25*(2), 169–184.

White, M. (1988). Saying hullo again: The incorporation of the lost relationship in the resolution of grief. *Dulwich Centre Newsletter,* (Spring), 29–36.

White, M. (1990). Family therapy and supervision in a world of experience and narrative. *Dulwich Centre Newsletter,* 27–38.

White, M. (1995). *Re-authoring lives: interviews & essays.* Adelaide, Australia: Dulwich Centre Publications.

White, M., & Epston, D. (1991). *Narrative means to therapeutic ends.* New York: W.W. Norton.

Wilson, E.O. (1998). *Consilience: The unity of knowledge.* New York: Knopf.

Witelson, S.F. (2007). Sex and the single hemisphere: Specialization of the right hemisphere for spatial processing. In E. Gillian (Ed.), *Sex and the brain.* (pp. 541–4). Cambridge, MA: MIT Press.

Witelson, S.F., Glezer, I.I., & Kigar, D.L. (1995). Women have greater density of neurons in posterior temporal cortex. *Journal of Neuroscience, 9*(5 Pt 1), 3418–28.

Wolin, S.J., & Wolin, S. (1993). *The resilient self: How survivors of troubled families rise above adversity.* New York: Villard.

Woods, V.D., King, N., Hanna, S.M., & Murray, C. (2012). *"We ain't crazy! Just coping with a crazy system": Pathways into the Black population for eliminating mental health disparities.* Sacramento, CA: California Department of Mental Health.

Yarber, W.L., & Sayad, B.W. (2013). *Human sexuality: Diversity in contemporary America.* New York: McGraw-Hill.

Zak, P.J. (2008). The neurobiology of trust. *Scientific American, 298*(6), 88–92.

Zak, P.J., Kurzban, R., Ahmadi, S., Swerdloff, R.S., Park, J., Efremidze, L., Redwine, K., Morgan, K., & Matzner, W. (2009). Testosterone administration decreases generosity in the ultimatum game. *PLoS One, 4*(12), e8330.

Zak, P.J., Kurzban, R., & Matzner, W.T. (2005). Oxytocin is associated with human trustworthiness. *Hormones and Behavior, 48*(5), 522–7.

Zak, P.J., Stanton, A.A., & Ahmadi, S. (2007). Oxytocin increases generosity in humans. *PLoS One, 2*(11), e1128.

Zeig, J.K., & Lankton, S. (1988). *Developing Ericksonian therapy.* New York: Brunner/Mazel.

Zellner, M.R., Watt, D.F., Solms, M., & Panksepp, J. (2011). Affective neuroscientific and neuropsychoanalytic approaches to two intractable psychiatric problems: Why depression feels so bad and what addicts really want. *Neuroscience and Biobehavioral Review, 35*(9), 2000–8.

Index